FRONTIER ENCOUNTERS

The Russia-China-Mongolia border

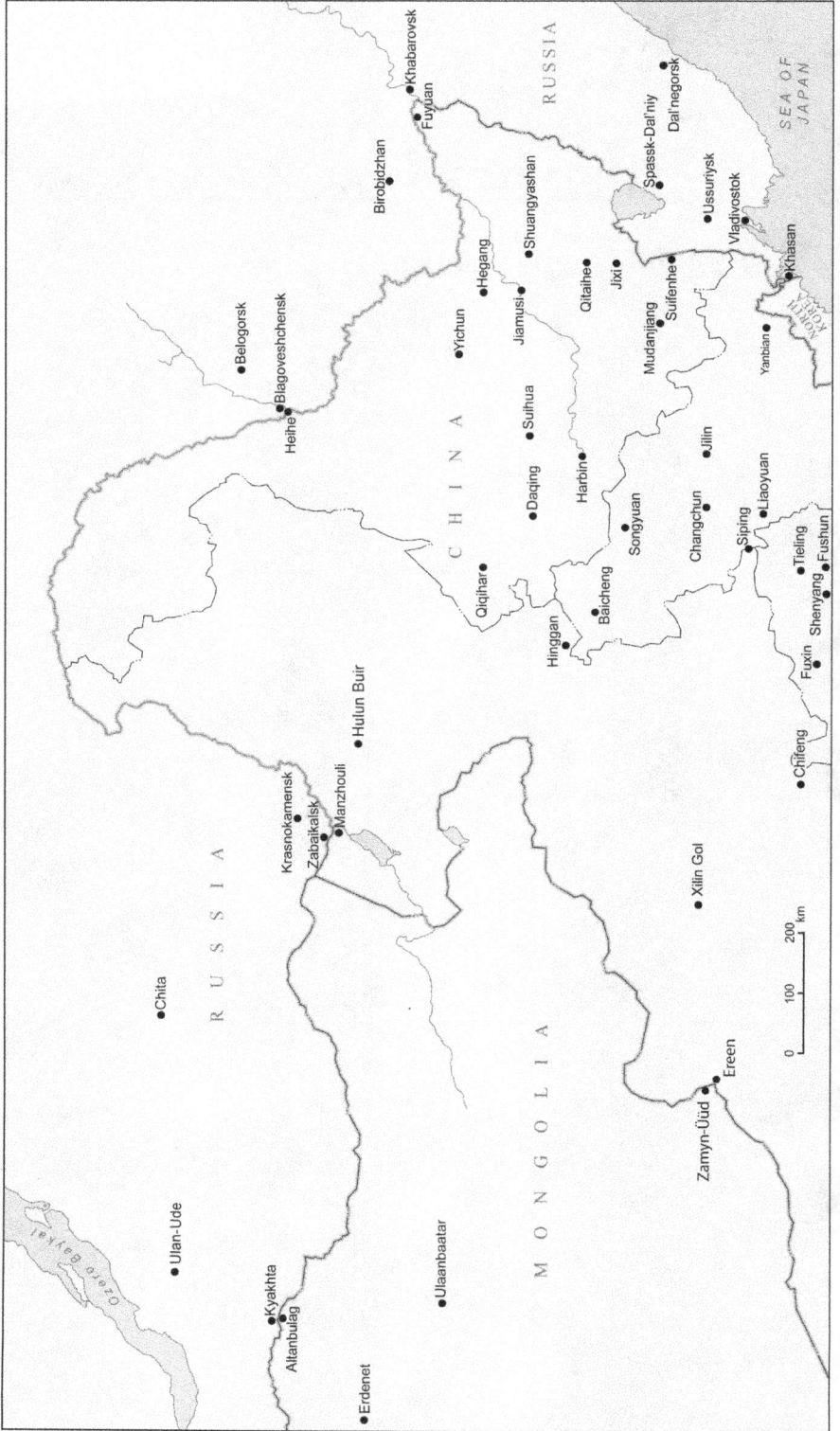

FRONTIER ENCOUNTERS

Knowledge and Practice at the Russian, Chinese and Mongolian Border

Edited by

Franck Billé, Grégory Delaplace and Caroline Humphrey

OpenBook
Publishers

http://www.openbookpublishers.com

Digital material and resources associated with this volume are available from our website at: http://www.openbookpublishers.com/isbn/9781906924874

ISBN Hardback: 978-1-906924-88-1
ISBN Paperback: 978-1-906924-87-4
ISBN Digital (PDF): 978-1-906924-89-8
ISBN Digital ebook (epub version): 978-1-906924-90-4
ISBN Digital ebook (mobi version): 978-1-906924-91-1
DOI: 10.11647/OBP.0026

Cover image: Chinese frontier guard at the Manzhouli-Zabaikalsk border © John S.Y. Lee http://www.flickr.com/photos/38760691@N03/4905791767/

All paper used by Open Book Publishers is SFI (Sustainable Forestry Initiative), and PEFC (Programme for the Endorsement of Forest Certification Schemes) Certified.

Printed in the United Kingdom and United States by
Lightning Source for Open Book Publishers

Contents

Contributors

Franck Billé is a post-doctoral researcher at the Department of Social Anthropology, and member of the Mongolia and Inner Asia Studies Unit, University of Cambridge. He is the coordinator of an ESRC-funded project (2012-2015) entitled 'Where Rising Powers Meet: Russia and China at their northeast Asian border'. He previously carried out research in Mongolia where he investigated the prevalence of anti-Chinese sentiments. His manuscript *Spectral Presences: Anxiety, Excess and Anti-Chinese Speech in Postsocialist Mongolia* is currently under review, and his second book project, *Phantom Pains: National Loss, Maps and Bodily Integrity,* is in progress. Franck Billé can be contacted at franck.bille@gmail.com.

Grégory Delaplace is a social anthropologist, working as a lecturer at the Université Paris Ouest Nanterre. His most recent research concerned the political dimension of the invisible in Mongolia today (or the invisible dimension of politics), whereby ghosts, or spirits, are led to play a role in the postsocialist nation building process. His publications include *L'invention des morts. Sépultures, fantômes et photographie en Mongolie contemporaine* (2009), and *Parasitic Chinese, Vengeful Russians: Strangers, Ghosts and Reciprocity in Mongolia* (2012). Grégory Delaplace can be contacted at gregory.delaplace@mae.u-paris10.fr.

Caroline Humphrey is an anthropologist based at the University of Cambridge who has worked in Russia, Mongolia, China, India, Nepal and Ukraine. She has researched a wide range of themes including Soviet and post-Soviet provincial economy and society; Buryat and Daur shamanism; Jain religion and ritual; trade and barter in Nepal; environment and the pastoral economy in Mongolia and the history and contemporary situation of Buddhism, especially in Inner Mongolia. Her recent research has concerned urban transformations in post-Socialist cities. Caroline Humphrey can be contacted at ch10001@hermes.cam.ac.uk.

Ross Anthony is in the final stages of a PhD in social anthropology at the University of Cambridge and is a member of the Mongolia and Inner Asia Studies Unit, Cambridge. His recent work focuses on issues of urbanisation and ethno-politics in the Xinjiang Uyghur Autonomous Region. He currently holds a research fellow position at the Centre for Chinese Studies at the University of Stellenbosch in South Africa.

Marina N. Baldano is the head of the Department of History, Ethnology and Sociology, Institute of Mongolian, Buddhist and Tibetan Studies at the Siberian Branch of the Russian Academy of Sciences (Ulan-Ude, Russia). Her research analyses the changes brought by modernisation in Inner Asia, nation-building, panmongolism and cross-border migrations. She is the coordinator of a number of research projects including "Civilizational Dynamics and Modernization Processes in the Baikal Asia" and "Border, Transborder and Migrants in Central Asia: Strategy and Practices of Mutual Adaptation". She can be contacted at histmar@mail.ru.

Valentin Sergeevich Batomunkuev is a researcher at Baikal Institute of Nature Management SB RAS, Laboratory of Nature Management Economics. His current scientific work investigates the use of mineral resources, desertification and trans-boundary issues between Buryatia and Mongolia. Previously he carried out research on the management of subsurface resources and the development of transport crossing in the border territory between the two countries. He can be contacted at bvalentins@yandex.ru.

Uradyn E. Bulag is a reader in social anthropology at the University of Cambridge. His interests span East Asia and Inner Asia, especially China and Mongolia, nationalism and ethnic conflict, cosmopolitics, diplomacy, and statecraft. His works include *Nationalism and Hybridity in Mongolia* (1998), *The Mongols at China's Edge: History and the Politics of National Unity* (2002), *The Mongolia-Tibet Interface: Opening New Research Terrains in Inner Asia* (co-editor, 2007), and *Collaborative Nationalism: The Politics of Friendship on China's Mongolian Frontier* (2010), which has won the International Convention of Asian Scholars 2011 book prize. He can be contacted at ueb10@cam.ac.uk.

Victor I. Dyatlov is a professor at the Faculty of World History and International Relations of Irkutsk State University, Russia, and Director of the Research Center on Inner Asia (Irkutsk). He published widely on cross-border migrations in modern and late imperial Russia, on the role of ethnic migrations in the formation of settlers communities in the East of Russia and on the comparative study of diasporas. He can be contacted at dyatlov@irk.ru.

Gaëlle Lacaze is an assistant professor at the Department of Ethnology of the University of Strasbourg. Her research focuses on the anthropology of the body relating to Mongolian people and Turkic populations, including Kazakhs. Her current research investigates patterns of international migrations of Mongolian citizens. She is the author of *Le corps mongol: techniques et conceptions nomades du corps* (2012), the editor of "Migrations in Central Asia and Caucasus" (*Revue europeenne des migrations internationales*, 2010–13) and a number of articles in the field. She can be contacted at gaelle.lacaze@misha.fr.

Sayana Namsaraeva is a Research Associate in the Division of Social Anthropology, and member of the Mongolia and Inner Asia Studies Unit, University of Cambridge. During her recent post-doctoral research at the Max Planck Institute for Social Anthropology she conducted extensive fieldwork on border regions of the Russian, Chinese and Mongolian territories. Her current project focuses on local society that straddles the Sino-Russian border in the twin cities of Zabaikal'sk and Manzhouli. She has published a number of articles in Russian, English and Chinese languages and is currently working on her book on the Qing frontier administration in Inner Asia. She can be contacted at namsaraeva@gmail.com.

Ivan Peshkov is an assistant professor at the Institute of Eastern Studies at the Adam Mickiewicz University in Poznan, Poland. His current research focuses on the political dimension of quasi-indigenousness on the Russian-Chinese frontier. He has carried out research in the Chinese, Russian, and Mongolian border triangle and investigated the main economic and historical processes that characterize this area. He can be contacted at i.peshkov@wp.pl.

Natalia Ryzhova is the director of the Amur Laboratory for Economic and Social Studies at the Economic Research Institute of the Far Eastern Branch of the Russian Academy of Science. She specialises in regional economics and economic sociology with particular focus on informal economics. In recent years she has focused on the interactions between Russian-Chinese frontier people, firms and authorities and on the issue of "border openness" in China. She is a member of the Cambridge Mongolia and Inner Asia Studies Unit's Network for the study of the border zones between China, Russia and eastern Mongolia. Her publications include *Trans-border Exchange between Russia and China: The Case of Blagoveshchensk and Heihe* (with G. Ioffe, 2009); *The Case of the Twin City of Blagoveshensk-Heihe* (2008) and *The Political Economy of Trade Openness Reform: Consequences of Reform for Russian Border Regions* (in Russian, 2011). She can be contacted at n.p.ryzhova@gmail.com.

1. A Slightly Complicated Door: The Ethnography and Conceptualisation of North Asian Borders

Grégory Delaplace

This book presents a collection of ethnographic essays on the border region, in North Asia, where the territories of China, Russia and Mongolia meet across the contrasted landscapes of the Siberian taiga, in the northwest, and the Manchurian plains, in the south and the east.[1] The aim of the present volume is two-fold. On the one hand, it seeks to provide fresh material to a field of research still heavily dominated by studies of the United States and Mexico border. On the other, it intends to challenge a tendency in anthropological research to frame analysis in terms of "culture" and "identity" when dealing with issues relating to social life in the borderland areas. Drawing on the material provided throughout the eleven chapters of this volume, this introduction proposes an alternative, and underlines the benefits of a *technological approach* to the study of borders.

---

1   This introduction is the outcome of a collective reflection carried out with Caroline Humphrey and Franck Billé during the process of editing this volume. It greatly benefited from the insightful suggestions of two anonymous reviewers, and from repeated discussions on border studies with Morten Pedersen while we were both doing fieldwork in Ulaanbaatar during the summer of 2009.

           DOI: 10.11647/OBP.0026.01

International borders have attracted an increasing amount of interest in the social sciences over the past three decades, resulting in the creation of research centres (e.g. the Centre for International Borders in Belfast or the Nijmegen Centre for Border Research in the Netherlands), academic networks (e.g. the Association for Border Studies, which edits the *Journal of Borderlands Studies*), and in countless publications in the fields of Geography, Political Sciences, Economy, and History, to name only a few (for a useful yet now outdated overview, see Donnan and Wilson 1999, chapter 3). While it has not been a trailblazer in this domain, Social and Cultural Anthropology has not lagged behind either. Although the anthropology of borders has not yet been recognised as one of the discipline's "big topics" (it is rarely mentioned in specialised encyclopedias, e.g. Barnard and Spencer 2010), anthropologists have contributed to this field of research in numerous and important ways. Highlighting the processes by which borders are "socially" or "culturally" constructed, some have insisted on the growing number of challenges posed by globalisation to the notion (e.g. Migdal 2004), while others have emphasised the enduring significance of borders at a local level in a context of global political and economic transformations (e.g. Donnan and Wilson 1998; Martinez 1994).

Overall, and at least since Renato Rosaldo's early and seminal contribution to the field (1988), the idea has been that the specific expertise anthropologists could provide in relation to borders concerned "culture", "identity" or "ethnicity" in borderland areas. Is there an "identity" specific to the "borderlands milieu" (Martinez 1994: 10), stemming from the simultaneous distance from political centres and the daily immersion in transnational flows that characterises these areas? How is "ethnicity" used as a border marker between neighbouring peoples, in borderlands (Vila 2005) or elsewhere (Bretell 2007)? What kind of "culture" does the presence of an international border produce, and what kind of cultural practices, in turn, constitute borders between territories and people? These, roughly, have been the questions on which the anthropology of borders has thrived.

One could hardly fail to notice, however, that a particular subfield of anthropology has remained remarkably absent from this debate: material culture, or *technology*, that is the study of techniques spearheaded by Mauss' seminal essay (1979 [1934]), "the particular domain of human activity immediately aimed at action on matter" (Lemmonier 2010: 684–85). Of course, recent technological developments in border control processes, in particular the introduction of biometric identification devices, have not escaped the researchers' attention: philosophers of sciences, jurists, and criminologists have provided valuable expertise on the implications of this technology in terms of conceptions of the body, conditions of international migrations and notions of citizenship (van der Ploeg 1999; Pickering and Weber 2006; Dijstelbloem and Meijer 2011).

Nevertheless, when scholars have considered the question of technology in relation to the border, they have limited themselves to the study of how it was *involved* in the process of crossing a particular border (often the one delimitating Schengen space). The concern of these authors lies in the way technology is becoming *constitutive* of European borders, indeed in ways that cannot but call to mind Agamben's famous warning on exceptions becoming the rule.[2] While these developments are certainly cause for concern, and one can only encourage research into the political implications of borders' technological turn, it seems possible to conceive of a more comprehensive understanding of technology in relation to the border.

So far, indeed, it seems that anthropologists, just like other social scientists, have neglected the analytical benefits of considering the border *itself* as a technique. Yet, it seems hardly possible to overlook that a border is first and foremost a technical object: in fact, what is a border but a *slightly complicated door*?

Doors and the (unsuspected) relations between office colleagues, cats, and gulls

In the opening essay of a small book entitled *Petites leçons de sociologie des sciences* Bruno Latour (1993: 14–24) finds an unlikely ally in Gaston Lagaffe, a Belgian comic strip character created by Franquin, to introduce his notion of a technical "programme".[3] Gaston Lagaffe is famous for the sympathetic blend of naive humanism and laziness that constitute his personality, as well as for the simultaneous taste for DIY methods and perennial clumsiness that characterise his daily activity (his surname means "the blunder" in French). The setting of Gaston's adventures is an office, actually the editorial offices of *Spirou*, the very magazine in which the comic strips were originally

---

2   The reader will find in the volume edited by Sharon Pickering and Leanne Weber (2006) several chapters developing Agamben's concept of "exception" in relation to border control (see, for example, the one by Pickering herself, and the one by Dean Wilson).

3   *Petites leçons de sociologie des sciences* was originally published under the title *La Clef de Berlin, et autres leçons d'un amateur de sciences*.

published. Gaston appears in many situations as the modern-time, office version of a trickster, and the particular example chosen as an illustration by Bruno Latour for his essay is a case in point.

Gaston keeps a cat in the office, to the dismay of several of his colleagues who have to endure the animal's every whim. In this particular scene, Gaston's immediate superior, Prunelle, is upset about constantly having to open the door for the cat that keeps meowing in front of it when it is closed. When Gaston naively suggests to leave the door open for the cat, Prunelle becomes even angrier, saying he refuses to be exposed to draughts while working. Seizing this opportunity to avoid doing actual office work, Gaston takes it upon himself to improve the door and solve the problematic situation. Cutting out a rectangle in the lower part of the door, he reattaches it with hinges to create a cat-flap. Prunelle is concerned with Gaston's tampering with office equipment, but there is nothing he can say: as a result of this technical improvement, the door can now both keep cold air out, and let the cat through. Of course, Gaston being Gaston, the story does not end there – Gaston *also* happens to own a sea-gull that he likes to keep in the office too... The gull, of course, is jealous of the cat's newly (re) acquired freedom, and is now eager to go through doors as well. No sooner said than done, Gaston readily cuts out an opening for the gull in the upper part of the door – the gull is happy, Prunelle has a heart attack.

Thus, concludes Latour, with Gaston's cunning invention, the "programme" of the door, its purpose as a technical object, has changed. Originally the door, like most doors, was a rather simple device allowing humans to go through – since they are able to depress the handle (or turn the knob) that commands the opening of the door – while keeping cold air and animals out – at least those who cannot depress handles (we all know cats who can). Following Gaston's intervention, the door has evolved into a more complicated mechanism, one that can, in addition to humans, let two kinds of animals through, yet two kinds only: those that are small enough to crawl through the lower opening, and those that are able to fly through the upper one. It continues to keep all other kinds of animals out: Gaston's horse, had he had one, would still be unable to proceed through, as well as draughts, if we assume cold air will not flow through the upper opening.

Hopefully the reader will see by now the relevance of this lengthy prologue to the question of borders. Like a door, and most of all, like Gaston's door, a border is a device whose "programme" is *to let certain people and things through, while keeping others out*. Borders, of course, are slightly more complicated than doors – even Gaston's – and it is precisely the purpose of this volume to show *how*. What are the specific devices regulating border crossings (we will see that identification technology is not the main one in the region), and how might these be challenged, or circumvented, by local populations? The starting point of this volume is thus a technical one: what, exactly, is the programme of a border? Or rather, more modestly, what are the programmes of North Asian borders, in the area where China, Russia, and Mongolia meet? How, and how successfully, are they implemented?

North Asian borders: where empires meet

This volume and the chapters that compose it emerged from two conferences held at the University of Cambridge as part of a research project funded by the Economic and Social Research Council.[4] The motivation for this research project was that the geophysical dividing line where the Siberian taiga abuts the steppes of Manchuria is also the place where the territories of two of the world's largest countries, Russia and China, meet along a common border extending over a thousand miles. What is interesting here is that these two gigantic political formations, which are also major players in the world economy – two empires, as it were – meet *at their confines*: one of the most sensitive areas of their territory, where their land meets that of their rival, is actually located far away from their political centres. And while a great amount of information is available on each country taken separately, far less is known about the practicalities of their interactions locally, on the border they share.

Lodged in between these two giants, Mongolia is of crucial strategic importance to both of them: in recent history, Mongolia has served as a frontier area both to the Qing Empire (1644–1912) against Russia, and to the Soviet Union (1922–1991) against China. While more modest in both size (yet still more than six times larger than the United Kingdom) and economic stature, Mongolia is also heir to one of the largest empires that ever existed. Given this geopolitical context, the regional history is rich with dramatic displacements of population, with peoples pushed and

---

4   The project, entitled Where Empires Meet: The Border Economies of Russia, China and
    Mongolia (RES-075–25_0022), ran from 28 January 2010 to 27 January 2011. The first
    conference held in Cambridge on 6 July 2010, was entitled "Trading, Smuggling and
    Migrating across the Border between China, Russia and Mongolia". The second event,
    "Politics, Concepts and Practicalities at the Chinese Russian Border", was held on 17–18
    November 2010, in Cambridge as well.

pulled from one side of the border to another, as wars broke out and the balance of power changed between these empires.

The Buryats, in this respect, are a case in point. The recent history of this Mongol group bears the mark of most of the twentieth-century upheavals that affected the region. Victims of exactions during the Russian Civil war (1917–1923) following the Bolshevik revolution, they fled to neighbouring areas in North Mongolia and North-East China, where they lived as exiles throughout the hardships that struck these regions during the Japanese invasion, and the Chinese Cultural Revolution (see Sayana Namsaraeva's chapter in this volume). As described by Marina Baldano (chapter 10), post-socialist attempts of repatriation to Russia for some Buryat groups were often a mixed success as the returnees strove to find a place on either side of the border. Ivan Peshkov (chapter 9), tells a similar story for the "Cossack" (Guran) population that migrated to China and Mongolia as a result of the Soviet regime's hostile "decossackization" policy after the revolution. Contrary to those who stayed in Russia, and who remained attached to the defence of Russian territory, as shown by Caroline Humphrey in her own contribution (chapter 4), these exiled Cossacks have become, through acculturation and intermarriage with other local groups, peoples who belong to the borderland rather than to a particular political formation.

Several contributions to this volume thus broach the well-researched topic of "identity" and "ethnicity" of borderland peoples. However, instead of taking notions such as "identity", "ethnicity" or "culture" as a point of departure and a frame of analysis, as anthropologists working on borders are wont to do,[5] this book considers them only as one possible component of the border apparatus. Adopting a technological approach, this volume starts off with very simple questions: what are North Asian borders made of? What are they supposed to do? What, and how do they actually perform on the ground? Although "culture" and "identity" might be *part* of the answers to these questions, a concern shared by the following

---

5   The introductory chapter in the book by Hastings Donnan and Thomas M. Wilson is perhaps the most elaborate, and the most often quoted, theorisation of this approach. The authors contend that major changes have affected border areas in the face of the "twin threats of supranationalism from above, and ethnonationalism and regionalism from below" (1999: 1). Anthropologists can contribute to the understanding of these tremendous changes with their expertise on "the role which culture plays in the social construction and negotiation of these borders" (ibid.: 3). "Anthropologists provide the data to explore the cultural bases to ethnic, racial and national conflict at international borders, a task made all the more urgent by the resurgence of ethnic and nationalist violence at many of the world's borders" (ibid.: 12).

chapters is really to avoid *framing* these answers in terms of "culture" and "identity" from the outset.

On this basis, and as mentioned at the beginning of this introduction, this book intends to provide fresh material in a field still heavily dominated by research on the border between the United States and Mexico. Of course, this is not the first attempt at doing so: in addition to European ones, borders of northern India have attracted a great deal of scholarly attention (e.g. van Schendel 2005 and Gellner Forthcoming), as have those of Africa (Asiwaju and Adenyi 1989), and even Amazonia (Goulard 2005).

Undoubdtedly, phenomena observed in other regions also concern this border, or have concerned it in recent history: forced migrations (Baldano, Namsaraeva, Peshkov), transnational trade (Lacaze), anxieties over illegal immigration (Billé, Dyatlov), and attempts to limit the latter while fostering the former. Some issues, however, such as the development of informal networks of transnational poachers (Ryzhova) and smugglers (Namsaraeva), might appear more clearly here than in other border areas.[6] In addition, the states that meet in this region see themselves not only as nations, but also as "civilisations" (Humphrey, Billé), whose encounter on the ground cannot be as simple, if it ever can be (see Williams 2006 and Ettinger 2009), as drawing a line between them.

How (slightly) different a border is from a door: overview of the volume's content

In this context, surely, a border can only be more complicated than a door. But how exactly? This is precisely what the following chapters demonstrate. Each contribution, in its own particular perspective, provides us with ethnographic evidence on how the border works, as a device of *passage*.[7] Which elements is a border composed of, what programme is it supposed to perform, and how is it able to do it in practice? These are some of the questions the following chapters could help to answer and which I propose

---

6 This does not mean that smuggling is absent from other borderland areas: for a detailed study of cross-border informal trade in South-Asia at the turn of the twentieth century, see Tagliacozzo 2005.

7 The relevance of Arnold Van Gennep's theory of "Rites of Passage" (1909 [1991]) to the study of border crossing has been noted by several authors (see, for example, Rösler and Wendl 1999: 2). This is especially relevant here given Van Gennep's heavy reliance on the metaphor of doors and thresholds to illustrate his theory.

to develop in the rest of this introduction, in order to give an overview of the volume's content.

The fuzzy materiality of the border

First of all, and from a material point of view, a border is obviously made of far *more elements* than a door. It is a well established idea in the literature that a border is not just a line. Donnan and Wilson (1999: 15), for example, list three constitutive elements to a border: it is composed, according to them, of a "juridical borderline which simultaneously separates and joins states", but also of "the agents and institutions of the state, who demarcate and sustain the border" as well as "frontiers, territorial zones of varying width" stretching away from the borderline itself. If several chapters in the present volume confirm the relevance of these three components to North Asian borders as well, some contributions also show that the materiality of the borderline – the infrastructure marking the "juridical borderline" – is itself composite.

A survey of the border crossing infrastructures between Russia and Mongolia, compiled by Valentin Batomunkuev, is presented in an appendix to this volume. In addition to the border checkpoints themselves, we see that the technological apparatus that ensures border control is made of custom buildings and warehouses, roads and a railway network surrounding and crossing the border, as well as various installations ensuring water and electricity supply. Robin Grayson and Chimed-Erdene Baatar (2009), using satellite images available on Google Earth, had already inventoried the infrastructures that constituted the border between China and Mongolia. Grayson and Baatar showed that not only crossing points, but also the line of separation itself was of a composite nature: on the one hand, satellite images reveal a multitude of ancient border vestiges in the form of wall ruins, which leave in the landscape the mark of previous territorial delimitations (what Prescott, quoted in Franck Billé's chapter, called a "relict boundary"); also, and more significantly, newly erected fences on the Chinese side are doubled with a large ploughed area, of 40 to 100 metres wide, running along the border with Mongolia over more than 1,300 kilometres.

The border, from a material point of view, resembles a double-door system more than a single one: rather than just a fence, it often takes the form of an assemblage of walls and spaces (the no man's land being only one type of border space), that constitutes a *zone of separation* between two different territories.[8] Yet, walls are not the only way by which the border zone is delimitated: the list of its constitutive elements also includes the "regulations" that frame the legal regime specific to the border area (Billé, Batomunkuev). In chapter 4, Humphrey reveals that this strip of land is managed directly by the FSB, Russia's Federal Security Service, which regulates access to this zone.

Other material components in this border assemblage might be located at a distance from the actual borderline. Thus cities might be an essential factor in connecting or keeping apart neighbouring states: Manzhouli, located near the border between China and Russia, is as much part of the border device as the actual checkpoint, and more of a zone of encounter between the two sides than an instrument of demarcation (see Manzhouli city map in the appendix section).[9] In chapter 7, Gaëlle Lacaze looks at the city of Ereen, on the Chinese side of the border with Mongolia: comparable to a modern caravanserai, where Mongols stop and trade, the city is the place where cross-border relationships involving all sorts of business, including sex work, actually occur. Chapter 12 provides further examples of elements in the Mongolian border apparatus that are actually located outside of the frontier area: I show in this chapter that memories attached to material and immaterial vestiges of foreign presence in Mongolia – abandoned Russian towns, resilient Chinese ghosts – are used by Mongolian people to qualify and manage their relationship with their neighbours.

Finally, Uradyn Bulag, in chapter 3, reminds us that populations have often been deemed more efficient than walls to protect the border from unwanted intrusions. Thus the Qing dynasty, in China, has relied on the presence of the Mongols to protect their Northern confines from the expanding Russian empire. Likewise, entire ethnic groups have been put in charge of border control by centralised political formations: the Cossacks, famously, were tasked by the Tsar to guard the Russian border. Caroline Humphrey (chapter 4) describes the central place that the border continues to hold in contemporary Cossack identity: although no longer officially in charge of its defence, Cossacks continue to patrol the border and create rituals to celebrate their involvement in the protection of the "integrity" and the "purity" of Russian land.

---

8   Moreover, as was already noted by Weber (2006) for the Australian border, the borders between China, Russia and Mongolia often lack precise localisation: satellite images clearly show in certain places a succession of different lines of demarcations in space, none of which seem to be more prominent than the others.
9   For a similar perspective, see Vila's ethnography of the cities of Juárez and El Paso, respectively on the Mexican and on the American side of the border (Vila 2005).

Material and immaterial components in border assemblages

Yet, clearly, border assemblages are not only composed of material elements. In some cases the border between populations may be of a "psychological" nature, and may not even need to be marked in the landscape. Uradyn Bulag, in chapter 3, shows that such is the case between Mongolian and Chinese populations in Inner Mongolia. Although they have been part of the same political formation for the past three centuries at least, their antagonism is the result of a divide-and-rule strategy carried out by Manchu emperors during the Qing dynasty (1644–1912). Having themselves conquered China thanks to alliances with Mongol groups, Manchu rulers made sure a similar alliance would never arise against them: in addition to erecting a willow palisade between Chinese and Mongolian territories, as an extension of the Great Wall, they made sure through strict legal regulations that Mongol and Chinese people would not intermarry, and that they would engage in as little interaction as possible, even actively fostering hostility between them. As a result, while the willow palisade no longer exists in a material form, it lives on locally as a psychological barrier between these populations.

Borders, or rather certain components of the border assemblage, might thus be invisible. This point is particularly well illustrated in chapter 11, in which Ross Anthony takes the reader to the Altai mountain range, in Xinjiang province, where China borders Kazakhstan. Building on ethnographic "episodes" taken from his fieldwork, Anthony shows that the way the border is envisioned by the local population is as important as its materiality to understand local practices in relation to it. Thus, a bear hunter has to imagine the invisible line demarcating the international border through the Altai range, in order to avoid trespassing and getting into trouble with the border guards. His hunting expeditions, and the path he follows to chase his preys are therefore modelled on an approximate idea of where the "line" actually lies. Meanwhile, for the Uygur youth in the border town of Jimunai, the border is pictured as a wall obstructing their dreams of self-accomplishment in Kazakhstan, and one that needs to be overcome. Anthony argues that borders are suffused with "technologies of imagination", a term he borrows from David Sneath: pictured as single lines, borders thus become part of a broader imaginary whereby the territory of the nation-state is enclosed within clear-cut demarcations.

Racial stereotypes could also be seen as a technology of imagination which extends and reinforces the border between two countries. In chapter 5, Viktor Dyatlov retraces the history of anti-Chinese sentiments in Russia. Whereas the rhetoric of the "Yellow Peril", at the turn of the twentieth century, pictured Chinese people as parasites ("locusts", "midges") emerging from a political void, fears of Chinese expansion nowadays envision them as the tentacles of a threateningly powerful and imperialist state. Yet, stereotypes do not only concern interethnic relationship: Ivan Peshkov (chapter 9) and Marina Baldano (chapter 10) show respectively for the "Cossacks" (Guran) and the Shenehen Buryats, that such prejudices also emerge within ethnic groups that have been kept separate as a result of forced migration. The repatriation campaigns carried out in Russia to encourage the return of these populations is rendered difficult by the cultural distance that has accrued, in the space of a few generations, between them and those that stayed behind. Echoing a well established idea in the anthropological literature (Donnan and Wilson 1998: 5), Baldano thus contends that the border "represents the interrelations between individuals, groups of people and states".[10] This idea finds an unexpected, yet undeniable echo in Lacaze's contribution, which looks into a characteristic component of border interrelations: prostitution.[11] Through a detailed description of the life of Mongolian sex workers at the Chinese border, Lacaze shows that prostitution is not only an important aspect of cross-border trade, but also a regime of relationship suited to the characteristic liminality of borderland areas.

Borders and regimes of openness

Another reason why borders are more complicated than doors is because contrary to the latter, the former are *always open and closed at the same time*. In a philosophical essay on bridges and doors, Georg Simmel reflects on the contrast these technical objects offer, as visualisations in space of human

---

10   The idea that "borders are spatial and temporal records of relationships between local communities and between states" (Donnan and Wilson 1998: 5) also finds an echo in Janet Carsten's point, mentioned by Franck Billé in his chapter, namely that states were defined on "ties of fealty between persons, not on the unambiguous mapping out of space" (Carsten 1998: 218) before becoming delineated by international borders. Of course, several authors (e.g. Anderson 1983: 170–78) have stressed that the conceptualisation of states as territorial units delimited by lines, emerged with specific and relatively recent mapping techniques.

11   In his ethnography of the Mexican border-city of Juárez, Vila analyses the narratives portraying it as a "city of vice" bustling with prostitution, and excessive alcohol consumption (2005: 113 *et passim*). According to Vila, the pervasiveness of this idea in the imaginary about borders plays on an intuitive association of the limit of "social systems" with the limits of the body (ibid.: 114).

fundamental ability and urge, to "separate the connected or connect the separate" (1903 [1997]: 66).[12] Whereas the bridge, argues Simmel, is the perfect instance of permanent connectedness between two points that were initially kept apart by nature, the door always carries both possibilities: it can *either* be closed, thus separating an inside from an outside, *or* open, thus allowing passage and communication between the two spaces. In Simmel's own words:

> Whereas in the correlation of separateness and unity, the bridge always allows the accent to fall on the latter [...], the door represents in a more decisive manner how separating and connecting are only two sides of the same act (67).

Yet, although the door might offer both possibilities simultaneously to intellectual contemplation, its "open" and "closed" modes never occur at the same time in practice. This stands in sharp contrast with borders: while a door is *either* open *or* closed, a border is *always both at the same time* – it is closed to certain people and things, while remaining open to others. In this respect, borders are more akin to Gaston's door than to ordinary ones. Following Gaston's intervention, as we saw earlier, the door became permanently open to animals, while remaining closed to draughts: the door's new conformation transformed it into a *discriminating device of passage*, which is what, fundamentally, international borders are meant to be.

Borders look different depending on who you are, and crucially, where you come from: while to some migrants they are a mere administrative formality (a procedure only slightly more time-consuming than depressing a door handle), to others they will never be anything else than fortress walls, the crossing of which is made at the risk of one's life. This contrast is particularly striking in the case of European borders (see the contributions to the volume edited by Dijstelbloem and Meijer in 2011), but it is also true of others: Leanne Weber (2006: 24), drawing on Daniele Joly, has aptly compared the border to a "porous dam", "expected to allow a steady and lucrative flow of welcome visitors, while holding back the floods of unwanted Others".[13]

---

12 For another use of the same reference in relation to borders, cf. van Houtum and Strüver (2002).

13 Peter Andreas, meanwhile, stressed the performative dimension of border management: showing the border as both open to legal flows of people and goods and closed to illegal ones is a matter of political "face work". The US and Mexico, as well as the

Borders, however, not only discriminate between different kinds of people, they also impose certain conditions to their crossing: borders are not open to everybody, and *not to everybody on the same conditions*. Some nationals will need specific authorisations, in the form of visas, or even specific forms of monitoring (such as the biometric database established for asylum seekers, van der Ploeg and Sprenkels 2011), while others will only need their passport, or even their national ID. Meanwhile, borders are not open to any commodity under any circumstances: the particular goods, as well as their quantities, that an individual can take across the border is often subject to limitations, and such limitations, of course, do not apply in the same way to imports on a national scale.

The particular conditions set to border crossing for individuals and goods vary from one country, even from one border, to the other. Therefore, rather than the opposition between a "closed" and an "open" mode, like ordinary doors, what characterises a border is a specific *regime of openness* – i.e. a set of conditions under which it is open to certain people and to certain things, while closed to others. The modulation of this regime according to economic needs, anxieties about migration, and international political agendas, is of crucial importance in a state's "governmentality", as shown by Michel Foucault in his famous 1978 lecture series on "Security, Territory, Population". With the advent of mercantilism in the eighteenth century, the "problem of population" – its management and its discipline – became a central concern (*the* central concern) for the sovereign. However, Foucault continues,

> The population can only be the basis of the state's wealth and power in this way on condition, of course, that it is framed by a regulatory apparatus (*appareil*) that prevents emigration, calls for immigrants, and promotes the birth rate, a regulatory apparatus that also defines useful and exportable products [...] (2007: 69).

Borders, as the main device of migration control, cannot but have a central role in this "regulatory apparatus". Of course, the situation has changed since the eighteenth century, and the concern now, at least in Euro-American countries, is not so much to prevent emigration than to control immigration.

European Union, take the border as a stage where image management, rather than the actual deterring of illegal crossings, is at stake: "What makes the border a particularly challenging stage is that the actors are involved in a double performance, having to assure some of the audience that the border is being opened (to legal flows) while reassuring the rest of the audience that the border is being sufficiently closed (to illegal flows)" (2000: 10).

Yet, the border has kept its role as part of the regulatory apparatus by which a sovereign state seeks to ensure *security* and manage its *population*, through an "efficient" administration of its *territory*. This is also true of North Asian regions: the data presented in appendix A shows that Russia produces a huge amount of statistics (one of the main tools in the art of governement, says Foucault, 2007: 104) concerning borders, in order to evaluate the way these perform as a device that fosters economic exchanges while regulating migration.

In this respect, contrary to doors, and against a widespread rhetoric in Europe and Anglo-American countries, there is no such thing as a "closed" border: there are only varying degrees of openness. Indeed, it would be unheard of for a state to choose to close its borders to *all* incoming migrants; would it decide to do so, it would probably not wish to close its boundaries to the circulation of its *own* population – even North Korea, to a certain extent, receives some visitors, and sends some of its population abroad.[14] "Closing borders down" is thus a political fiction, which really means an increasingly discriminatory migration policy – a particularly restricted regime of openness. In other words, the border is never closed, it might just be open to a smaller proportion of migrants – to those who are "chosen", as well as to "deserving" refugees.[15] "Closed border" policies are nothing but a smoke-screen for a dryly utilitarian migration policy taking economic efficiency, centrally and unilaterally engineered, as the only possible justification for incoming migration. Moreover, rather than closing the border this kind of policy only makes it more difficult, and more dangerous, for refugees to cross it (Fassin 2005; Weber 2006), for it is a well known fact that candidates for migration will *always* find ways to circumvent the official programme of a border that restricts their access.

Subverting the border

This brings us to the final point of this introduction, the third main reason for which a border is more complicated than usual doors: while, in the absence of cats and gulls, everybody more or less agrees on how to use a door, *borders might be simultaneously defined in a number of different*

---

14   Mongolia, actually, is one of the countries with which North Korea maintains student exchange programmes: Mongolians, moreover, are allowed to enter North Korean territory, for short visits, without a visa.

15   For an analysis of the shift in French immigration policy, from a legal framing of migration control to the rhetoric of "chosen immigration", see Fassin 2005.

ways. Of course, when cats and gulls come into play, like in the comic strip described earlier, the use of doors too starts to be at the centre of diverging conceptions: Bruno Latour, to this end, proposes to add to his concept of "programme" the notion of "anti-programme" (1993: 19). An "anti-programme" is simply a programme that contradicts or impedes the realisation of a given programme. Thus according to Prunelle, Gaston's cold-sensitive superior, the door's initial programme is challenged by the cat's anti-programme. Thanks to the cat-flap, however, Prunelle and the cat can share a single programme for the door, while the sea-gull still has its own anti-programme, etc. In a similar way, the following chapters show how border programmes may be subverted by all sorts of anti-programmes. Of course, given the multiplicity of actors meeting at the border, and given also the different levels at which the border might be considered, the situation is never as simple as a binary opposition between a programme and its contradiction.

First of all, at an international level there are often disagreements about what the border is, and about the tasks it is supposed to perform. Even when the exact location of the border is not in question – there are no major border disputes between China, Russia and Mongolia – there may still be discrepancies between two states' understanding of what a border actually *is*. The next chapter, by Franck Billé, shows through a comparative analysis of the terminology that ideas of the border in China and Russia are expressed in drastically different ways. While Chinese terms tend to describe the border as a "frontier" – a zone radiating from the centre – Russian vocabulary conveys the idea of a definite line. The contrast is appealing, and yet Billé warns us that this opposition is somewhat misleading: understandings of the border as a frontier also exist in Russian, and the Great Wall is here to testify that Chinese imperial formations, at times, have also conceived of the limits of their territory as firm lines. Interestingly, Billé shows that the way Chinese people are believed to think of the border causes a great deal of anxiety in Russia. Fears of "Chinese expansion", also considered by Dyatlov in chapter 5, are based precisely on this idea that Chinese allegedly conceptualise borders as concentric circles radiating outwards, rather than as an unambiguous single line.

What Billé highlights, therefore, is an anxiety about the "enemy's point of view" (Viveiros de Castro 1992) on the border: *what if my neighbour had a completely different border than mine*? What if our practices at the border could never match, and what if *her* conception of the border actually included *my* territory? The main reason why a border is different from a door, perhaps, is that while the latter separates an inside from an outside, the former, in a way, delimitates *two competing "insides"* – the "outside", or the "beyond" of a border, is often if not always, someone else's inside.

Most contributions, however, tackle less dramatic misunderstandings about the border, whereby the official programme enacted through state regulations and central ideology enters in contradiction with the multitude of anti-programmes that underlie daily practices in borderland areas. Caroline Humphrey (chapter 4) thus shows that Russian ideology of "civilisation", based on an idea of purity and permanence of the border, is shared both by Moscow's intellectuals and by local Cossack populations of Buryat and Evenki descent, in spite of starkly diverging notions of what actually constitutes the border's "purity". In a way, the rituals performed by Cossacks at the border to celebrate its purity fly in the face of the nationalist discourse – which is combined with pragmatic realpolitik and interaction with China – produced in the metropolis.

In chapter 6, Natalia Ryzhova provides an unprecedented account of informal networks of salmon poachers and smugglers. After a close examination of the legal framework of fishing rights and cross-border trade, Ryzhova illustrates the multiciplicity of tactics – among which bribing is only one example – whereby informal associations of local fishermen with Russian and Chinese traders manage to circumvent official regulations. Highlighting that both sides are actually involved in these illegal activities, Ryzhova proceeds to propose solutions to improve the way these "Common Pool Resources" might be managed across the border.

In chapter 8, Sayana Namsaraeva shows how Buryat exiles who settled in Mongolia and China following the Russian civil war challenged officially closed borders in order to visit their kin and what they still see as their "homeland" on the other side. Namsaraeva reviews with a wealth of details the imaginative ways in which split families were able to maintain contact despite separation on two sides of a "sealed off" border. Wearing deer hooves on their soles to leave only animal prints behind, or adjusting their boots backwards to convey the impression that they were actually walking away from the border, some could trick border patrols, crossing through and back again. Even when it proved impossible to physically cross the border, Buryat migrants found ways to subvert it in other ways: if nothing else, a shaman could still let her spirit run through, in an animal form, and deliver a message to a distant and longing kin.

There is little doubt that the wealth of fresh material provided in this book will foster reflection within the emerging field of border studies. Although this introduction might have appeared to try to tie the following chapters into a single approach, through the idiom of techniques and the metaphor of the door, the reader should not assume that this is the sole contribution the papers bring to the theorisation of borders. On the contrary, scholars working on borders or not, whether they are specialists of North Asia or work in other regions, will certainly welcome the refreshing diversity of perspectives proposed by the contributors to this volume.

2. On Ideas of the Border in the Russian and Chinese Social Imaginaries

Franck Billé

Following Liberation and the installation of a communist government in 1949, China set out to resolve numerous border disputes with neighbouring countries. Between 1960 and 1963, China settled outstanding territorial disagreements with North Korea, Mongolia, Myanmar, Nepal, Pakistan and Afghanistan. A number of other border disputes have been resolved more recently, particularly with territories formerly included in the Soviet Union. In 1991, China signed the Sino-Soviet Border Agreement, which brought to an end longstanding territorial disputes with Russia and led to a final agreement in October 2004 (Foucher 2007: 33). Delimitation agreements have also been signed over the last two decades with Central Asian countries adjacent to China, namely with Kyrgyzstan in 1996, Kazakhstan in 1994 and Tajikistan in 1999 (Pan 2009: 95).

If in several of these agreements China frequently flexed her political muscles – claiming as hers significant areas of Tajik, Kazakh and Kyrgyz territory in the process – these demarcation efforts also index a willingness to put to rest outstanding disputes and to normalise border relations with her neighbours. Indeed, if normalisation of borders is essential to the development of border trade, and therefore financially advantageous (Simmons 2005: 842–43), China's participation in territorial resolutions clearly signals her desire to portray herself as good-neighbourly (Lukin 2009, Tang, Li and Acharya 2009). As Fravel notes, "China's compromises have often been substantial, as it has usually offered to accept less than

DOI: 10.11647/OBP.0026.02

half of the contested territory in any final settlement. In addition, these compromises have resulted in boundary agreements in which China has abandoned potential irredentist claims to more than 3.4 million square kilometres of land that had been part of the Qing empire at its height in the early nineteenth century" (2008: 2). Yet, despite China's insistence on her commitment to a "peaceful rise" (*heping jueqi* 和平崛起), many of her neighbours continue to look at her progress with ambivalence and anxiety, and frequently suspect imperialistic designs.

In Mongolia, for example, all anxieties relating to continued cultural and political independence are focused on China (Batbayar 2005): the spectre of a Chinese takeover of the country remains pervasive and rumours of Chinese malfeasance omnipresent (Billé 2008). Popular discourses in the far eastern provinces of Russia are strikingly similar. Scholars writing on Russian perceptions of Chinese migrant workers (Dyatlov 1999, 2008; Larin 2005; Alexseev 2001, 2006) report widespread fears that the Chinese are coming in vast numbers and that they attempt to stay behind illegally (see Dyatlov, this volume), thereby introducing significant demographic shifts that may eventually lead to a balkanisation of the region and the secession of the eastern regions of Russia to the benefit of China. While it is likely that such fears are grounded, in part, in the demographic imbalance between China and eastern Russia, I wish to suggest here that suspicions of Chinese imperialistic designs may also have emerged in response to differences in Russian and Chinese conceptualisations of the border. Despite China's efforts to settle border disputes and to normalise relations with all her neighbours, Chinese current approaches to the issue of borders appear to be at odds with Russian, or Mongolian, understandings.

Definitions of the word "border" are notably difficult to agree upon since the term can refer both to the political boundary of a state and to the limits of cultural regions, two entities that are hardly, if ever, coextensive. English makes a useful distinction, however, between "border" and "frontier", with the former denoting a formal line of demarcation between states and the latter the process of expansion of a political entity, such as the frontier of America's westwards expansion in the eighteenth and nineteenth centuries, or indeed the similar eastwards expansion of the Russian state into Siberia.[1] According to Wilson and Donnan, "frontiers"

---

1   The English word "frontier" comes from the French *frontière* which etymologically is related to the word "front" in a military sense. The "frontier" was thus the line that

are "territorial zones of varying width which stretch across and away from borders, within which people negotiate a variety of behaviours and meanings associated with their membership in nations and states" (1998: 5). Indeed, the disconnect between the apparent arbitrariness of political boundaries and the reality of the numerous cultural regions that straddle these lines has proved a fertile terrain for anthropological research, since the very existence of borderlands, of liminal regions "bisected by the boundary line between states" (Donnan and Wilson 1999: 50) helps disrupt the national fantasy of complete geophysical and cultural separateness.

The focus of this paper is on this conceptual tension between "border" and "frontier" and its relevance for the Sino-Russian border. As I will illustrate shortly, the difference between the two concepts gains palpability when a linguistic comparison is made of the terms currently used in Russian and Chinese to speak of borders: if in Russian there is a relative paucity of terms to refer to borders, Chinese lexical wealth suggests a much wider set of spatially overlapping concepts. Indeed, while in Russian the border tends to be conceptualised as a firm line, Chinese perceptions are significantly more zonal and frontier-like. I suggest however that the predominance of one particular model is not necessarily culturally specific but that both models coexist and fluctuate in a dialogical process.

A strong differentiator in the way Russians and Chinese currently visualise their common border is the emotional quality they attach to it. While for Chinese the north-eastern border with Russia appears to be seen, predominantly, as a frontier of opportunity where commercial ties can be created and valuable contracts concluded, in the Russian media the border is most often associated with illegal migration and criminality (see Ryzhova, this volume) and tends therefore to be perceived as a source of anxiety. This divergence, whereby the Chinese display more proactive and entrepreneurial attitudes while the Russians remain on the defensive, is in fact also played out in the linguistic realm, with more Chinese proficient in Russian than the other way round.

Undeniably, Russian fears of Chinese encroachment are linked to China's demographics and fast-developing economy. Russians routinely imagine masses of Chinese pressing against their border, encouraged to migrate through state incentives. These perceptions are also escalated by the situation at home: at the same time as China is imagined bursting at the

---

separated the polity from the enemy, by definition an eminently mobile line of both contact and separation.

seams and hungry for land, inhabitants of Russia's Far Eastern provinces see their region as becoming depleted, weaker, and increasingly abandoned by the state (Hill and Gaddy 2003). It is precisely this combination, these feelings of abandonment in the face of a populous China allegedly eager to recapture lost territories, that proves so anxiogenic. Dyatlov (2008) notes that the arrival of Chinese migrant workers has been described as a "second coming" (*vtoroe prishestvie*): the continuation of prerevolutionary migration trends that had been stemmed by the Soviet government.[2] In other words, the presence of Chinese individuals on Russian territory is seen as indexing both the raw demographic power of China, and the weakness of a Russian government no longer able to keep them out. Alexseev (2006a: 46) provides a similar explanation for these Russian anxieties. He argues that the perceived uncertainties about the government's capacity to care turn exaggerated claims into a sensible psychological coping strategy.

And these concerns do, indeed, appear to be widely exaggerated. Research carried out by local scholars suggests that prevalent fears are not supported by facts (see Alexseev 2006a: 2–15). While Russian media assert that Chinese migrants routinely evade immigration restrictions and stay behind, data tell a different story. In Primorskii Krai in 2000, only 82 Chinese failed to return home, i.e. a proportion amounting to 0.03 per cent of the total number of Chinese visiting the region that year. The following year, in 2001, the number had dropped further, to 15 people, i.e. 0.01 per cent (Larin 2005: 51). Instead of the tidal waves and invasions described in the Russian media (see Dyatlov 2008), the majority of the Chinese working in the Russian Far East typically stay for the duration of their contract and then return home. Indeed, surveys carried out among them indicate they do not consider the region an attractive prospect for long-term settlement (Hill and Gaddy 2003: 181). For their part, Chinese scholars are careful to distinguish them from traditional migrants (*yimin* 移民) and sojourners (*huaqiao* 华侨), preferring to refer to them as overseas workers (*waipai laowu* 外派劳务) instead (Wishnick 2005: 80).

While demographic imbalance and socioeconomic factors go a long way to explain these sentiments, similar fears of Chinese expansion are also prevalent on Sakhalin Island, despite the presence of only a few hundred Chinese there (Larin 2005: 58),[3] suggesting that the cause of these anxieties

---

2   Dyatlov points out that these perceptions have often been consciously manipulated by "interested parties" for various personal and political reasons.

3   In Sakhalin's capital, public demonstrations against Chinese encroachment led to sweeping raids being carried out, but these raids produced barely a dozen Chinese

might be located elsewhere. In fact, the dangers thought to originate from China are largely associated with a phantasm of China pertaining to the realm of the imaginary, a "would-be China" as Lomanov (2005: 71) has phrased it. Given that China is not making any territorial claim,[4] and is on the contrary trying to resolve outstanding issues, and given that despite fears of being overrun by the Chinese, actual numbers are hardly threatening (the total annual percentage of Chinese workers employed in the RFE has never exceeded 0.2 per cent of the total work force there,[5] Larin 2005: 55), the issue appears to be less one of actual socioeconomic threat than a misalignment between official statements and imagined intentionality.

This misalignment may be due, in part, to the different concepts of the border held by Russians and Chinese. Specifically, what does elicit Russian anxieties may be less a matter of aggressive and imperialistic designs on the part of China than her considerably more supple understanding of "borders". Before I go on to develop this argument, it may be useful to draw a brief comparison between the two sets of lexical resources available to Russian and Chinese speakers to refer to borders.

In modern Russian, the concept is expressed by two terms, largely synonymous: *granitsa* and *rubezh*. *Granitsa* is etymologically related to *gran'*, meaning "facet" or "edge", while *rubezh* comes from *rubit'* (to cut, chop) and was previously synonymous with *zarubka*, meaning "cut" or "notch" (Shanskii and Bobrova 1994). The semantic fields delineated by the two terms show some similarity with the opposition found in English between "border" and "frontier" with *granitsa* indicating a linear demarcation and *rubezh* denoting a fuzzier differentiation between Self and Other. However, in most linguistic contexts *rubezh* appears to be losing ground in favour of *granitsa*.[6] In other words, a shift in the semantic landscape concerning borders, and specifically a "linearisation" of the concept, is discernible in the lexical resources available to Russian speakers. This linearity is also visible in the adjectival forms of the term *granitsa* like *pogranichny and prigranichny* and particularly in words derived from both *granitsa* and *rubezh*, such as "foreign" (*zagranichny*) and "abroad" (*za granitsei, za*

---

nationals (Alexseev 2006b: 142).

4   Although this is not China's official position, some Chinese groups do make such territorial claims.

5   Since 2005, changes in the calculation methods have increased this percentage to 3 to 4% for the Amur *oblast* (Ryzhova, personal communication).

6   The term *rubezh* is never used for instance to speak of an actual border with another nation. Its use is virtually limited to set expressions such as *za rubezhom* (abroad).

rubezhom), with the preposition *za* (over, across) which clearly constructs the border as a line rather than a zone.

This makes for a stark contrast with modern Chinese where the lexical landscape referring to borders is much broader (see Table 1). The principal lexemes used to refer to borders are *jiè* (界), *jìng* (境), *jiāng* (疆) and *biān* (边) and these are used in combination with each other as well as with other characters to form a wide array of words. While *jiè* and *jìng* unambiguously denote a linear concept of boundary and limit, *jiāng* and *biān* are more polysemic. On its own, *jiāng* can mean both "boundary" and "dominion" (as in Xinjiang 新疆, literally "new dominion"). Similarly, *biān* translates in various ways depending on context. Its primary meaning is that of "side", but it can also mean "border", "boundary", "edge" or "margin" when combined with another character (i.e. *biānjiè* 边界: territorial boundary; *biānjìng* 边境: border area; *biānjiāng* 边疆: borderland, frontier; *biānmín* 边民: frontiersman; *biānqū* 边区: border region). Thus the lexical wealth of Chinese points to conceptualisations of the border that extend beyond a linear perspective and are significantly more zonal. While in Russian (like in French or German) no clear lexical distinction exists between the concepts of "border" and "frontier", the numerous Chinese terms convey a range of images of a border – as a line, as a liminal zone, as a margin.[7]

边 (*biān*: side, edge, margin, border, boundary)	
边界	biānjiè – territorial boundary, border
边境	biānjìng – border (area), frontier
边境线	biānjìngxiàn – borderline, demarcation line
边疆	biānjiāng – border area, borderland, frontier
边缘	biānyuán – edge, fringe, periphery
边沿	biānyán – edge, fringe, margin
边民	biānmín – frontiersman
边区	biānqū – border area, border region
边塞	biānsài – frontier fort/fortress

---

7   The linguistic landscape I have sketched here focuses on the terms used in Russian and Chinese, however along the lengthy Manchurian border numerous minority groups are found whose concepts of "border" may not necessarily dovetail with those of the dominant groups. The Mongolian cairn system (*oboo*) that dots the landscape for instance functions as a mark of physical as well as spiritual boundary.

界 (jiè: boundary, scope)	
国界	guójiè – national boundary
疆界	jiāngjiè – border, boundary
分界线	fēnjièxiàn – border, boundary
界限	jièxiàn – demarcation line
境 (jìng – border, boundary)	
国境	guójìng – national territory/border
国境线	guójìngxiàn – national boundary
边境	biānjìng – border (area), frontier
境界	jìngjiè – boundary; realm
疆 (jiāng – border, boundary, dominion)	
疆域	jiāngyù – territory
边疆	biānjiāng – border area, borderland, frontier
疆界	jiāngjiè – border, boundary
缘 (yuán – margin, edge)	
边缘	biānyuán – edge, fringe, periphery
塞 (sài: strategic pass)	
边塞	biānsài – frontier fort/fortress

Table 1: Overview of the Chinese semantic landscape for the term "border"[8]

This, I suggest, has an important resonance for the ways in which speakers conceptualise the border and it may help understand the customary visualisation by Russians of the border as a national and ethnic fault line susceptible to be crossed and requiring protection[9] (see Humphrey, this volume), while the Chinese imagine it as a more supple zone, at times rich in opportunities, at other times as regions of danger.

---

8 The headings in the table are morphemes rather than words *stricto sensu*. The semantic neighbourhood they delineate is refined through association with other morphemes, creating words, given as examples underneath.

9 This may help explain the defensive attitudes frequently displayed by Russians and their reluctance to enter into collaborative ventures. Alexseev (2006a: 238) notes for instance that Russian fears about Chinese poachers stealing Russian frogs have not translated into business opportunities. Yet, the breeding and harvesting of frogs to meet the huge demand of the Chinese market could potentially turn into lucrative opportunities for local inhabitants.

The formation of the Chinese state has often been described as a process of gradual expansion outwards, slowly incorporating lands on its margins (Fairbank 1968, Tu 1994) in a process of Sinicisation or "cooking" of surrounding barbarian groups (Fiskesjö 1999). From a cultural centre located in the North China Plain, China is perceived to exist "at the centre of an ever-widening series of concentric borderlands" (Potter 2007: 240). The centre, or "core", noted Sinologist Owen Lattimore (1967: 41–42), was known as "central plain" (*zhongyuan* 中原) or "inner China" (*neidi* 内地) and referred to the densely populated, ethnic Han region running from north to south along the coast. The periphery, also known as "frontiers" (*bianjiang* 边疆) or "outer China" (*waidi* 外地), enveloped this Han heartland to the north, west, and southwest.

While the process of Sinicisation is somewhat problematic since it assumes a unidirectional transformation and assimilation (Crossley, Siu and Sutton 1991: 6; Billé 2009), what interests me here is the assumed survival of this model. In fact, a large share of anxieties about China gravitates precisely around this idea, namely that China continues to perceive itself as a cultural centre radiating outwards, and that formal demarcation (and resolution) of her national borders continues to exist in parallel with an ever-advancing cultural front.

Earlier, I defined "borders" as the territorial limits of a nation state and "frontiers" as the process of expansion of a political entity. Ethnographic data from various parts of the world, like South-East Asia (Carsten 1998) or Europe (Wilson and Donnan 1998: 8–9) suggest that nations were defined historically by their centres and that they articulated on "ties of fealty between persons, not on the unambiguous mapping out of space" (Carsten 1998: 218). It is only later, as nations expanded and unclaimed lands shrank, that attempts were made to "resolve these difficulties by delimiting a precise boundary" (Prescott 1987: 46).[10] From a people-based understanding, what was then witnessed was a gradual "territorialisation" of the state (Sahlins 1998: 37), i.e. a decline in relationships-inflected views of the nation and a progressive isomorphic identification between the physical and cultural extent of the state.

Traditionally, China's views of her borderlands were predominantly negative: borderlands were places of banishment as well as spaces

---

10   The Peace of Westphalia, signed in 1648 and signalling the establishment of the modern state system, has generally been seen as the critical event in this conceptual shift (Pan 2009: 20).

generating cycles of crisis and catastrophe (Woodside 2007: 21–22). But if these territories formally included within the nation were seen, and frequently continue to be seen, as not quite Chinese and peopled by non-Han groups, the misalignment between political boundaries and cultural frontiers also has a formative impact on common perceptions of territories lying outside the current borders of the PRC. Regions such as Mongolia or parts of the Russian Far East, notably the Maritime region (*Primorskii Krai*), are not considered Chinese yet remain perceived as somewhat less foreign (Billé 2012).[11] Frequently described by Chinese nationalists as regions that have broken away (see Zhang 2005: 110–11), these are liminal regions, not currently under Chinese control but with strong cultural and historic ties to China (see Nelson 1995).

Given China's use of history as a dominant state narrative and its routine insistence on being the country with the longest unbroken existence, historical and archaeological claims suggesting that these outlying regions were previously "Chinese" (in a national rather than ethnic sense) are frequently understood as territorial claims.[12] Russians living in the Russian Far East have often perceived the Chinese presence as a political and strategic phenomenon rather than a social, economic or cultural one (Larin 2005: 48). Hostile intent is also frequently ascribed to the existence of Chinese names to refer to local (Russian) cities (Alexseev 2006: 111). Traditionally the Chinese name for Vladivostok was *Haishenwei* 海参崴, Khabarovsk was called *Boli* 伯力, and Ussuriisk was known as *Shuangchengzi* 双城子. While these locales tend today to be referred to by their Russian names, i.e. *Fuladiwosituoke*, *Habaluofisike* and *Wusulisike*, these transliterations have not wholly displaced former names. As historian James Stephan (1994: 19) noted, in the 1970s, Soviet archaeologists and historians were careful to cleanse the territories included within the Russian borders from Chinese historic presence by renaming over a thousand locales.

The attempt by Soviet, and later Russian, government to draw a sharp separation from China and to remove all ambiguity from the border has

---

11   The fact that, during the Ming dynasty, titles were bestowed upon tribal units as far north as the Uda River and the shore of the Sea of Okhotsk (Waldron 1990: 75) has provided a historical rationale in China for considering vast expanses of Siberia as "historically Chinese".

12   There also tends to be some confusion between the claims of the PRC and those of the nationalist government in Taiwan, the latter indeed laying claim to Outer Mongolia, Tuva and some parts of the Russian Far East.

also left its traces on the physical landscape. As is clearly visible on aerial and satellite pictures of the border (see map of the Manzhouli/ Zabaikalsk border crossing, Appendix II: 245), the Russian state border is paralleled by additional markings and lines of defence, reinforcing further this sense of separation. Specifically, two kinds of demarcation are seen at this particular point: a no-man's land (*dublirovanie pogranichnoi polosy*) that frequently includes ploughed out strips and which, at some points along the border, may extend to widths of several miles; and a zone of fortification (*ukreplennye rayony*), which typically includes obstructions and/or minefields.[13] Also visible on aerial photographs is the so-called "Chingis Khan's Northern Wall" (Severny Val Chingis-Khana), a 340-mile long demarcation line established by Jurchen rulers during the Jin dynasty (1115–1234) in the first and unsuccessful attempt to insulate themselves from the Tatar and Mongolian tribes to the north (Logvinchuk 2006). Today, this line has become a "relict boundary", defined by Prescott (1987: 14) as a boundary that has been abandoned but endures through the differences in the landscape that have developed during its lifetime.

On the Chinese side, by contrast, there does not appear to be such an aspiration to hermetically insulate the national body from Russia or to expunge all traces of former Russian presence. In Harbin, for instance, numerous Russian buildings remain in the old quarters and several Orthodox churches have survived the Cultural Revolution (see Lahusen 2001). In fact, in recent years, the city has actively tried to capitalise on its Russian heritage: today, Harbin is one of the largest centres in China for the study of Russian and it is also there that the main Russian-language news website in China operates.

I argued earlier that the concept of border in the Russian and Chinese imaginaries differ in significant ways, as is suggested by the lexical categories used in these two languages. While in Russia the border is usually visualised as an inflexible boundary line, the limits of the nation in the Chinese national imaginary are much less rigid. Of course, at an official political level, the boundaries of China are just as fixed and subject to policing practices as the Russian ones. However, another dimension also exists in which the extent of the nation is much fuzzier. When speaking with Chinese citizens outside Inner Mongolia for instance, Mongols often

---

13   This particular fortification zone in the vicinity of Zabaikalsk was implemented in March 1966, as a result of the Sino-Soviet split.

note that their interlocutors are never quite sure whether Mongolia forms part of the nation or not. While these responses may be due in part to confusion between "Mongolia" (Mengguguo 蒙古国) and "Inner Mongolia" (Neimenggu 内蒙古) – the latter being a province of China – and also to a general lack of interest about those neighbouring nations that are perceived as less economically developed, I suggest that it also indexes a certain disconnect between the physical extent of the nation and the cultural realm.[14]

However tempting it may be to see this fuzzy conceptualisation of frontiers as something specifically Chinese, it is important to note that Chinese ideas of the border have fluctuated significantly throughout history. At specific times, like during the Ming dynasty, the northern border was perceived as more linear and less ambiguous than during the preceding dynasty (see Waldron 1990). Indeed, my overall reading of Chinese borders as zonal may feel somewhat counterintuitive given the commanding presence of the Great Wall as signal of political and cultural discontinuity.[15]

In the same way, if Russian ideas of the border with China appear to be more rigid, this has not always been the case. In addition to the two words discussed earlier, *granitsa* and *rubezh*, a third term, *krai*, is also occasionally used that comes even closer to the more fuzzy delimitation evoked by the English "frontier". Etymologically, the word is related to the term *krayati*, a dialectal variant of *kraiti* meaning "to cut". Historically, *krais* were vast territories located along the periphery of Russia and the term is still used in the name of administrative divisions, notably those bordering China. And if today *krai* is never used to refer specifically to the border, the concept remains embedded in names like Ukraina, literally "on the edge" [of Russia].

While traditional scholarship on borders has tended to see frontiers chiefly as pre-modern phenomena, to be later superseded by borders (see Prescott 1987), it would seem that the process whereby one particular model gains prominence cannot be simply attributed to a historical process

---

14   Waldron notes that in the earliest period of its history, the idea of clear boundaries was not a particularly strong one in the Chinese tradition: "Early texts were rather vague about China's borders: they described not a single frontier, but rather a series of zones". Similarly, "differences among the peoples were not of quality, but of degree" (Waldron 1990: 42).

15   On ideas of the Great Wall as a transition zone, see Lattimore (1967). See also Waldron (1990) on the cultural construction of the Great Wall as a singular structure.

of development from a pre-modern political system to that of a nation-state, nor indeed to cultural specificities. If Russian concepts of the border appear to have changed over time from a zonal to a more linear understanding, the fluctuations seen in the Chinese cultural region suggest that the two models can, and do, coexist side by side.

I argued earlier that Russian concerns about the Sino-Russian border are inherently tied to the increasing economic and political power of China, and that these fears are exacerbated by the feeling that the RFE is economically and demographically weak, compounded by a pervasive sense of having been abandoned by a geographically distant centre.[16] In this sense, it would appear that the predominance of one particular conceptual model of the border is highly contextual and that it emerges in dialogue with the other nation beyond the boundary line but also with the indigenous minority of peoples residing in the borderlands.

Consequently, boundaries with different neighbours are likely to be conceived differently. If Russia's boundary with China is conceptualised as an inflexible line, other Russian borders, and particularly borders that previously demarcated republics within the Soviet Union, will not necessarily share the same rigidity. Over the last two decades for instance, Russia's border with the Ukraine has gradually been transforming into a "proper" state border, equipped with complete border-crossing infrastructure such as customs posts and border guards (Popkova 2001). Nonetheless, it remains a highly porous border, and, importantly, does not elicit the kind of anxiety seen at the border with China.[17] Similarly, if China's view of her northern border with Russia may appear in many ways to be akin to a frontier, this is not necessarily true of her other boundary lines, notably in Xinjiang (see Anthony, this volume). In that part of the country, in stark contrast to the restoration and packaging of Russian architectural heritage for tourism purposes, the modernisation of Uyghur cities has sought to efface all traces of otherness. This difference is also played out in the realm of social exchanges: while at the Sino-Russian border more Chinese usually speak Russian than Russians speak Chinese, at the border with Kazakhstan and Kyrgyzstan Chinese businessmen and traders tend

---

16   In fact, this very sentiment of distance may index a continued conceptualisation of the nation as radiating from the capital.

17   Attitudes are of course eminently unstable. Thus a recent article reports the increased sense of threat associated with neighbouring Belarus, currently ranking fifth among countries perceived as constituting a risk for Russia, ahead of Iran, Iraq or Chechnya (Smirnov 2011).

to rely on local Kazakhs and Kyrgyz as cultural and linguistic mediators (Babakulov 2007).

In fact, if political geographers and International Relations scholars are quick to describe frontiers as older concepts that have faded in favour of the more linear understanding of borders, certain state practices suggest the survival of a more complex and multifaceted outlook.[18] This coexistence is visible for instance with respect to coastal waters, conceptualised primarily as an outward extension of a given country's territory but considerably complicated by diverging, and at times conflicting, definitions. Thus, due to the existence of offshore islets (some of which may be submerged at high tide) and underwater geography (such as the position of the nation in relation to the continental shelf), zones of ownership occasionally overlap, with one country owning fishing rights over the seabed and another the rights to the mining activities and to the harvest of sedentary species of fish (Prescott 1987: 24).

To conclude, rather than view "borders" and "frontiers" as mutually exclusive regimes that are culturally-embedded or specific to certain modes of governnmentality (see Foucault 2004), I suggest that the two in fact frequently coexist. If current Russian and Chinese terminology indicates significant variation in the ways in which the nations' boundaries are conceptualised, it is crucial to look at how these concepts and understandings play out at various endpoints of the nation and how they fluctuate in time and space. As cogently pointed out by Pavel Baev in reference to Russia, when "some parts of the state start to drift away, borders are declared sacred and inviolable, but when there is a chance to add a piece to the state – then borders are taken as conveniently expandable" (Baev 1996: 4, quoted in Kuhrt 2007: 3).

In other words, frontiers are not merely phenomena that gradually become superseded by borders. Rather, the two concepts denote different attitudes about Self and Other, attitudes that are inherently variable and shifting. Even after borders have ossified into rigid and linear boundaries, relict frontiers such as the "Chingis Khan's Northern Wall" or the

---

18   As Delaplace (Introduction, this volume) nicely illustrates with the story of Gaston
      Lagaffe, a border is rarely conceptualised by the state as two-dimensional. A border is
      in fact a line of demarcation with infinite depth, both subterranean and aerial. Indeed, a
      crucial factor in territorial disputes has consistently been the resources the soil is known
      or believed to contain. Similarly, with the advent of air transportation and the emergence
      of the concept of "national airspace", the boundaries of the nation have also extended
      upwards.

"Willow Palisade" (see Bulag, this volume) frequently leave their imprint on the geographical and social surroundings. These physical traces of past national and imperial incarnations, like tidemarks, enframe liminal zones where national identities and values routinely find themselves reinforced, contested and challenged.

3. Rethinking Borders in Empire and Nation at the Foot of the Willow Palisade

Uradyn E. Bulag

Prologue: stony wars at the foot of the willow palisade

Every year, on the fifth day of the fifth lunar month, i.e. the traditional Duanwu Festival (also known as Dragon Boat Festival or Double Fifth Festival), people in Wangsiyingzi and the neighbouring village Sifangtai, just about one and half kilometres to the south, would climb atop a small mountain that lies between the two villages. Instead of racing dragon-headed boats as is the practice in south China, where the tradition first started more than two thousand years ago, people in these two villages, and their supporters from as far as Shenyang city, threw stones at each other. In this annual fight, called *kezhang doushi*, many were injured, some even seriously, but apparently no one ever died. Curiously, as soon as the fight was over after dusk, the warring sides resumed normality and visited each other as if nothing had happened. This tradition was, however, banned by the Liaoning provincial government a couple of years ago for having allegedly attracted large numbers of armed gangsters from outside the villages.[1]

---

1   Violence is endemic in dragon-boat festival. See Hsin-Yüan Chen (2008/09).

                                    DOI: 10.11647/OBP.0026.03

On a late summer day in 2010, Burensain and I drove to Wangsiyingzi for a quick visit, hoping to learn a bit about the fight.[2] The two villages belong to two separate counties, which in turn are under the jurisdiction of two different prefecture-level municipal cities in Liaoning Province. Under Heishan County of Jinzhou City, Sifangtai has about 1,500 people, half Manchu, half Chinese. Wangsiyingzi, on the other hand, is a village under the jurisdiction of the Fuxin Mongolian Autonomous County, Fuxin City. Originally a pure Mongolian village called *Norsan Ail*, today the Mongols constitute only one fifth of the village's population of 1,100 people; the rest are Chinese and Manchu, the latter making up one fourth of the total. As we roamed the village, we encountered a few Mongols chatting in fluent Mongolian. The Mongols, they told us, occupy the north-eastern corner of the village, and they do not normally interact with the Manchu or Chinese. Pointing at the nearby mountain, they recounted the fight in vivid terms, dismissing the government ban as nonsensical.

The mountain, about a kilometre south-west of Wangsiyingzi, is called Norsan Oroi (Norsan Hill), after the village name. In Chinese, however, since the mountain has two connected mounds, the northern one is known as Ma'an Shan (Horse-Saddle Mountain) and the southern one Wangbao Shan (Treasure-Watching Mountain). There is a *bianqiang* nearby, they said, and the two villages fight over it. *Bianqiang* is the Chinese term used by local Mongols for *Liutiao Bian*, the Willow Palisade (lit., willow-branch border).

We drove up to the foot of the mountain and walked on the ridge from the northern end to the southern end, which is about two kilometres long. A grass-covered water gully runs between the two mounds, so we thought it must be the ruins of the famed Willow Palisade. We were wrong. Qu Yanbin, a Chinese folklorist, writes that the ruins of the old palisade are actually at the foot of the southern mound, Wangbao Shan (Qu 2007: 158). Unfortunately we missed it, as this information was not available then and we did not have enough time to do more explorations.[3] In the fight, Sifangtai villagers occupy Wangbao Shan, and Wangsiyingzi villagers Ma'an Shan, and they try to conquer each other's mountain, stoning the "enemies" off, for fun, according to the Mongol villagers we talked to.

---

2   Burensain Borjigin is a Japan-based Inner Mongolian historian. See Burensain 2007.
3   We made the excursion on the last morning of our three-day visit to the Fuxin Mongolian Autonomous County.

The previous day, at a banquet with several retired Mongolian cadres from the Fuxin Mongolian Autonomous County, one of them pronounced proudly to us that the Mongoljin[4] Mongols in Liaoning Province still maintain their Mongolian identity well, and they have been serving as a Great Wall (*chang cheng*) protecting Inner Mongolia. Another elder, having learnt that I am from Ordos, said that the Ordos Mongols speak Mongolian with a strong Shaanxi Chinese accent, whereas the Mongoljin Mongols speak the most authentic Mongolian. I admitted readily that we in Inner Mongolia are not holding our cultural ground as well as we should. Afterwards, Burensain, who has been studying the region for more than a decade, confided that the Mongoljin suffered heavily during the Jindandao cult rebellion in 1891, when they lost more than 10,000 lives at the hands of the Han Chinese tenants who tilled Mongol land (see Borjigin 2004; Dai 2009; Wang 2006). Today, these Mongolian retired cadres, known as local elders, *nutgiin övgöd*,[5] run three associations: the first pertains to the promotion of Mongolian culture, the second to the study of China's ethnic autonomy laws, and the third to the study of tourism. Sophisticated in political skills, they have been relentless in their pursuit of justice, making use of every bit of China's Constitution and laws, especially the *Regional Nationality Autonomy Law*.

In the past decade, these elders have campaigned effectively against the term *Menggu Daifu* (Mongolian doctor), a Chinese ethnic slur which characterises Mongolian doctors as low-skilled and cruel veterinary surgeons.[6] More recently, they have successfully challenged the Han-dominated standing committee of the autonomous county Party Committee, by persuading the higher authority to make it a Mongol majority committee to reflect the Mongolian titularity of the autonomous county. This was no small feat, and in fact unheard of anywhere else in China.

Remarkably, deep inside China, in the thick of the Chinese population, the Mongoljin Mongols are still fighting at the foot of the Willow Palisade to defend their identity and interest. In this chapter, I re-examine the borders in empire and nation in China and Inner Asia.

---

4   The Mongoljin Mongols used to be part of the Tumed Tumen, one of the six Tumens of Central Mongols ruled by Chinggisid princes. During the Qing, they were organised into the Tumed Left Wing Banner, belonging to the Josotu League of Inner Mongolia. In 1958 the banner was re-organised as Fuxin Mongolian Autonomous County in Liaoning province (see Bao and Xiang 2008).

5   The Mongoljin Mongols used to have an elders' assembly, *övgödiin chuulgan*, which led a major rebellion against the Qing in 1860–1864 (see Tai and Jin 2008: 238–49).

6   A cursory discussion of the campaign can be found in Bulag 2008.

Rethinking imperial and national borders

The Willow Palisade is a ditch and embankment planted with willows; its construction started in 1644 and was completed in 1681. Resembling the Chinese character 人 (*ren*, human), the palisade starts from the Shanhaiguan Fortress, at the eastern end of the Great Wall, and terminates at the western end of the Korean border. This was the old palisade (*lao bian*), built to prevent the Mongols and Koreans from entering the heartland of Manchuria. A new palisade (*xin bian*) was added, starting from Weiyuanbaomen gate and ending at Fadiha gate, which was built from 1670 to 1681. This palisade was built to prevent the so-called wild Jurchens from entering interior Manchuria (see Edmonds 1979; 1985).

The Willow Palisade was not the only border the Qing instituted. The Qing dynasty also demarcated arguably the world's first international border with the Russian Empire, as documented by Peter Perdue (1998). This is extraordinary and interesting because the builders of these borders and walls were not the sedentary Chinese, but the Manchu, a semi-nomadic Inner Asian people,[7] and this fact alone goes against much of current thinking on borders in empires and nations, a point I will elaborate below. I am tempted to call the Qing dynasty a border-building empire.

Conventional studies of Chinese nationalism focus almost exclusively on extraterritoriality and unequal treaties that gave western powers enormous privileges in China after the first Opium War (1839–42). Liu Xiaoyuan, a Chinese-American historian of Chinese and Inner Asian international relations, argues, however, that we pay more attention to Chinese obsession with territoriality. For him, Chinese nationalism is marked by China's territorial expansionism and incorporation of "Inner Asian borderlands into the territories of the Chinese republic" (Liu 2010: 233). While this is correct, I think he errs in claiming that a clearly demarcated border was the product of nationalist modernity as a result of what he called "cartographic modernisation" during the last decade of the Qing dynasty, i.e. 1902–1911. Before that, he argues, "although China has a long history of using maps, ancient Chinese maps did not demarcate China and its neighbours as bordered geo-entities. In the ancient world of China, border demarcation was occasionally practiced but was not institutionalised, for systematic border demarcation would have contradicted the universalistic ideology

---

7   David Sneath (2003) made an acute observation of this fact and attributed it to the Khitan Liao tradition of dual administration.

of 'all under heaven' and misrepresented the political reality of China's shifting frontiers" (ibid.). His theory, insightful as it is, in fact resonates with the recent movement in social science theorisation about borders, and some popular Chinese views on borders.

Largely, in social science literature, borders have become a vantage point to critique nation-state. Borders and borderlands are "sites and symbols of power" (Donnan and Wilson 1999: 1). The US-Mexico borders and the Israeli-Palestine borders are characterised as emblematic "wild zones of power" where the state authority exercises extralegal violence to defend them (Morris-Suzuki 2006). As such, borders are seen as what define a nation-state, which is largely represented as a gigantic prison with wired fences, preventing free movement of goods and people. Empires, once denounced and overthrown, have now struck back; they are re-imagined as a cosmopolitan space without borders, imbued with hospitality, welcoming and hosting strangers. Deleuze and Guattari's "nomadology" reigns over the post-national global imagery: nation-states are sedentary and bound whereas empires are nomadic and open (Malkki 1995).

This pro-empire theoretical movement in the West mirrors debates on borders and walls in modern China. In the early 1960s at the height of the ideological tensions with the Soviet Union, the Chinese Communist Party (CCP) openly defended Chinggis Khan and the Mongol Empire, celebrating them for sweeping away all the petty kingdoms lying between China and Europe, thereby spreading Chinese civilisation to Europe, including Russia (Farquhar 1967). *Pax Mongolica* was appropriated as *pax Sinica*. During the liberalist movement leading up to the Tian'anmen protests in June 1989, many Chinese intellectuals denounced the Great Wall, not only for its ineffectiveness in defending China from repeated nomadic invasions, but more importantly for its historical role in creating a closed frame of mind in the Chinese people while what they longed for was the blue ocean, where they could sail toward freedom. *Heshang* (Deathsong of the River), a six-part television documentary series made in 1988, celebrated as a Chinese version of *The Closing of the American Mind*, and one which led to political radicalism, has the following to say about the Great Wall:

> By the time that Genghis Khan's [1162–1227] fierce horsemen had swept down like a tide, not even natural barriers like the Yellow River and the Yangtze, let alone the Great Wall, could stop them (Su and Wang 1991: 127).

> In direct contrast to the now-forgotten Great Wall of the Qin, the Great Wall of the Ming which retreated a thousand *li* backwards, has been the object of incomparable reverence. People pride themselves on the fact that it is the

only feat of human engineering visible to astronauts on the moon. People even wish to use it as a symbol of China's strength. And yet, if the Great Wall could speak, it would very frankly tell us, its Chinese [*huaxia*] grandchildren, that it is a great and tragic gravestone forged by historical destiny. It can by no means represent strength, initiative, and glory; it can only represent an isolationist, conservative and incompetent defence and a cowardly lack of aggression. Because of its great size and long history, it has deeply imprinted its arrogance and self-delusion in the souls of our people. Alas, O Great Wall, why do we still want to praise you? (ibid.: 130)

Here, the Great Wall was imagined as the Berlin Wall, a symbol of closed mind and cowardice. Today, leading Chinese writers such as Yu Qiuyu (1995) laud the Kangxi Emperor of the Qing dynasty for his decision not to repair the Great Wall when he received a report from Cai Yuan, the governor of Gubeikou Pass in May 1691 about the derelict state of the Wall. In numerous contemporary Chinese writings, the following from Kangxi's reply is quoted to prove that the Qing was an open Empire:

> Emperors and kings had their own ways to rule all under heaven; they did not simply rely on perilous nature. After the Qin built the Great Wall, the Han, Tang, and Song dynasties often repaired it, but had they ever been free from border troubles? At the end of the Ming, my grandfather [Hong Taiji] led his great army, riding straight in, defeating all [Ming] armies; nobody could stop him. It is obvious that the way to defend a state is really to promote good morality and let people live in peace. If people obey happily, then the state is legitimate and the border will be solid automatically... In the past the Qin launched a large scale project to build the Great Wall. Our dynasty bestows favour to the Khalkha, allowing them to defend the North [against the Russians]; this is more solid than the Great Wall (Qingdai Guanxiu 1985: ch. 151, pp. 19–21).

It is fascinating that contemporary Chinese scholars have taken the perspective of their former conquerors who *ipso facto* would not need a Great Wall to block themselves from conquering China. In their political romanticism,[8] Chinese intellectuals have turned the Manchu conquerors into staunch enemies of smallness, the best practitioners of *da-yi-tong*, the highest Chinese political ideal of grand unity. A Li Zhiting (2005) romanced the following:

---

8   See Schmitt's discussion of political romanticism: "In the romantic it is not reality that matters, but rather romantic productivity, which transforms everything and makes it into the occasion for poetry. What the king and queen are in reality is intentionally ignored. Their function consists instead in being a point of departure for romantic feelings. The same holds for the beloved. From the standpoint of romanticism, therefore, it is simply not possible to distinguish between the king, the state, or the beloved. In the twilight of the emotions, they blend into one another" (1991: 126).

The Kangxi emperor decided to abandon the Great Wall, so that henceforth there was no more division between the south and the north, no more distinction between the Chinese and barbarians, genuinely becoming "one family", endowing "Central Kingdom" with contemporary meaning of China. Abandoning the Great Wall was tantamount to dismantling a barrier wall that segregated the great masses of the Han from the "three northern" minority nationalities, rapidly forming an unprecedented multi-nationality state of "grand unity". This decision of the Kangxi Emperor, while abandoning the earth and stone Great Wall, built instead a national Great Wall of "collective will", which was no doubt an epochal breakthrough of the theory of "grand unity", a great pioneering undertaking!

The admirers of the Kangxi Emperor's grand political philosophy ignored what he might have really thought; they conveniently forgot or did not realise that he in fact lied about his dynasty needing no wall. It is true that the Manchu did not repair the Great Wall, but it was in 1681, during Kangxi's own reign (1662–1722), that a different kind of wall, the Willow Palisade, was built, which had been initiated by his father the Shunzhi Emperor (Lee 1970: 6) well before he boasted about "consolidating the empire without relying on the perilous mountains and rivers" in 1691, a year when the Khalkha Mongols submitted to the Qing.

The main arguments that I will elaborate on in the remainder of this chapter are the following. Contrary to conventional assumptions, empires built by nomads or semi-nomads did have a sense of border and boundary. The Manchu Qing, and for this matter the Mongol Yuan, had a strong sense of border, using it as a political technique to manage the disparate populations within the empire. One of the distinct characteristics of Inner Asian conquest dynasties was the dual rule instituted to administer the conquered Chinese population separately from their own ethnics. The Mongols in fact created a native chieftainship (*tusi*) system to rule non-Mongol and non-Chinese populations in the Yuan separate from the Mongols and Chinese who were administered in provinces (*xinsheng*), another Mongol invention (Bulag 2010a).

This proposal that empires have borders is by no means a novel idea. After all, one of the key techniques used by rulers, imperial or otherwise, is "divide and rule". What I suggest is special about the Qing is the enormous degree to which internal borders had been codified and policed, and the severe consequences such borders have had for the post-imperial communities. The histories of nationalism of both the Mongols and the Chinese are deeply intertwined with border maintenance and border dismantlement. I propose therefore to take a closer look at the internal borders within the Qing Empire and the nationalist backlashes. Below I will first look at the Mongolian and Chinese internal borders separately before examining the common border between them.

Inter-Mongolian borders

The Manchu Qing governance of the Mongols has had a profound long-term impact on the Mongols. On the one hand, the Manchu unified all the disparate Mongolian groups by alternate means of alliance and conquest. It was under the Qing administration that the ethnonym *Mongol* was used to override such ethnonyms as Oirad and Horchin, expanding the name that had earlier been monopolized by the Chinggisid six *tumens* (see Crossley 2006). Almost all the Mongols, except the Buryats in southern Siberia and the Kalmyks who migrated to the Volga region, were administered by the *Lifan Yuan* (Board of Colonial Affairs, M. *yadayadu mongyul-un törü-yi jasaqu yabudal-un yamun*), inculcating a sense of unified Mongolian identity as opposed to the Manchu, Tibetans, Muslims and Han. Segregation, according to Mark Elliott, was a key Qing mode of governance, that is, segregating the Manchus from the conquered and/or subordinate peoples in order to maintain what he calls "ethnic sovereignty".[9] The Qing segregation policy was, in his view, partly responsible for the institutionalisation of ethnic groups, each of whom was not only named, but also segregated from others.

On the other hand, this ethnically-unified Mongolia was not to be a unitary political entity.[10] Instead, they were subdivided into numerous smaller units, from *aimag* (tribes) and *chuulgan* (leagues) to *hoshuun* (banners). The six leagues of inner *jasag* (later known as Inner Mongolia) were divided into 49 banners, and the Khalkha (later known as Outer Mongolia) were divided into 81 banners. There were also numerous other banners outside the two large entities. Borders were demarcated and policed between tribes, leagues and even between banners. *Karun* (M. *Haruul*, C. *Kalun*) border control stations were set up along borders, and stone cairns called *oboo* were built between *karuns*. At strategic places, each *karun* was manned by 30–40 soldiers from Manchu garrison armies stationed in Suiyuan, Ningxia, Uliastai and other places; they would patrol along

---

9   The Manchu segregated themselves from the Chinese wherever they set up garrison cities.

10   See Johan Elverskog (1996) for the transformation of the Mongol polity from *ulus* to banner.

the border every day to the *oboo* between *karun*s, where they exchanged information with patrols from the other *karun*. This was called *khaich yavakh*, scissor-walking, a metaphor implying that the soldiers were cutting the borderline like scissors, making a radical partition. These *karun*s and *oboo*s would be checked by Manchu garrison generals once a month and they would be inspected by officials from the Lifan Yuan in Beijing occasionally. No tribal, league, or banner nobles and subjects were permitted to cross banner borders, nor were they allowed to marry across banners without authorization. The *karun* guards would make their record every day and the inspection report would be sent to Beijing regularly (Baoyinchaoketu 2003).

Punishment was severe for any violations of borders, trespassing either into *"neidi"*, that is, inland China, or into other's territory. For instance, *Daqing Huidian Shili*, published in the twenty-third year of Jiaqing reign (1814), recorded the following: "Originally, should there be border violations from Mongolia, a prince would be fined 10 horses, *zasag*, *beile*, *beizi*, and *gong* 7 horses, *taiji* five horses, and commoner, a cattle". By the second decade of the nineteenth century, the fine had been increased tenfold for aristocrats, and a commoner would lose all his property, including himself, which would be awarded to the whistle-blower (Huidianguan 2006: vol. 979, pp. 237–39). The fine soared further towards the end of the Qing, betraying an increase in violations and their seriousness.[11]

Such stringent prohibition of trespassing borders was to mould a divided unity of the Mongols under the Qing *gurun* or state. All Mongols were to identify with the Qing state, not as a politically unified nation (*ulus*), but through the banner system. It was intended to prevent the Mongols from realigning with each other and challenging the Qing, as it categorically prohibited princes from conquering each other, which was the classical mode for the rise of power among the nomads. Consolidation of the banner administrative system was designed to ensure political stability in the backyard of the Qing.

The long-term effect of the Qing governance was that there remained a general sense of "Mongolness", aided by a historical memory and maintained by the Qing administration, and yet, the Mongol groups

---

11   Border clashes increased over years, sometimes escalating into major incidents. In 1937, without the Qing imperial border control, the Otog and Ushin banners of the Yekejuu League resorted to an all-out war over border violations, lasting for a year, and inviting mediation from the Chinese Communist Party. See Lifanyuan (1998).

were deeply divided and suspicious of each other. This was the imperial legacy. After the collapse of the Qing, Mongolian nationalists did not find themselves facing a group of ethnically unconscious herders who could be easily molded into a Mongol nation, as Eugen Weber's (1976) peasants would turn into Frenchmen; instead, they were confronted with a unified Mongol people with a clear consciousness of who they were, and yet who were deeply divided institutionally. In 1925, when the Kharachin Mongol nationalist leaders of the Inner Mongolian People's Revolutionary Party came to Ordos, they were largely rejected by the Ordos members of the Party who formed the bulk of the Party's army. This Party was perhaps the first ever Inner Mongolian effort for a united action, but failed ignominiously thanks to the deeply entrenched banner division (Atwood 2002). Mongolian institutional division also frustrated the earlier effort for unification between Outer Mongolia and Inner Mongolia in 1911–1915. So did it lead to the internal split of Prince De's Mongolian autonomy movement in 1936, not of course without external pressure by the local Chinese warlord Fu Zuoyi (Bulag 2010b).

Nationalist Mongolian frustration at internal division was conducive to mythologising any sign of unity. Thus the "April the Third 1946 Meeting" (*4.3 Huiyi*) between Ulanhu and Hafenga/Tümürbagan has attained a huge significance in the historiography of modern Inner Mongolia, celebrated as the first success in the unification of Eastern and Western (Inner) Mongolia. With unity thus becoming the highest ideal of the Mongols, it is not surprising that the Inner Mongolia Autonomous Region has been characterised as a unitary or unified autonomy (*tongyi zizhi*), not only for overriding and demolishing Chinese provincial boundaries, but also for establishing a Mongol polity in which Mongols from different banners, leagues and tribes, for the first time in the history of Inner Mongolia, could come together (Bulag 2010c).

This is not to say that internal divisions have disappeared: far from it. What I am suggesting is that modern Mongolian nationalism has been built upon the historical Mongol identity created in the thirteenth and fourteenth centuries, and institutionalised during the Qing Empire, and yet it is also a violent protest at the Qing imperial partitioning of the Mongols into numerous small groups. Mongol nationalism works on two sets of imperial legacy: first the boundary created and policed by the Manchu between the Mongols and the Chinese, which has been accepted as national border of the Mongols and which they fight to defend, but not always successfully;

second, the borders between Mongol banners, which they think illegitimate and which they vow to dismantle or overcome, but not always successfully, either. The ethnic groups the Manchu helped maintain – Manchu, Mongols, Tibetans, Muslims, and Han – were internally divided groups. It is true that all communities show "a degree of unity to the outside world while simultaneously remaining a site of internal tension" (Bellér-Hann 2008: 16). But the ethnic groups that emerged out of the Qing Empire were intended to be so, and this has been recognised by nationalists. This recognition gave rise to border-breaking political programs.

Breaking down provincial borders

The Manchu segregationist border building was not limited to non-Han peoples; even the Han Chinese were segregated from each other largely along provincial lines. The Qing provincial administration followed Ernest Gellner's (1983) classical agrarian political structure, that is, a pyramid structure with the emperor at the top who ruled, through literati officials, vertically insulated communities, which were not allowed mutual communication without authorisation from the centre. In the Qing dynasty, this was done through provincial governors appointed by the imperial court. Qing-created provinces became cultural communities with distinct dialects, mind-sets, local cuisines and customs, even though they were unified by literary high culture and the imperial court.

One of the sagas of Chinese political modernity was a fight between nationalism and provincialism. Towards the end of the Qing dynasty, as the Manchu rulers began to rely on the Chinese for both defending China against western powers and for quelling Muslim rebellions in Gansu, Chinese provinces emerged as autonomous political entities, eventually defying the Manchu-dominated Qing centre when the latter was weakened by the western powers. Provinces were not initially granted any autonomy from the central authority, as were Mongolian banners. However, once the ideal of self-rule was introduced, especially in relation to a perceived alien empire, it was the Qing-created provincial lines that became the natural divisions for the new political articulation of self-rule. In 1908 the Qing court officially recognised and even promoted provincial self-rule as a new governmental measure to salvage the crumbling empire, thereby opening Pandora's Box. "Hunan for the Hunanese", "Guangdong for the Guangdong people" and so on became the slogans of the epoch, and provinces became the most important bastion for anti-Manchu activities. And yet the provincial divisions had become equally entrenched, challenging a unified action among Han anti-Manchu revolutionaries. Sun Yatsen's *Xinzhonghui*, established in 1894, was an exclusivist Guangdong organisation, and the leading revolutionaries were divided into provincial factions, each insisting on their own provinces as the basis for launching the anti-Qing uprising (Liu 1999; Su 2009).

However, once the Qing was overthrown, leading Chinese nationalists envisioned that China's power must come from a unitary and centralised state, an ideal stemming from their observation of the rise of modern Japan. In this vision, provincial autonomy was deemed a challenge to the new national centre, fragmenting the new nation into numerous local kingdoms ruled by military strongmen. Thus, prior to the 1927 northern campaign by the Chinese Nationalist Party (Guomindang), China was beset with wars among provincial strongmen, which contributed to the Guomindang's desire for a unitary and centralised polity. The debate between a unitary state model and a confederate state model was ultimately won on the battle front, with the nationalists militarily unifying China in 1928, discrediting the provincial strongmen as "local warlords", and local provincial autonomy as feudal separatist rule (*fengjian geju*) (Duara 1995; Fitzgerald 2002).

The Guomindang dream for a unitary state was realised by the CCP in 1949. In the first four years of the People's Republic until 1954, province was made a second tier administrative unit, below *da xingzhengqu*, great administrative region, of which China had six, plus one autonomous region, i.e. the Inner Mongolia Autonomous Region.

As this cursory examination of provincialism shows, Chinese nationalism has had to grapple with internal borders instituted by the Manchu, and this continues to be a thorny issue. Provincial identity often contributes to political factions in the ruling Communist Party, and the Party seldom appoints a provincial native to the position of the province's party secretary. The autonomist tendency of Chinese provinces and the stringent measures adopted against it challenges one of the political mythologies of China that a unified China was achieved as early as the Qin dynasty two thousand years ago. It also behooves us to remember that provinces were first set up by the Mongols during the Yuan, abolished by the Ming, and restored by the Qing, which divided the Chinese regions into eighteen provinces, which were together called "China Proper" by Westerners.

Inter-ethnic border or international border?

As we have shown, nationalists reject internal borders; Chinese and the Mongol nationalists are in agreement that the Qing imperial governance was predicated on a divide and rule policy. What they do not agree on, however, is what to do with the inter-ethnic borders erected between the Mongols and the Chinese.

By the end of the Qing dynasty, Chinese nationalists had largely accepted the eighteen provinces created by the Qing as *Zhongguo Benbu* (China Proper), and their original ambition was no more than to drive the Manchu out of these provinces. The nationalist flag used during the Wuchang Uprising on the 10th October 1911 was called "flag of the iron blood and eighteen stars" (*tiexue shibaxing qi*) – eighteen stars representing eighteen Chinese provinces. Although on the 1 January 1912 the Republic of China instated a five-colour striped flag symbolising a newly declared union of five races (*wuzu gonghe*), the flag of iron blood and eighteen stars was retained; it was used as flag of the army until 1928, when the Guomindang established a new National Government. Small China-ism died hard.

Until the 1930s, even the Chinese Communists regarded the Great Wall as the border between the Han and the Mongols, as was evidenced in Mao Zedong's proclamation to the people of Inner Mongolia on behalf of the Central Government of the Chinese Soviet People's Republic on the 10 December 1935, avowing to return Mongol land occupied by the Chinese to the Mongols:

> First, Baotuwan, which was occupied by Jing Xiuyue, and the area which was occupied by Gao Shixiu, along with the two salt ponds, will be returned to the Inner Mongolian people. Moreover, the area along the Great Wall, including places such as Ningtiaoliang, Anbian, and Dingbian, is designated as a commercial area, in order to promote bilateral trade between you and us (Mao Zedong 1992 [1935]: 72).

Mongol nationalists also accepted the Qing ethnic border along the Great Wall and the northern part of the Willow Palisade as the national border of the Mongols. In 1913–14 the government of Bogd Khan Mongolia sent five columns of cavalry to liberate Inner Mongolia only to lose its own independence in 1915, becoming an autonomy recognising China's suzerainty. In 1945 the Mongolian People's Republic army marched into Inner Mongolia against Japan, and briefly entertained the idea of unifying

Inner Mongolia with the MPR only to gain formal recognition of its independence by the Republic of China in 1946 (Liu 2006). Henceforth, pan-Mongolism died as a political programme, and Inner Mongolia was to emerge as an autonomous region within China. When the region took its current shape in 1956, it lost a quarter of the Mongolian population, including the Mongoljin, to the neighbouring provinces, and most of its land along the Great Wall and the Willow Palisade.

However, while the Mongols continue to think in terms of the borders created by the Qing, this "national geography" has been challenged by the Chinese. In the early 1990s Lin Gan, arguably the most prominent Chinese historian of the northern peoples, furiously debunked the idea that the Great Wall and the Willow Palisade should be seen as the national border of China. He was careful not to criticise the independent state of Mongolia, but blame two external imperialists, the Japanese and the Soviets, for introducing this idea. He denounced the Soviets for following the Japanese assertion of "Beyond the Great Wall is no longer China" by quoting the following passage, a statement issued by the Soviet government in June 1969, at the height of the Sino-Soviet confrontation:

The border of China in the north is marked by the Great Wall. Prior to China's conquest by the Manchu, the northern border of China proper ran along the Great Wall. In the west, China's border did not go beyond Gansu and Sichuan provinces. The Willow Palisade of the Qing dynasty was the northeastern border of China at that time (Lin 2007: 50).

In challenging this statement, Lin Gan advanced a new argument that all the nomads that had appeared in Chinese history, and all those who had invaded China, were *a priori* "northern nationalities of ancient China". Borders and divisions were thus internalised or nationalised and dismissed as of little or no political and international significance. This argument somewhat resonates with the theory of Fei Xiaotong (1989), China's foremost anthropologist, who famously claimed in 1989 that non-Han peoples in the past were Chinese except that they were not aware of that identity, and their consciousness as Chinese became apparent only after the invasion of imperialists, i.e. Europeans in the mid-nineteenth century. In this discourse, Inner Asian conquests were rendered no more than a domestic violence between brotherly ethnic groups of the newly-imagined Chinese nation – *zhonghua minzu*.

Gehe: inter-ethnic psychological barrier

The domestication of the non-Han peoples as sibling ethnic groups of the Chinese nation is of course characteristic of nationalism in general, but the vehemence in Chinese hostility toward inter-ethnic boundary requires further commentary. For what is at issue is not necessarily the physical border, which has long crumbled, but rather the psychological barrier, that is, the refusal of the Mongols (and some other groups) to identify with the Chinese even though they have been incorporated into China. This psychological barrier is best denoted by the Chinese concept of "*gehe*", referring not just to a barrier, but an estrangement, a tendency to move away, thereby having an effect on someone from whom one moves away. More importantly, *gehe* between two persons or entities is often attributed to a third party; as such, it may not be just an innocent lack of communication, but may be conducive to realignment of relationship. *Gehe* must be acted upon if it is not to adversely affect oneself. *Gehe* is a triangular effect.

Robert Lee is, in my view, correct in arguing that the Willow Palisade was erected not just for preventing Chinese immigration into the naturally better endowed Manchuria and for preserving the Manchu culture and identity. It was primarily designed to prevent an alliance between the Mongols and the Chinese, minimising their contact. "The Manchus had conquered China by forging an alliance composed of themselves, the Mongols, and dissident Chinese. As rulers of China, they were determined not to let such an alliance be formed again" (Lee 1970: 21). One may add that the Manchu rulers must have remembered that their former dynasty Jin was annihilated by none other than an alliance between the Mongols and the Song dynasty in the thirteenth century.

If we accept this thesis, then, the Qing segregationist policy was to prevent alliances and the Willow Palisade was a wedge driven between the Mongols and Chinese, who were pit against each other. This was because in the heartland of Manchuria there were already significant numbers of Chinese prior to the Qing, and many remained during the Qing period. I am thus tempted to suggest that the *kezhang toushi* ritual fight mentioned at the opening pages of this paper is a historical memory of a Mongolian perimeter defence against encroachment from land hungry Chinese migrants or famine refugees. The Willow Palisade was only part of an elaborate Qing segregation measure. Indeed, throughout Mongolia, while the Manchu bannermen policed the internal Mongol borders, the Mongols were charged to defend the Qing-Russia border, and the numerous *karuns* along the Willow

Palisade were manned by soldiers of the Chinese eight banners under the close supervision of Manchu bannermen. It was a classical imperial mode of playing off one party against another.

A far greater *gehe* between the Mongols and the Chinese was created on the cultural and psychological front. The prohibitions of communication between the Mongols and Chinese prescribed in *Lifan Yuan Zeli* were unprecedented and comprehensive:

1.   Mongols were not allowed to marry Chinese (Lifanyuan 1998: 249).
2.   Mongol nobles of all ranks were prohibited from hiring Chinese to teach Chinese language or use them as scribes.
3.   Chinese language was prohibited in writing the Mongol official documents, memorials or letters.
4.   Mongols were prohibited from using Chinese names (ibid.: 365).

This was radical "multiculturalism". Most commentators have viewed this segregationist policy as a Manchu fear for Chinese "polluting" the Mongols and undermining their military prowess, rendering them useless. Today the predominant Mongol nationalist assessment of the Manchu promotion of Tibetan Buddhism among the Mongols is pathological, believing that the Manchu deliberately tried to weaken the Mongols. The following passage from Qianlong's "*Lama Shuo*" (*On Lamas*) is quoted by Sechin Jagchid (1988) to this effect:

> The Yellow Religion of the interior and the outside was generally governed by these two persons, the Dalai Lama and the Panchen Erdeni. All the Mongolian tribes whole-heartedly submit themselves. The development of the Yellow Religion is intended to pacify the Mongols. This matter is not insignificant and therefore should be protected but is not a policy similar to that of the Yuan Dynasty, which deviously flattered the Tibetan monks.

A huge contradiction can be detected in the interpretations of the Qing approaches to the Mongols: the Manchu did not want the Chinese to weaken the Mongols, but the Manchu used Tibetan Buddhism to weaken them. If there is any logic in this contradiction, then, what is clear is that the Mongols were not barred from accessing Tibetan Buddhism and culture as they were from Chinese language and culture. I would argue that the Manchu measures were not necessarily intended for preserving the Mongol prowess or weakening them, but rather for rendering them "submissive" or loyal to the Manchu. Nothing would work better than entering the Mongolian religious system by making the Manchu emperor become Manjushri, one of the highest bodhisattvas (Farquhar 1978). As the Kangxi Emperor believed that the Khalkha Mongol defence against the Russians was "more solid than the Great Wall", so were Mongols expected to be more solid than the Great Wall in their defence against the Chinese. And nothing would be more effective than creating *gehe* between them, making them psychologically distant from each other but identify with the Manchu. As such, the Qing dynasty was not a simple segregationist Empire, hardening the boundaries of ethnic groups. It was also Georg Simmel's *tertius gaudens* (laughing third) (Wolff 1950).

The long-term effect of the Qing policy was a profound distrust and fear of the Chinese on the part of the non-Han peoples, to whom the Chinese often appeared like ghostly figures. I myself can remember vividly my own fear of Chinese strangers in the early 1970s. We were living in the countryside, and the closest neighbour was about three kilometres away. One night, my sister and I discovered huge footprints behind our house. For several nights, we huddled together with our mother, believing that the footprints must be those of a Chinese, who might have long daggers. This fear was as much a result of Chinese persecution of the Mongols during the Cultural Revolution[12] as a historical memory.

Perhaps an institutionalisation of this fear can be found in numerous Mongolian fables of *altan unag*, golden pony. In these fables, which can be found in many parts of Inner Mongolia, but not in Mongolia, the local *nutag* (homeland, allocated pastureland) is rich, lush with grass and animals. Many places are called *bayan*, rich: *bayangol, bayanbogd, bayantal* and so on. These places have treasures, which are represented by golden ponies that peacefully graze the pasture, but disappear when there is turmoil. In some regions, golden ponies or golden calves are said to reside in the lake. Some fables have it that the golden animal is stolen by an alien, usually Chinese, and sometimes yellow-haired Russians (Chen 2001; cf. Bulag 2010b: Ch 5). The morals of the fables are that the Mongols should engage in both "perimeter defence" and "social boundary defence" (Cashdan 1983) against the Chinese and Russians – which was indeed the historical role assigned to the Mongols by the Manchu in the Qing dynasty.

The deeply entrenched Mongol fear and distrust of the Chinese, long nourished by the Manchu, did not bode well for the Manchu who identified with the Chinese towards the end of the Qing. In 1902, the Qing opened the Mongolian border to allow Chinese to settle in Mongolia as the Manchu did

---

12   The most authoritative book on the subject is Qi (2010).

to their own homeland Manchuria, a policy deeply resented by the Manchu's former Mongol aristocratic allies. Violence and turmoil induced by massive Chinese settler colonialism prompted the Mongols to declare independence in December 1911 before the Qing abdication, turning to none other than the Manchu's nemesis, the Russians. Subsequently, the Chinese nationalists' solution to the so-called "Mongolian question" was none other than measures of dismantling Mongolian administrations, further Chinese settlement and promotion of Chinese language and cultural assimilation on all fronts. This is politicide *par excellence*.[13] These measures were to eradicate the alienation of heart or *gehe*, which was blamed on the Manchu imperial segregation policy, and external imperialists such as Russia and Japan. Nationalist China was now out to bring down all physical, cultural and psychological barriers and borders between the Mongols and the Chinese. Unfortunately for the Guomindang, this pushed the Mongols further away into the fold of the Japanese and the communists, both Russian and Chinese.

Concluding remarks: toward a triangular conceptualisation of border

In this paper I have argued that Chinese and Mongolian nationalists have reacted strongly against – and continue to grapple with – the borders and boundaries instituted by the Manchu in late imperial China and Inner Asia. I have mentioned two kinds of borders, one physical and the other cultural and mental. While the old physical borders such as the Great Wall, the Willow Palisade, or the border posts of *karun*s and *oboo*s may have long become defunct, the cultural and mental borders die hard. They continue to frustrate both Mongol nationalists and Chinese nationalists.

The ideal of any nationalism is of course to build a homogeneous nation. What is new in the case of China and Inner Asia is that nationalists are confronted not with "a plate of loose sand", to use Sun Yat-sen's famous metaphor, not with rural communities who could be easily moulded into nations, but rather with ethnic communities whose borders have been demarcated and maintained, and yet who are internally divided. In this regard, the Qing dynasty does not fit the popular image of an empire maintaining loose control over various communities. It bears all the hallmarks of a European colonial state whose governance of diverse populations was predicated on

---

13   For the use of "politicide" instead of "genocide" in the Chinese context, see Bulag 2010a.

divide and rule. Anthropologists and political scientists have long noted the European colonial production of cultures and ethnic groups.[14] And yet, unlike a modern European colonial state that instituted indirect rule, the Qing did not stand aloof and above all groups as a disinterested sovereign. Rather, Qing emperors tried to win the loyalty of the subject groups by identifying with their cultural and religious systems, and drove wedges between the subject groups making them checkmate each other, so that they could sleep soundly at night, laughing in their dreams.

We thus find a unique border or boundary formation in China and Inner Asia. Boundary or border is both closed and open. For instance, the internal boundary either among the Chinese or among the Mongols was closed to their fellow ethnics, but open to the Manchu. The closed border was an antagonistic one, with both sides treating each other as foes, engaging in both perimeter defence and social boundary defence. These defences were as inter-ethnic as intra-ethnic. The open border was one erected between the Manchu and each of the ethnic groups within the Empire. This border was not symmetrically guarded as in the case of closed border. Since the border around the Manchu was erected for the purpose of maintaining the "ethnic sovereignty" of the Manchu, it was closed to non-Manchus who were prohibited from crossing borders. The Manchu, on the other hand, as the master race of the Empire, had access to every inch of territories "under the heaven" – *tianxie* – as it were, which were simultaneously territories of "our great Qing" (*wo da qing*).

I am now close to proposing a new conceptualisation of border. Instead of seeing the border as simply lying between two groups, border in the Qing was often triangulated and as such they were politically *affective* borders. Invested with legitimacy or illegitimacy, morality or immorality, affective borders are targets of either radical closure or opening up. If this conceptualisation is valid, then borders in China and Inner Asia are not simply arbitrary demarcations preventing free movement of goods and people, where states exercise their maximum power. An affective border defines the existential essence of a group, which may see it as legitimate so as to defend it with all its might, or as illegitimate to so as to dismantle it.

In this light, we may go beyond the initial argument advanced in this paper that nationalists have had to grapple with borders set up by

---

14   The most devastating critique comes from Mahmood Mamdani (1996; 2002), who attributed the African tribalism at large and the Rwandan Tutsi-Hutu mutual genocide in particular to European colonial policies.

empires. Nor should we stop at saying that nationalists reject internal borders and only accept external borders. To the extent that we are dealing with multi-ethnic political entities, borders and boundaries are actually a political technology not specific to imperial conquerors. If the essence of the political lies in the distinction between friend and enemy (Schmitt 2007), imperialists or nationalists or communists must attend to organisational matters if they were to build a community. Collaboration, as I have argued elsewhere, is endemic in nationalism. Collaborative nationalism is never binary; it is at least triangular. Knowing when and how to open and close boundary and with which partner is an art that is essential for one's political survival.

In a similar way to the Manchu, the Chinese Communist Party (CCP) made an alliance with non-Han ethnic groups in its struggle with the Chinese Nationalist Party. In this collaboration, the CCP insisted that the minorities maintain boundary with the Guomindang, and for this purpose, the CCP advocated ethnic self-determination and promised ethnic autonomy. The Inner Mongolia Autonomous Government established in 1947 was supported and led by the CCP; its border was open to the CCP. However, it closed its border to the Guomindang, against whom the Mongol autonomists fought heroically, supporting the CCP. This collaboration was mutually beneficial, as it helped the CCP to win the Civil War, and helped the Mongols to secure an autonomous region.

However, the CCP alliance with the Mongols and other non-Han peoples were predicated on a discourse of presenting themselves as Good Han and denouncing the Guomindang (GMD) as Bad Han (Bulag 2012). This was an effective strategy insofar as the CCP won the minorities to its side. What the CCP did not realise was that they had subjected themselves to the judgement of the minorities whose trust of the CCP depended on whether it could continue to be Good Han. Any Han chauvinism, which the CCP is often susceptible to, is thus seen as blurring the boundary between the CCP and its nemesis the GMD, thereby incurring strong resentment from the minorities who feel betrayed. Minority criticism of the CCP trespassing its own line with the Guomindang had thus been blamed by some within the Party as a result of the very autonomy the Party had awarded to minorities. From the late 1950s, and especially during the Cultural Revolution, minorities were openly attacked for distancing from China, from the CCP and for splittism.

Today, although the CCP upholds the system of regional nationality autonomy as a result of the catastrophe during the Cultural Revolution, some within and without the Party, and especially those in academia, including many anthropologists, fear that the autonomy system and the category of nationality itself have not achieved the original purpose of integrating minorities with the Chinese in the form of *minzu tuanjie*. Rather, they have induced more *gehe*, estrangement between Chinese and minorities. They are said to have entrenched internal ethnic borders, which are in the process of externalisation, being turned into the border of China. A Chinese nation, it is now asserted, needs no internal borders, either ethnic or administrative-cum-territorial. The Chinese nation is imagined as a national cosmopolitan space, in which no bound autonomous nationalities have any room for existence. Ethnic groups are no longer allowed to have any line of demarcation (*jiexian*) with the Chinese. Chinese intellectuals now openly embrace Deleuze and Guattarian nomadology, using it to urge the descendants of nomads to live up to this ideal. To the ears of the Mongoljin Mongols at the foot of the Willow Palisade, this nomadological argument sounds so alien. They have rolled up their sleeves ready to fight the last ditch of battle of defence, a battle they have been fighting since the first years of the Qing dynasty. In Xinjiang, while the political (autonomy) boundary has long been trespassed, the ethnic boundary is most vehemently maintained by both the Han Chinese and the Uyghurs (Topin 2011).

Today, inter-ethnic *gehe* is as deep as ever, perhaps deeper, not because there is lack of emphasis on national unity. To the country, this *gehe* has gone deeper precisely because of the overwhelming Chinese nationalist attempt at breaking down all boundaries to create a national empire. A new Chinese national empire by necessity will not need a Great Wall to block its conquest, but there is no reason to believe that it will not erect new boundaries even as it tries to pull down old ones to achieve its purpose.

4. Concepts of "Russia" and their Relation to the Border with China

Caroline Humphrey

If one thinks about what is distinctive about the Russian eastern border with China in comparison to other international borders, two elements are striking: first, that this is a centuries-old border between two post-imperial states with markedly different cultures; and secondly, that the peoples indigenous to the frontier regions, such as Buryats and Evenki, belong to the respective large "civilisations" only by a process of (incomplete) incorporation. In many respects they have more in common with their fellows immediately across the border than they do with the metropolitan centres (see Namsaraeva, this volume). One task therefore would be to characterise the social forms of frontier and cross-border populations, paying attention to their elusive features such as transient networks and non-national kinds of identity. But another task, the main focus of this paper, logically takes precedence – since the border was created in the seventeenth century by the two states of Russia and Manchu China and not by local ethnic groups – is to understand how the overarching and contrasting political cultures have respectively conceived the state and constructed its borders. This chapter, focusing on Russia, will suggest first that the existence and positioning of international borders, in particular that with China, have played an active role in certain influential conceptualisation of "Russia" as a political formation; and second, it will make the reciprocal argument that the historical evolution of notions of Russia, through the

 DOI: 10.11647/OBP.0026.04

Tsarist Empire, the USSR, and the Russian Federation, has then impacted on how the border has been treated by the state.

The anthropology of borders has broadly taken two directions, either to emphasise the people living in frontier regions and moving across borders, or to focus on how borders are conceived as more or less powerful presences of the state (see discussion in Radu 2010: 419–10). A fruitful synthesis by Peter Sahlins makes the point that the political boundaries imposed by states have to be actualised in practice by diverse local actors with their own various interests. He argued in the case of the border between France and Spain that the presence of politically-divided ethnic groups living across the boundary "makes the problem of nation building all the more salient" (1989: 22) – and that in frontier zones of "cultural bilingualism" the process of creating French or Spanish citizens involves the agency of the people inhabiting frontier zones as well as central state projects.[1] This perspective is particularly useful for former empires like Russia and China, which both have large and heterogeneous minority populations in frontier areas.

This chapter will focus on one specific input in such processes, the role of national imagination – the changing conceptions of "what Russia is" as a civilisation – in the construction of the eastern border with China, and it attempts to explain thereby the ideological load on this border and its self-defining, other-excluding quality. I should be clear that this paper does not itself attempt to erect a model or "ideal type" of Russia,[2] but rather to point to the main streams of Russian thought on this matter, particularly in the present day. They are relevant to political policy because countless Russian (and non-Russian) writers, officials and politicians have expounded on the theme normatively, i.e. with the intent of making interventions in political projects. Yet, as I shall suggest in line with Sahlins (1989), the *local interpretations* of such ideas are currently at least as striking (if not more so) than those of the state centre.

The body of social thought that interprets Russia as a civilisation is not of course the only one in existence. Not just western but also many Russian commentators have rejected such an approach to understanding the country. For in this case "civilisation" implies not just an assemblage of mobile traits that adhere over geographical space (as was proposed by Marcel Mauss in 1930), but a cultural structure based on certain essential

---

1   The notion of "cultural bilingualism" comes from Yuri Lotman (1984: 3–35) quoted in A. J. Reiber (2003: 27).
2   See critique by Roberts Crews (2010) of such modes of historical writing.

values. There are plenty of critiques of contemporary attempts to prolong nineteenth-century debates about such an "idea" of Russia, exposing them as academically bankrupt, out-dated and ideologically isolationist (e.g. Miller 2008). But it is easy to see why, with the demise of the Soviet Union and consequent radical border changes, the question of what would constitute the unity of the resulting country would urgently present itself to its rulers – especially for generations used to there being such an idea in its Soviet version. They see that the global market economy into which Russia has plunged not only fails to provide such a notion but would tend to obscure it. Consequently, as Kaganskii has observed, there is a renewed demand for schemes and analogies for "a great united state power" (2004: 201). From an anthropological point of view, the normative character of such civilizational models is what makes them interesting.

This chapter will first describe some historical and contemporary models of Russia as a civilisation, along with Russian critiques of them that nevertheless keep the discussion within the civilisation paradigm. The last section of the paper discusses the implications of such ideas at the Russo-China border itself.

Changing ideas of Russia as a Eurasian country

In the wake of the defeat in the Crimean war in 1856 Russian governmental elites rejected the earlier Petrine vision of Russia as an essentially European country and turned their attention toward its Asian hinterlands beyond the Urals. Even before this, Russia had been envisioned as having a "manifest destiny", both to tame wild Siberian Nature and to civilise the stagnant Asian societies of the East. In the 1840s, Russia was already described as having a "particular mission among humanity... Russia is an entire Europe unto itself, a Europe that is intermediary between Europe and Asia, between Africa and America: a marvellous, unknown, and new country" (Balasoglo quoted in Bassin 1999: 86). Such were the grandiloquent terms in which "Russia" was discussed, but at the same time strategic and practical opportunities beckoned. General Murav'ev's campaigns to the east were impelled on the one hand by fear that Russia's Far Eastern interests were threatened by the imperialist European moves into China, and on the other by a desire to join with them in appropriating Chinese spoils. He fashioned a grand plan to overturn the border agreed in the seventeenth century and move decisively into the Amur region, eventually annexing this weakly-controlled and under-populated area in

1858 and 1860 (Bassin 1999: 116–19).[3] Not content with this success, military voices still spoke of a further expansion southwards into Manchuria. With explicit and warm reference made to the "manifest destiny" of the United States (to push westwards), the sentiment was "you will not hold back Russia's universal destiny" (Bassin 1999: 116, 218).

Such visions of Russia as rightfully present *in* Asia were not transformed into an explicit *Eurasianist* doctrine until the 1920s. The émigré authors of the movement put forward the idea that Russia is not a European country, nor an Asian one, but is "Eurasia", a separate civilisation located between the two. Russian nationalism was not distinct from, but aligned with, an imperial vision of the entire country. According to this theory, while the West was in decline, Russia, including its diverse native cultures, would experience an imminent rise and bear a civilising mission towards the East. The Eurasianists argued that the continent must develop its own independent, self-reliant, non-maritime economy; they believed that the Soviet Union could transform into this harmonious utopia, and that it was capable of evolving away from atheist and proletarian doctrines to become a national, Orthodox Christian country. A bridge between this movement, which had died away by the 1930s, and the Neo-Eurasianism that is influential today, was the work of Lev Gumilev (e.g. 2002 [1989]). His books began to be published in the 1980s and are still immensely popular.[4] Like the earlier Eurasianists, Gumilev also emphasised the "natural" determinism of continental geography. Abandoning the previous emphasis on Christianity, Gumilev extolled the strength of the great steppe empires that flourished (achieved "passionary" vigour) on the basis of their fitness with particular ecological-historical-geographical conjunctions.

Contemporary Neo-Eurasianism, whose most noted leader is Aleksandr Dugin, has taken these basic ideas, re-infused them with Russian nationalism and Orthodox Christian messianism,[5] and extrapolated them into contemporary global conditions. Dugin writes that Russia is God-chosen and destined (*obrechena*) to become the leader of a new

---

3   In 1858, at the conference at Aigun, Russia acquired the territory on the north bank of the Amur, and at the Treaty of Peking, signed in November 1860, exclusive rights over previously jointly held territory from the Ussuri east to the ocean (Bassin 1999: 218).

4   An indication of Gumilev's popularity among Central Asian leaders is that the Kazakh president Nursultan Nazarbaev ordered the L. N. Gumilev Eurasian University to be built opposite his palace in the new capital, Astana.

5   Neo-Eurasians have resurrected the idea that Russia is the "Third Rome", or successor to the Roman and Byzantine empires (Sidorov 2006).

planetary (Eurasian) alternative to the Western version of global relations: unipolar globalism (Dugin 2002: 13; see also Bassin 2008: 294). The idea of Empire (*Imperiya*) is central to Eurasia and the Russian people who "in their essence *are* the empire-building process, the willful geo-political factor in creating the State of the Absolute Idea" (Dugin 2004: 348–49). Dugin's geo-political vision, Bassin argues, diverges from the prewar versions of Eurasianism, since its principle is opposition to the global project of the United States after the Cold War. One of its early, more extreme, forms envisages a burst to the South, i.e. beyond the former Soviet borders, to assure the "natural-historical line of development and preservation of the territorial integrity of Russia" (Zhirinovskii 1993: blurb), while Dugin has rhetorically sought to rally the "brotherly" people of the Eurasian *landed* continent struggling against the hegemony of the *sea-born* hegemony of the Atlantic powers (Dugin 2004: 422–33). Neo-Eurasianism must be seen as a strategic response to the *post-Soviet* political environment (Bassin 2008: 283–85).

At the same time, there are strains in Neo-Eurasianism that return to certain themes of the nineteenth century: the civilising mission, the "organic" harmony that melds together the diverse peoples of Russia, the anti-mercantilism, the idea that Russia must flourish in a different, spiritually pure way. Such views have influential contemporary proponents, such as Mikhail Titarenko, director of the Institute of Far Eastern Studies, who writes that Eurasianism espouses "the principles of collectiveness (*sobornost'*), interdependence, mutual aid, co-operation of individuals and peoples, dialogue based on equal rights, of co-development, of harmony and of mutual complementarities in the relations between the civilisations and peoples of Russia, with a united common historic destiny" (Titarenko 1998: 27). This vision is implicitly opposed to the rationalist, competitive, individualistic zone of "the West" and its eastern flank is bounded by the discursive void of the other zone that is alien, China.[6]

It is not difficult to see, at a very basic level, why such a doctrine must assign great – but one-sided – importance to borders. If "geography is the fate of Russia" (Dugin 2004: 272), if "Eurasia" is defined first of all by what it is not (that is not "the West" and not "Asia") and it is conceived as a unitary, autarchic civilisation, then its external contours are *constitutional*

---

6   I have been unable to find a reference to China in the 507 pages of Dugin's volume outlining his geo-political strategy except as an un-named "zone of strategic interest" to both the Eurasian and the Pacific Ocean belts (2004: 181).

in what "Eurasia" is. Let us now, however, look at some Russian critiques of the idea to gain some further insights into how borders are conceived in a broader civilisational analysis.

Russia as a "border civilisation"

Accepting Russia's interstitial Eurasian position, though not the Eurasianist doctrine, some writers have argued that the whole of Russia is a border (*pogranichnyi*) type of civilisation (Shemyakin and Shemyakina 2004). Such a civilisation, balancing itself between alien "barbaric" others, manifests the restlessness of borders. Being defined primarily by the in-betweenness of its position, it accords priority to natural conditions and to maintaining the wide spaces of its realm. Because of its interstitial character, this civilisation has a constant tendency to extend, to overstep the mark, or more generally to excess. Consisting internally of countless varied elements, a "border civilization" is its own world, but one that is intrinsically heterogeneous and allows a greater role to chaos than other kinds of polity. The influential conservative thinker Il'in has indeed written that Russia is a whole cosmos – and not just a cosmos but also chaos – a "chaocosmos" (1997: 60).

In such an imaginary, there is no monolithic culture that penetrates throughout the entirety of society. Rather, as Shemyakin and Shemyakina write, the principle of border civilisation is multiplicity and the coexistence of different ways of resolving existential problems (2004: 36). Nevertheless, despite the lack of a monolithic culture or stylistic unity, Russia – albeit from different standpoints – has always seen a search for absolute good. The content of transcendental ideals may have changed through history, but the tendency to value them extraordinarily highly and to attempt to put them into practice in daily life is a constant. This has resulted in repeated attempts to broaden the sphere of the sacred and to impose liturgical time on events. With this attitude comes a corresponding lack of attention to the profane sphere of Russian life (2004: 40–41). The rest of the world, not partaking of the same holy goals, is seen as antagonistic, and self-defence against external materiality-profanity is therefore a constant preoccupation (2004: 56–57). As this chapter will show, the notion of sacred space was to become important on the Russian-Chinese border.

Russia is not only itself a "border civilisation" but also has its own frontiers, where the "chaotic" combination of restlessness, expansion and defensiveness appears even more strongly. Shemyakin and Shemyakina point to the contradictions this has engendered, for example in the case of the Cossacks (2004: 59–60). Initially made up of rebels and runaways, they were held to manifest the ancient Russian sacred values of wilful liberty (*volya*), autonomy, and freedom without limits. It was Cossacks who launched the initial forays into Siberia and later into Manchurian lands. Indeed, they became crucially important frontiersmen along most of Russia's most precarious borders. As soon as the border with China was demarcated they established landed settlements and communities along the frontier and became its guards. From having initially set out as barely controllable freebooters, they transformed, symbolically and in practice, into a closed hereditary estate and one of the most reliable supports of the autocratic state – a point to which I shall return.

Critique of Neo-Eurasianism

Many sober Russian observers take civilisational analysis seriously because they realise the influential role it plays in political attitudes, and they are therefore all the more anxious to point out its contradictions and defects. Kaganskii (2004), for example, castigates Neo-Eurasianism for sanctioning messianistic, anti-Western, and essentialist attitudes. He writes that the concept of Eurasia proposes a macro-region that because of its vast size and variation is suitable for autarchy. But this is an idea of self-determination through space, by the occupation of territories and places, and, whatever the proclamations, in fact does not establish the values of a civilization realised through history (thus Gumilev's promotion of the Mongolian Empire as a Eurasian prototype for Russia is, in Kaganskii's view, pure nonsense, since the two are quite different in structure and culture, 2004: 205). Preoccupation with extent goes with lack of attention to the *content* of Eurasia, the reality of its internal complexity and diversity of parts. For the Neo-Eurasianists it is enough to hold that great size indicates the greatness of the state. Eurasian space is sacralised and given a mythic vertical (an allusion to a magical hierarchy of power). But Eurasia is actually manifest only horizontally, that is again extensively (2004: 206).

Kaganskii maintains that this spatial kind of self-definition, given fundamentally by the position of Eurasia, and therefore by what is not Russia, is quite different from ideas found in either the main European nations or in China. There, countries define themselves positively, by their ideals, achievements and special values, and space does not play such an important role. China as the Middle Kingdom never sees itself as "not India", for example; and its relation to the people of the steppes is one of bearing a coherent civilisation to a hazy barbarian periphery. In other words, the centre in the Chinese case, does not define itself in space; rather it defines space (2004: 206).

The Neo-Eurasian vision, by contrast, insists on the *naturalness* of Russian borders. Not only is this a delusion, Kaganskii writes, which ignores the history of border indefiniteness and changeability,[7] but it becomes a mythology based on unacknowledged contradictions: for the theory proposes absolute laws of the spatial rightness of states but simultaneously holds that it (Eurasia) is higher than and supersedes such laws when they are applied to any other region than itself. Finally, Kaganskii observes, if we ask ourselves the question "What type of space does [Eurasianist] Eurasia correspond to?" the answer has to be cartographic space. This is a simple representation of contours and colours on a map, like a schoolroom map, or one that may indeed hang on the walls of prominent politicians or appear as background for television programmes (2004: 213), and all that the Eurasianists add to the schoolroom version is a notion of natural global zonality, on which rests their geo-political strategy (2004: 209–12).[8]

We cannot say, Kaganskii writes, whether such maps are ever used as working documents, or whether they are just "mental maps" – in all probability the latter. Nevertheless, the mental freeing of Russia from Empire has not led to construction of a non-imperial Russia. The systematic imaginative overriding of "cultural" spaces, such as demographic, land-use, ethnic, confessional, linguistic, etc. spaces, by a "natural" one, has facilitated confusion over whether what is represented is Russia as an Eternal Empire or Russia itself. It is to this confusion that the present political system corresponds, with its mono-centrism and stratification, rent-resource economic orientation, the low role given to provinces and the high importance given to external and internal boundaries (2004: 211–13).

The salience of civilisational perspectives for the Russia-China border

The ideological aspect of the Russian-Chinese border can be related to nationalism, or in this case to the conflation of the nation-state with

---

7   Kaganskii's critique on this point would find support in Zatsepine's study of the Amur River, which highlights the shifting and secretive character of even this, seemingly most obvious, dividing line (Zatsepine 2007).

8   Kaganskii observes that these maps, which ignore alternative projections that would reduce the size of Russia, are immediately understandable to people with Soviet education, but difficult to recognise for people brought up in other systems (2004: 211).

the post-empire. As John Dunn (2011 n.d.) has pointed out, "the two primary presences of nationalism in contemporary political life, each with protracted pasts, are as strategies for political leaders (incumbent or aspirant), and as more diffuse imaginative susceptibility to such strategies, dispersed to varying degrees across populations". There is a large literature on the influence of Eurasianism on the foreign policy of Russia's current leaders – significant according to some (Berman 2001; Sidorov 2006), negligible according to others (Schmidt 2005; Leonard 2010), and relevant primarily as a factual geography that underpins Russia's legitimate role in East Asia affairs for yet other writers (Rangsimaporn 2006).[9] I would point out only that both of Dunn's two locales for nationalism, i.e. not only among political leaders, are pertinent in our case, for contemporary Russia combines autocracy with a version of electoral democracy in what Henry Hale has called a "hybrid regime". In such a regime, public opinion, ratings and more generally the "popularity" of leaders has an important and distinctive role (Hale 2010: 35). Thus the fact that Putin has courted Eurasianist support among dispersed domestic audiences (electorates), while eschewing them in international arenas, is relevant.[10] If we are to look for *where* in Russian society the more strident versions of Eurasianism are popular, it seems that two locales are especially prominent: first among the military and security apparatuses (Rangsimaporn 2010: 382), and secondly among Asian minority intellectuals (Humphrey 2002). The former may be concerned with Russia's Great Power status and the latter with something quite different, enhanced attention to non-Russian nationalities and the promise of harmonious relations. But in either case, these two very different social constituencies relate to borders, since both of these social groups are key actors in frontier zones.

With the end of the Cold War and the healing of the Sino-Soviet split, the frontier with China has ceased to be a place of overt confrontation. On political and national security issues Russian relations with China seem excellent. Leaders meet congenially, and in July 2001 Presidents Jiang Zemin and Vladimir Putin signed a joint statement of friendship and cooperation over a wide range of issues. The treaty included recognition of the legitimacy of current borders and ratification of earlier reductions

---

9   Rangsimaporn points out that different nuances in the meaning of Eurasianism are reflected in Russian vocabulary. The pragmatic, factual sense is employed in official communications, using *Evroaziatskaya* to describe the country, while *Evraziiskaya* is employed by Neo-Eurasianists and by some of the civilization analysts (2010: 373).

10   For example, Putin publicly praised Gumilev at the celebration of the city of Kazan's one thousandth anniversary in 2005 (Shlapentokh 2005).

on troop numbers at the frontier. Through the relatively small number of crossing points, massive trade now flows in either direction (Davis 2003: 88–92). Today, Russian and Chinese border guards carry out joint training exercises to combat terrorist incursions, illegal migration, gun and drug running, smuggling and poaching.

Nevertheless, the Russian side of the border is still massively securitised. Adjacent to the border itself, and along its length, there is a restricted zone, to which access is limited to citizens having special passes issued by the Federal Security Service (FSB). This strip has varied in breadth through the years, sometimes limited to 5km, but sometimes and in some places expanded to include villages and well-used roads. The Border Guard Service argues for it to be widened, local inhabitants object to the inconvenience.[11]

It is along this strip of land, which is on the one hand managed centrally from the border directorate of the FSB in Moscow and on the other subject to all kinds of local practice and interventions that ideologies lay their hand, and the complex relation between the centre and the periphery becomes evident. The view of Russia as a civilisation extending its order to the brink of the wild terrain of "the other" appears, for example, in the outputs of the contemporary border guards (who belong to a Federal institution and are not necessarily local people). For example, posted on YouTube is a video that seems to be a home-made effort by the border guards: starting with an image of a frontier post against a mountain sunset, with the title "The Russian border is sacred and inviolable", it proceeds to a guards' song along with scenes of resolute military-type activity in barren landscapes. The song's repeated refrain is "The border strip eternally was and will be" and the verses frequently evoke the longing to return "home to Russia" – as though this home is indeed a civilization away from these wild parts.[12]

Inside and near to the restricted zone are many Cossack settlements, formerly the "stations" (*stanitsa*) of the Transbaikal, Chita, Amur and Ussuriisk regiments. In 1916, the Cossack population of the Transbaikal Cossack Host numbered 265,000 people, 14,500 of which served in the military.

During the Soviet period, the Cossacks were disbanded and repressed – for many of them had opposed the communists during the Civil War – and their border guard duties were taken over by the NKVD,

---

11   See http://chekist.ru/article/1292. Sept-Oct 2006 (accessed 4.11.2010).
12   In Russian "The border strip eternally was and will be" reads as *"Pogrannichnaya polosa vechno byla i budet"*.

later KGB-FSB. However, in post-Soviet times, Yeltsin encouraged the revival of the Cossacks and a "brotherhood" (*zemyachestvo*) was formed among the some 6.5 million self-proclaimed Cossacks scattered in across the border regions of the Russian Federation (Galeotti 1995: 55–56). In the turbulent 1990s, Russia's leaders turned to the Cossacks for internal and external security, permitting local administrations to hire them as vigilantes and the FSB to recruit them alongside the border guards and customs officials in frontier duties (Davis 2003: 114).[13] Today, Cossacks, many of whom are still part-time soldiers, patrol the border areas close to their villages. In 2006, a conference organised by the FSB in Ulan-Ude called on the rights and duties of local militias, patrols and Cossack units to be enhanced and regularised. All of this indicates recognition by the state of the need to involve the inhabitants of the frontier region not only in making the border secure but also in participating in the work of the state. As the FSB official stated at the conference, "We need to carry out wide explanatory work among the local population and return to the principle, 'the border defends the whole people'".[14]

The Cossacks have become a significant paramilitary, but also social and cultural, force along the Russian border with China, and they are particularly relevant to this paper for two reasons. First, they see Cossack rejuvenation as an integral part of the overall rejuvenation of Russia and they strongly support the state and the territorial integrity of Russia (Skinner 1994: 1019). Second, because their numbers grew to include non-Russians during the eighteenth and nineteenth centuries – around 10 per cent of the Transbaikal Cossacks are Buryats and Evenks – they embody the mixed ethnic heritage of the frontier regions and the very idea of "Eurasia". The existence of such a rejuvenated formation all along the border – hyper-loyal to the Russian political amalgam of nation and post-imperial federation – constitutes an

---

13 Davis writes that there are local militias in many regions of the Russian Far East, used mainly in response to rising crime rates and ineffectual, corrupt police (2002: 114–5). However, Cossacks themselves are not infrequently involved in crime and racketeering (Galeotti 1995: 58). In the early 1990s, Cossack units acquired a centralised main directorate. For border duties they are supplied with pay and weapons by whatever force employs them: the Border Guards, Ministry of Defence, municipal militias, or the Ministry of Emergencies (Davis 2002: 115).

14 According to the organisers of the conference, the need for extra vigilance was the consequence of illegal trade in arms, military supplies, drugs and psychotropic substances, the rise of illegal migration, theft of natural resources, and introduction of infectious diseases. Available at: http://chekist.ru/article/1292. Sept-Oct 2006 (accessed 4.11.2010).

important element in making it the kind of place it is.

The Buryat and Evenk Cossacks cannot totally ignore that they are not Russian, if only because they have a different appearance, but they are attached to the consolidated formation of Cossacks of Russia as a whole, which assimilated other nationalities in different border regions. In this way they separate themselves from the great majority of Buryats and Evenks who are of course not Cossacks (and have a long history of resenting the latter for their advantageous land settlements and wealth derived from customs duties at the border). The vision of "Eurasia" espoused by Buryat intellectuals is accordingly quite different from the Russian version popular among the re-emerged Cossacks. In the versions of indigenous elites, the implicit centre of the formation is no longer Moscow but shifted to their own territory, be that Kalmykia, the Altai, or the Baikal region (Humphrey 2002). The mystic aspect of "Eurasia", which in Dugin's version refers to a "world view" and a "spiritual movement" (2004: 185), is transmogrified into indigenous ancestral values of respecting/worshipping nature. The emphasis on the border shrinks away, and instead authors highlight the spreading, "super-ethnic" character of the great steppe empires along with their contemporary cultural heritage as a specific kind of ethics derived from living in a broad geographic-ecological zone (e.g. Urbanaeva 1994).

Let me return however to the views centred on the idea of "Russia". Since the Cossack revival is based on the historic role of the ethnically Slav freebooters in first conquering and then defending the border, the contemporary emphasis falls on recalling Tsarist-era social formations, values and traditions. The social, cultural and moral aspects are as important to them as the military, since it is in this way that the Cossacks assert their identity and pride in a specific way of life. Little is known of how the Buryat and Evenk members adapt to this situation.[15] Consultation of genealogies, tailors to make the correct uniforms, training in use of sabres and riding skills, well-rehearsed choirs, the swearing of oaths to serve the Fatherland, have sprung to life since the 1990s. The admission of new members is generally conducted by an Orthodox priest in a church, with each new recruit kissing the Gospel and the Cross (Skinner 1994: 1020–22).

---

15   It seems that there may exist a Transbaikal Cossack identity based on the experience of repression, punishment and forced dispersal under the Soviet regime. Such former Cossack families in Transbaikalia now refer to themselves in quasi-ethnic fashion as the Guran. But this half-hidden grouping is different from the public revival of Cossack institutions, which is heavily dominated by Russian cultural elements (Ivan Peshkov, personal communication).

It is in keeping with this trend across Russia that the Transbaikal Cossacks engage in ritual activities on the border with China. With this we return to the theme of sacred space and Christian civilisation that is so prominent in some versions of Neo-Eurasianism.

For the past few years, Cossack representatives have taken young people on a 1,000 km annual voyage along the rivers that form much of the border, the Shinka, Ingoda and Amur, to commemorate the exploits of the seventeenth century. They float down the rivers in self-made rafts, as did their ancestors, sometimes taking a priest aboard, sometimes mounting an antique cannon in the prow. They sing nostalgic songs and receive instruction in the moral ideals (honour, integrity) of the Cossack way of life. Along the way, they call in for religious services at local churches. The leader is quoted as saying earlier this year (2010), "in Russia there has accumulated much impurity (*mnogo nechisti*), which wants to forget the feats of the ancestors. But no way will they succeed".[16] The journey is called *pokhod* (campaign, march, crusade), which suggests that it is envisaged not just as a memorial but also as a contemporary enactment of what the border means – re-establishing Russia as a zone of purity demarcated by a militantly defended line. Meanwhile, the Chinese bank of the river is ignored.

The specifically Christian aspect of Cossack border imagination can be seen from further activities: the discovery, digging up and reburial with Orthodox rites, of the remains of the ancestors killed by Manchu forces in the seventeenth century at the fortress of Albazin on the Amur River. What is the history that the contemporary Cossacks are so determined to remember (if only selectively)? During the 1650s the Russian adventurers had built fortresses from which they induced the indigenous people – in this case Dahurs (Daurs), Buryats and Tungus (Evenki) – to pay tribute to the Tsar; at the same time they lived off the food supplies appropriated from Dahur farmers. The Manchus, who had recently come to power in Beijing, received complaints from the Dahurs. As a result, the Manchus allowed most of the Dahur to resettle on the River Nonni, well away from the Russians, causing near starvation to the conquerors of Albazin. Then, with fierce fighting, Albazin went back and forth between the Russians and the Manchus, being attacked, blockaded and razed twice, until the Treaty of Nerchinsk in 1689 settled its fate. According to the border treaty, the entire

---

16   '*V Rossii razvelos' mnogo nechisti, kotoraya khochet zabyt' podvigi pradedov. No u nikh ni cherta ne poluchit'sya*', quoted in http://portamur.ru/news/detail/64218.

Amur basin was to revert to Chinese suzerainty. Albazin was levelled to the ground and the remaining sixty-six Cossacks marched for Nerchinsk, where they arrived in 1690 (Serebrennikov 1997 [1922]).

In the nineteenth century, as mentioned earlier, the north bank of the Amur was retaken by Murav'yev. It is now identified unquestioningly as Russian territory, and the site of Albazin (today a Russian village) has been opened for archaeological investigation. It is the religious aspect of all this that is highlighted by the contemporary Cossacks, and even here it is only certain aspects of the story that are told. For, interestingly, some of the Albazin ancestors had given themselves up to the Manchus during the wars, while others had been captured, and these Russians being respected for their fighting qualities were taken to Beijing to form a small privileged regiment. Some of their descendants remained Russian Orthodox Christians well into the twentieth century (Serebrennikov 1997 [1922]). However, Cossack publicity in Russia does not recall this piquant episode. Rather, it focuses on the supposition that the Cossacks killed defending Albazin, had been buried, with wives and children, without Christian rites, although each body wore an Orthodox cross.[17] Christian reburial has recently been called for. The congregations of "pilgrims" travelled to the reburial rites from many regions, stood all night, and then participated in the funeral service, which lasted most of the following day. The border, along the river-bank, has been marked in several places by a Christian cross.

Conclusion

Let me return now to the point about the intermeshing of metropolitan and local constructions of the border made at the beginning of this paper. Today, Moscow and Beijing conduct high-level agreements on the huge two-way trade between the two countries. In the contemporary global context, the Cossack rites could seem merely a local eccentricity, an archaic defiance, a touching but pointless throwback; and the Cossack revival in general is now regarded with some caution by Moscow for its potential to disturb matters on the borders.[18] In fact something similar could be said, at least regarding the apparent distance between metropolitan and frontier

---

17   http://portamur.ru/news/detail/64218
18   Cossacks are present in, or have claims to, many volatile and disputed regions of the former Soviet Union, such as Moldova, northern Kazakhstan, and the north Caucasus, resulting in a complex relationship with the Russian state (Galeotti 1995: 56).

attitudes, about Cossack activities in the seventeenth century. Tsar Alexei Mikhailovich, in response to a note conveying Chinese displeasure at Cossack encroachments, went so far as to plead ignorance to the Manchus that his Cossacks had ventured into this region, adding "not knowing that the Daurian lands are part of your Dominion".[19] Bassin concludes that the Russians made it quite clear during the Nerchinsk negotiations in 1689 that they were "if not anxious in any event entirely willing to sacrifice claims to the Amur valley if by so doing they could facilitate progress towards a formal trade agreement with China" (Bassin 1999: 23). This seems like a pragmatism not so far removed from the benign high-level treaties of the 1990–2000s and the grand scheme of mutually beneficial rapprochement with China.

However, running counter to this is the intense urge for national self-definition, which surfaces openly in Neo-Eurasianism and other conservative political movements. By no means all Russian citizens share these preoccupations, but if they are distributed unevenly among the population – concentrating especially in the military and security services – then it is no surprise to find them expressed most openly and unblushingly by the Border Guards and by some of the Cossacks living along the frontier.

Local sensibilities, like those of the Border Guards and the Cossacks, and many others that I have not been able to describe, contribute to the complex assemblages of which borders are made. In the ethnography I have described here, the Cossack contributions have their own specific form, which I think can be related to the notion of Russia as "Eurasia". The Christian re-burial rites and especially the *pokhod* – the voyage along the length of the "natural" border without crossing it or addressing any action towards the "other side" – reflect the spatio-geographical character of "Eurasia" and the way it is imagined not as a bridge/gateway between East and West but as an autarchic spiritual bulwark between the two.

Emotional investments in borders are not unique to Russia – one only has to think of the song "The White Cliffs of Dover", popular ever since the Second World War, with its accompanying slogan on the video on YouTube – "They stand as a symbol of indomitable British pride", all of which is associated today with a particular social environment: ex-service

---

19   *Russko-kitaiskoe otnoshenya*, 1, p. 299, quoted in Bassin (1999: 23)

associations, conservative fetes, fly-pasts and show-biz performances. More generally and comparatively, what becomes interesting is the social distribution of these susceptibilities to nationalism, the variety of relations they may enter with governments (encouragement, disjunction, repudiation, covert support, etc.), and the way that their symbols tend to pile onto borders.

5. Chinese Migrants and Anti-Chinese Sentiments in Russian Society

Viktor Dyatlov

A border is much more than merely a line of contact between state sovereignties. It always constitutes a special form of human ties and relationships, a meeting place for people of different languages and cultures, a ground and resource for their aspirations, life strategies and practices. In this sense, cross-border migrations and migrants constitute a vital component of border conditions and phenomena. Bringing the border with them, as well as within themselves, migrants embody the very situation of contact and conflict.

It is no accident that the well-known Japanese scholar Akihiro Iwashita named his book about the Sino-Russian border *4,000 Kilometres of Problems* (Iwashita 2006): these are not simply problems relating to international relations. Nearly half a century of constant evolution in the region along the Russian border has led to the emergence of a particular lifestyle, psychology and economic practice and behaviour in the eastern regions of the country. This accounts for the difficulty in making the transition from seeing the border as a threat in the 1960s and 1970s, to perceiving it as a resource in subsequent decades. Chinese migrants have played a remarkable, and often paramount, role in this complex set of cross-border relationships.

                    DOI: 10.11647/OBP.0025.05

The analysis of the present chapter will focus on Chinese migrants to Russia and on Russian attitudes towards them.[1] A significant outcome of the relationship between the host society and migrants has been the formation of a complex set of stereotypes, misgivings, anxieties and phobias. At the same time, this particular constellation becomes a compelling factor in the formulation and management of migration policies, having an impact not only on migration trends themselves, but also on the economic, social and political development parameters of the host society.

Migrant phobia is an inevitable component of a host society's adaptive response to migration. It rapidly incorporates into an already xenophobic social context, occasionally borrowing from pre-existing ethnic, racial and cultural phobias, while modifying its nature and increasing its scope. At times, the category of the "stranger" (Simmel 1971) can also include more people than the representatives of other ethnic and cultural groups. Galina Vitkovskaya convincingly illustrated the existence of migrant phobia in its "pure form", during the process whereby resettled Russians and Russian refugees were rejected and considered as "outsiders" by the Russian host society (Vitkovskaya 1999: 151–91).

A necessary and inevitable mechanism of these ideas is the formation of stereotypes. A stereotype is first and foremost the elaboration of a relationship, less a heuristic evaluation than an appraisal and a way of classifying social information. It comes within the sphere of *a priori* knowledge and existing scientific knowledge. Consequently, stereotypes do not require critiques of sources of information, confirmations, internal logic, nor consistency in individual tenets. Yet it is stereotypes, rather than positive scientific knowledge, that shape social and governmental attitudes to migration processes and to migrants. Reflecting the prevailing attitudes to migrants, stereotypes predominantly articulate around xenophobic ideas.

Stereotypes are complex systems that evolve in time and space. It is therefore important to examine them from the inside, to observe their fluctuations and regional variations. Thus, the study of the dynamics and basic parameters of this set of factors represents a crucial scientific and practical task. In this regard, Russia constitutes a very interesting, and

---

1   The fascinating issue of Russian migration to China and of past and present Russian diasporas in that country warrants further analysis. While a large body of literature deals with Russian migration to China from the late nineteenth century to the middle of the twentieth century, contemporary migration flows have been undeservedly overlooked by researchers.

possibly unique, case to compare the formation of anti-Chinese phobias and stereotypes through the example of two different historical periods within a single country.

Beginning in the 1990s, it is possible to speak of a "second coming" of Chinese migrants. The first wave occurred in the second half of the nineteenth century and the first third of the twentieth century. The two periods were separated by the Soviet era, when the border was closed and the prohibition of seasonal migration led to the disappearance of the diaspora. Not only did the phenomenon itself disappear, but the very historical memory about this Chinese presence vanished as well. It also disappeared because entire social strata were eliminated – strata that carried historical traditions and memory. Consequently, the very image of the Chinese migrant was utterly effaced, and the 1990s witnessed a new encounter, a new and independent attempt to comprehend the phenomenon through the formation of stereotypes.

In both periods, migrants played a vital economic role in the host society and their presence was characterised by highly dynamic demographics. This led to tension and jealous attitudes towards them, and to negative reactions about the presence of migrants and local dependence on them. All this provides a unique opportunity to compare the response of the host society in radically different contexts, to identify similarities and differences within a constellation of prejudices and phobias that have formed independently of each other.

The "Yellow Peril" at the turn of the twentieth century: a Russian variant of a global syndrome

The motives of the emergence, levels of tensions and basic parameters of anti-Chinese sentiments in late-imperial Russia cannot be understood outside the context of a specific set of motives and circumstances. Russia, perhaps for the first time in her history, was faced with a spontaneous, massive and highly concentrated influx (or "salvo") of migrant workers. These migrants differed drastically from Russia's inhabitants in terms of cultural characteristics, structure and way of life, behaviours and habits. The main stream of Chinese (and Korean) migrants was directed to a newly attached and sparsely populated territory, poorly integrated into the Far East Empire. Further, this region bordered China – a "sleeping giant" in the representations of the time. This led to strong anti-migrant sentiments.

These local Russian circumstances were repeatedly strengthened through their juxtaposition with the potent global syndrome of "Yellow Peril". The modern period gave rise to a phenomenon of "great xenophobia": great both in terms of its global character and of its regulating impact on the behaviour and in terms of the number of people involved. I share Lev Gudkov's opinion regarding the emergence of mass phobias, namely that the "emergence and development of symbolic 'enemies' are becoming models of particular reactions to processes of mass creation, initiated by modernising transformations in traditional societies" (2005: 17). The enemy becomes an essential tool of consolidation "of a fundamentally new social form – a poorly-managed plasma of mass resentment and indignation..." (ibid.: 19) as a result of the destruction of social order.

At the turn of the twentieth century, the "Yellow Peril" syndrome emerged as a global phenomenon and gained its appellation (see, for instance, Schimmelpenninck van der Oye 2009). In the United States, its formation was motivated by concurrent factors. A massive influx of Chinese workforce provoked strong anti-immigrant sentiments, a wave of commonplace racial hatred and violence. These sentiments were amplified and shaped by a well-developed mass culture. The syndrome became part of an ideological and political process embedded in mass culture (comics, films, criminal and fantasy novels). A powerful trend formed within mass culture – from the caricatured hero of the Yellow Kid to the image, which survived throughout the twentieth century, of the "sinister Dr Fu Manchu", a character in a series of detective novels and several films.[2] Dr Fu Manchu was a mystical Oriental, cunning and crafty, who possessed both incredible intellect and vast erudition; having received a European education, this made him especially terrible (Nepstad 2000). He was an absolute villain, intent on destroying European peace. He was a creature rather than a man, but an individualised creature, a colourful and unique personality.

In Germany, the syndrome evolved without common and recurrent contact with Chinese immigrants or China. It formed part of a geopolitical

---

2   For more on the Yellow Kid, see Sasha Sherman's "Zheltyi malchik v zheltoi reke", in *InterNet Magazine*, 15, available at: www.gagin.ru/internet/15/index.html (accessed 11.5.2012). Sherman writes that "in 1896, the caricaturist Richard Felton Outcault drew a character called "Yellow Kid" [...] He was an odd character, bald, lop-eared and snaggletoothed. He grinned mockingly. An ancestor of the Simpsons and of Beavis and Butthead, he was probably one of the first drawn characters in pop culture. His yellowness is attributable to the Sino-Japanese war of 1895, drawing for the first time the attention of the West to Japanese militarism and causing a wave of jingoist hysteria, which he parodied".

doctrine, based on ideas of statehood and racial and civilisational categories, together with a global perception of a "war of the worlds". Emperor Wilhelm II actively and intensively developed and disseminated the geopolitically-constructed syndrome of the "Yellow Peril" (Perepiska 1923: 8–10, 42–48; Wilhelm II 1923: 38–39). Planned and commissioned by him, a drawing was created in 1898 where a "group of women, portraying the main European nations, look in horror at the terrifying figure of a Buddha rising in the East, while an angel, standing on a mountain top, points at the figure with a sword in his hand. The drawing was accompanied by the following legend: 'Peoples of Europe, protect your most precious wealth'". The drawing was presented to Nicholas II with a note: "I beseech you to kindly accept this drawing sketched by me, representing the symbolic figures of Russia and Germany standing guard on the bank of the Yellow Sea to preach the Gospel, the truth and the light in the East" (Remnev 2004: 66).

In Russia, the modes of stereotyping in the USA and Germany merged together, and were reinforced by a distinct sense of insecurity in the Russian Far East. This distant outlying region – barely assimilated into the rest of the country, and isolated from the metropolitan area – was on the edge of a giant China, which had the potential to invade. China was still "asleep", and was perceived as a territory rather than as a bearer of sovereign power. However, it was potentially strong on account of its large population and its nationalistic tradition. The Russians wondered: what will happen if the sleeping giant awakes? The notion of a "yellow" expansionist Japan emerged following the Russo-Japanese war. The frightening consequences of a unification of China and Japan on the basis of race and the prospect of their joint "yellow expansion" were actively debated. These ideas clashed when tens of thousands of (mostly temporary and seasonal) Chinese migrant workers arrived, without whom the economic life, development and protection of the Russian Far East were impossible.

An important part of Russian tradition was the attitude towards the Chinese as an undifferentiated mass into which individuality dissolved. Epithets such as "crowd", "ants", "locusts" or "midges" were used to describe the Chinese. The description of the Chinese painted by the political writer A. Verezhnikov in *Sovremennik* is filled with depersonalising imagery:

> A Chinese crowd in blue rags, with the same beardless, yellow faces, wandering as far as the eye can see. It does not plot, argue, nor contradict… speaking with the same sibilant, squeaking voice… In this crowd there is no leader, no ring-leader, no individual standing out from the rest… No proud, bold, daring voices…. Every figure in a Chinese crowd moulded the

same as the rest, like factory items... But in this indifference, half-sleep and somnolence one can detect an enduring patience for the right moment, a concealed suspicion. And it looks as if they are just about to start stirring all at once, that they will start moving their slanted eyes, rise and go. And they will go... dozens turning into hundreds, hundreds into thousands... and they will keep going, breeding and multiplying (Verezhnikov 1911: 124–30).

This sketch evokes complex feelings of contempt, fear, disgust and alienation as well as a little pity towards the Chinese. It does not promote relations to humans, but to locusts, to aliens – indeed, in another passage, the author notes they have "the look of creatures from a whole other planet".

All this led to the formulation of a phobia, combining the geopolitical element of the German variant, the results of extended competitive contacts with migrants, and the fear of losing the Far Eastern region as a result of "Sinicisation", as well as a sober awareness of the area's complete economic dependence on migrants. These various elements merged into forms of daily racism, migrant phobia and geopolitical fears, rising to levels of mystical feelings of an impending war. Vladimir Solovyev's complex philosophical constructions became the theoretical foundation for this (Solovyev 1990: 233, 635–762; Solovyev 1993: 233; Kobzev 1984: 189–91).[3]

These constructions also led to a powerful and highly effective metaphor – that of "Panmongolism". This image helped reinforce the syndrome of "Yellow Peril" through the concept of the "Mongolian yoke". From the nineteenth century to the present time Russian public consciousness, official ideology and school curricula have been dominated by the notion that the "yoke" would be the worst disaster in the country's history. Panmongolism does not relate in any way to actual Mongols. The mystical "Mongols" of Panmongolism are symbolic of ideas of "yellowness", "invasion" and "yoke", which coalesce into a general but pervasive fear of a "war of the worlds". Even propaganda leaflets, whose main idea was that, without foreign capital, Russia would lose the Far Eastern region, referred to the "impending Mongolian yoke" (Panov 1906). Within the discourse of the "Yellow Peril", a wide spectrum of opinions formed, but the mystical element, the fear of an impending mass war, was almost always present. Its typical symptom – an invasion of "yellow hordes" – became a familiar theme in the then popular genres of popular literature such as science fiction (Koshelev 2000).

---

3   These constructions rested on eschatological notions of "threat from the East" or "Yellow Peril" as instruments of future deaths in Russia and generally leading to the annihilation of the old world.

The widespread sentiment was that the Chinese are "too numerous" and that the "yellow" population of the Russian Far East was growing at a faster rate than the Russian. The authorities saw the presence of the Chinese as a threat to national security, and there was particular concern about the lack of order and planning of the migration process, the huge scale of illegal infiltration, and the actual extra-territoriality of nationals of neighbouring empires (Arseniev 1914). Amur Governor-general Gondatti put it in this way:

> As for the political dimension of the question, being firmly anchored in their national culture, maintaining spiritual ties to their homeland, raising on foreign lands the faithful sons of their fatherland, and not feeling an especially strong urge to assimilate into the surrounding population, the Chinese constitute, in this as well, an element of downright hostility" (Dvizhenie 1997: 69–71).

The Chinese were perceived as fertile soil for so-called *hunhuznichestvo* [Chinese banditry] on a large scale (Nadarov 1896: 183–204). They were accused of taking their vices to an extreme. Opium dens and gaming houses were frequently described as the centres of Chinese slums (Schrader 1897). These slums were seen as hotbeds of poor sanitation. L. Bogoslovsky wrote that norms of hygiene are "foreign to the undeveloped mind of the Chinese" and, given the cost of housing, inaccessible to them; this created diseases, high mortality and the constant threat of epidemics (Bogoslovsky 1913: 20–33). A huge concern was the smuggling of *khanshin* (poor quality millet-based alcohol). The Chinese were frequently accused of carrying out predatory plundering of the wealth of the Ussuri *taiga*, illegal mining and gold smuggling. Exploitation by Chinese traders, poachers and bandits was deeply resented by the indigenous population of the province, and examples abound of violence, torture, murders and various forms of servitude (Nadarov 1887; Arseniev 1914).

The majority of problems linked to Chinese immigration were assessed in terms of "yellow labour". Specialist publications contain a qualified analysis of this state of affairs: industrial and regional dynamics of the practices of the Chinese and Korean workforce, levels of remuneration, cost structure and scale of financial outflow from the country (L. G. 1916: 140–71; Mezhduvedomstvennoe; Grave 1912; Matsokin 1911: 1–20; Panov 1910: 53–116; Predvaritel'nye 1924). China was able to export a low-cost, disciplined and seemingly unlimited workforce that was capable of quickly mastering new trades and spheres of activity. It was believed that this hindered settlement of the region by Russians, and increased "Sinicisation", could lead to Russia's loss of the region. These beliefs existed in parallel with the understanding that without the "yellow" workforce, development of the region was impossible. This resulted in conflicts between various agencies and their specific interests.

The successful entrepreneur, public figure and political writer Spiridon Merkulov, argued that the official estimates of the number of Chinese in the region were too low (Merkulov 1911, 1911a, 1912). He suggested that the Chinese workers took their money back to China, which undermined the financial stability of the region. He also suggested that the "yellow labour" constituted an insurmountable barrier to the influx of Russian settlers. According to Merkulov, the extreme cheapness of the Chinese workforce was a result of its technical archaisms, particularly in the mining and manufacturing industries. He noted that Russian peasants and Cossacks lease out their land to the Chinese, and therefore reduce their own participation in productive labour. This leads to problems of parasitism, drunkenness and degradation among them. Chinese workers were becoming a source of social conflicts – strikes, and clashes with Russian workers. Part of the problem of a "yellow workforce" was also located in competitive relations in the sphere of commerce. Many authors noted that the Chinese, on account of their energy, entrepreneurship, work ethics and corporatism, monopolised a significant part of the small and medium retail business in a relatively short time.

Alarmism and the notion of a "Yellow Peril" were dominant but they were not the only approach to the problem under discussion during that time. There were authors who perceived the presence of the Chinese as a necessary part of life of the region. They sympathetically described the dire conditions typical of their life and work, disapproved of the arrogant and contemptuous attitudes displayed towards them by the authorities and by a significant portion of society, and protested against widespread abuses. Without this workforce, the fast and inexpensive establishment of the necessary infrastructure to ensure Russia's rule (cities, ports, roads, railways, agricultural and industrial production and mining) was impossible. Unless it was adequately developed economically, militarily and politically, the region would inevitably be lost by Russia. Such a position was taken by Merkulov's constant opponent, A. Panov (1910: 53–116; 1912: 241–82; 1912a: 171–84). In his writings, we find a sober and far-reaching thesis:

> Chinese influx does not present the spontaneous character with which it is usually credited. It is not the ineluctable aspiration responsible for the movement of glaciers, landslides, sea currents or the flow of lava against

which human will is powerless. It is merely the most natural of economic phenomena, regulated, like any other phenomenon, by the laws of supply and demand, and it is therefore both possible and necessary to deal with it on an economic basis – by changing the conditions of the labour market (Panov 1912a: 251).

Similarly, Maxim Kovalevsky generally believed that "currently Chinese labour is characterised by seasonal work, it does not threaten the region with permanent settlement of Chinese in our eastern regions and is, therefore, unable to inspire serious political concerns" (1909: 423–37).

This kind of approach is seen, most clearly and professionally, in a report by the representative of the Ministry for foreign affairs, Vladimir Grave (1912). The main conclusion of this report is that the use of "yellow labour" carries with it a host of problems and dangers, but that it is both inevitable and necessary. It is consequently essential to regulate and guide its use, creating and perfecting a legal framework for it, as well as providing public institutions, and preparing highly qualified staff. The anonymous author of the article "Siberian Collection" strongly opposed this view, arguing that:

> … the Russian population, who do not share anything with the Chinese in terms of character, way of life and culture, look at the Manzi, in their folk expression, as creatures without a soul and, to some extent, even standing outside the law.[4] Differences in so many dissimilar civic traditions, religion, civilization and character, such as between Russians and Chinese, are seen everywhere, in all countries, and are accompanied by most severe difficulties which everywhere must seriously be taken into consideration… It is necessary… to withdraw needless criticisms of the Chinese and show that they also are people and that they have the right, just like anyone else, to legal protection insofar as they are equal, as is recognised by fundamental laws and not popular arbitrariness. In other words, it is essential to remove the Manzi from this improper position, for his own sake as well as for the sake of proper living conditions in the colonies of the Russian Far East" (L.-n. 1904: 77–108).

Nonetheless, the negative outlook was clearly dominant, and was openly and unambiguously stated in the brochure by P. Ukhtubuzhsky:[5]

> It is well-known that the yellow peoples nourish an organic hatred towards Europeans, and to us Russians in particular… They dream… of conquering the world… Invasion by the yellow races of the rich region of Siberia has

---

4   "Manzi" was the name given to the Chinese in the Russian Far East in the nineteenth century.
5   "P. Ukhtubuzhsky" is a pseudonym. The author's real name was Nikolai Dmitrievich Obleukhov.

already begun. It is true that it is, as we say here, a 'peaceful' economic invasion, but through this peaceful invasion, Russians are being displaced by the yellow races who seize commerce, industry, wages, and so on… God guides people. Those nations who protect Good and Truth will be victorious. If Russia, carrying the light of Orthodoxy, faces in Asia the yellow races wallowing in the darkness of paganism, there cannot be any doubt as to the outcome of this struggle. Symbolising the 'Lord of the whole world', the Cross will overcome the Dragon (1913: 64–65, 75, 85).

Contemporary Russia: the threat of "Chinese expansion"

At the turn of the twenty-first century, Russia's inhabitants once again came into massive and regular contact with Chinese migrants. As a result of market reforms, openness to the outside world and the establishment of good neighbourly relations and cooperation with China, there has been a massive influx of Chinese migrants, accompanied by robust economic activity. Migrants play an important role in the small retail trade, construction and agriculture of Russia. They facilitate the import of Chinese consumer goods to Russia and the export of certain raw materials to China. Their role in the Russian economy clearly surpasses their physical presence, which varies in accordance with economic conditions and fluctuates between half a million and one million people a year. A more accurate assessment is made difficult by an imperfect census system, the important role played by illegal migration and the fact that this migration is predominantly temporary (seasonal and pendulum migration). Nonetheless, permanent Chinese communities are beginning to emerge in Russia's principal economic centres.

Due largely to a Chinese influx, Russia is gradually becoming a country of in-migration, and this may represent a radical turning point in its transformation. An intensive process of reflection and evaluation of the phenomenon is taking place in public consciousness in order to fill a "blind spot" through a radical transformation of worldviews. The sudden appearance of masses of migrants from China in the early 1990s was, for the vast majority of Russians, not just unexpected but an enormous shock. The presence of Chinese in pre-revolutionary Russia and the experience of living with them had been wholly forgotten. Despite the vast quantity of pre-revolutionary texts, still physically present in libraries, the intellectual tradition of research on the issue had been interrupted and had fallen into oblivion. The ideological atmosphere and the country's phobias were now radically different.

The image of Chinese immigrants formed anew. This image reproduced a number of components from the previous century: that the Chinese are hardworking, simple and adaptable, with a sense of entrepreneurship. However, these qualities, positive ones in principle, are often painted negatively: hardworking (but at the expense of us patriots); self-reliant (but clannish and, again, detrimental to us).

Despite the massive presence of Chinese migrants in Russia, locals have not yet formed daily routine relationships with them. There is no familiar neighbourly and professional interaction, and no common work activity. Regular communication occurs only over the counter. This is a highly specific position, especially in a post-socialist society still affected by a powerful anti-market bias. Few incentives still exist to ensure that an individualised image of the Chinese emerges. This may seem odd considering the vast number of journalistic publications, reports and statements by political leaders and officials, and the growing number of scientific studies that exist. Chinese migrants are also regularly featured in television programmes, newspapers and special films. Nonetheless, there are no *faces*, including on television. There is no interest in the individual person, his life or his destiny. Russia is concerned not so much with the Chinese as people, but merely in the problems they are seen to embody. Before the revolution, the image of the Chinese was significantly richer in detail (even if some of this detail involved stereotyping). Today, the Chinese migrant has become a function, an abstraction.

There is one aspect of the nineteenth and early twentieth-century image of the Chinese that remains: the vision of them as an undifferentiated mass. Their large numbers constitute the basis of the construction of various fears about "demographic expansion" and the "Yellow Peril". What has shifted, however, is the emphasis placed on the assessment of group loyalties. This is largely due to the radical transformation of the role of China. If at the turn of the twentieth century, China was considered as a space rather than the actual medium of a sovereign power, today such a view is essentially impossible: China is now a superpower whose economic and military might is primordially directed outwards (if only due to the pressure of a huge and rapidly increasing population and the general limitations of its own resources). Migrants are seen as an absolutely loyal and obedient instrument, as the tentacles of this giant state. By contrast, in the constructions at the turn of the twentieth century, the Chinese were perceived as less state-bound: they dissolved not into the state, but into the group, into the "race".

The term "yellow", which was dominant at the turn of the twentieth century, has fallen almost completely out of use. It survives in the phrase "Yellow Peril", but essentially as the component of an established term. This disappearance is unlikely to be due to political correctness. It is, rather, the outcome of a peripheralisation of the powerful racial discourse that prevailed at the end of the nineteenth and beginning of the twentieth centuries in analyses of social relations and problems. However, the transformation of "Yellow Peril" into "Chinese threat" does not signal the disappearance or weakening of a phobia as such: its cornerstones are concepts of "expansion", "exploitation" and "criminality".

The widespread notion that Chinese migration constitutes a crucial tool of expansion was a purposeful, planned and organised idea, implemented by the state and by a population completely mobilised and organised through the state. In this construction, migrants themselves do not appear as individuals possessing their own motivations, free will and choices, but as integral organic extensions of the state. The old and widespread metaphor of "ants", implying mass, innumerability, orderliness and subordination of the individual will of the Chinese, remains.[6] This metaphor conveys another dimension: ants, while intelligent creatures, are not human. They are not guided by human logic and morality, and therefore attitudes towards them can be built outside of this context. An extreme expression of this approach is seen in the assessment of the problem of Chinese migrants and Chinese in general in terms of "biomass".

There is a widespread notion that Chinese authorities have a "plan" concerning migratory expansion into Russia. This plan allegedly includes a system of state organisation, planning and regulation, and is implemented through coercion and incentives (including the financial reward to the migrant obtaining permanent leave to remain in Russia). This thesis is widely represented in the media as well as in statements by officials and politicians, and in scientific work. Leonid Rybakovsky, Olga Zakharova and Vladimir Mindogulov played an enormous role in the shaping of this view:

> China has huge territorial claims against Russia and stimulates in every possible way the penetration of her citizens into Russian territory, building a basis for their legal presence. At the same time, the economic activities of these Chinese citizens bring colossal profits... The main goal of China's entry into Russia, regardless of its forms and channels, is its integration

---

6   On "Chinese ant-hills" see, for example, A. I. Gertsen (1967: 67–68).

into economic activities, acquisition of property and land, i.e. the creation of economic and legal preconditions for the legal seizure of territory… In spite of the fact that, currently, Chinese immigration into the Russian Far East is predominantly of an illegal nature, the existing system of penetration provides a process for the settlement and legalisation of illegal migrants (Rybakovsky, Zakharova and Mindogulov 1994: 35–36).

The phrase "small groups of a hundred thousand people each" is an old Soviet joke from the time of Sino-Soviet military confrontation, and represents one of the principal notions of demographic expansion. The question of Chinese migrants cannot be a small affair, since there can never be few Chinese. Therefore, given the scarcity of the Russian population in general, and in the east of the country in particular, there is a sense that the Chinese will simply absorb the local population and will become the majority group. Strictly speaking, they have already absorbed it. And further away from the Chinese border people, Siberian and far eastern cities are thought to have been already settled by the Chinese.

Over the years, the most discussed migration-related question in Russia has been: how many Chinese people live here? No accurate statistics exist and none are anticipated. Reasons for this are obvious: illegality, inefficiency of state structures designed to count migrants, and lack of interest in obtaining authentic information. Estimates range from 300,000 to six million a year. The maximum estimates, which appeared in the early 1990s, have consistently been quoted in newspapers, speeches of officials, and even in scientific journals. The calculations of serious scientists and statements by border authorities, which indicate that the gap between entry and exit numbers is only a few percent (and this means that the illegal portion is not as great as is frequently imagined), are simply ignored. Estimates of several millions of migrants are already ossified, and form the basis of mass ideological constructions as well as solutions by the authorities. They confirm the authority of scientific and government experts.

"The Chinese can only give birth to Chinese" is a phrase by the popular writer of the Soviet period, Peter Proskurin. Part of the threat of Chinese migration is the potential for mixed marriages as an instrument of demographic expansion. Especially threatening is the strategy of "naturalisation though marriage", through which many illegal immigrants (as well as their children and relatives) acquire legal status through marriage, including bogus ones. On the implications of this phenomenon,

Leonid Rybakovsky and his co-authors write, unequivocally yet somewhat incorrectly:

> Historical experience shows that, at various stages in the development of the Far East, the specificity of the population of the Russian Far East, and particularly the specific policy of neighbouring countries, including Japan, give a real chance to a positive outcome of these long-term, well-costed actions for the natural assimilation into the population (Rybakovsky, Zakharova and Mindogulov 1994: 23).

Available estimates suggest that the number of such marriages is negligible – however, this is of no significance for the authors of these constructions. What is important – although no one has demonstrated that culture is based on "blood" – is the idea that the Chinese gene is powerful and spreading. This is a recent fear: in pre-revolutionary times, the overwhelming majority of Chinese migrants were seasonal so did not start families and did not settle.

As early as the start of the 1990s, a persistent myth about the existence of compact settlements of Chinese in the Russian Far East started to emerge, claiming that numerous settled areas are already populated predominantly by Chinese. The further one goes from the Far Eastern region, the more stable these representations. A large number of journalists, politicians and officials write and speak of these settlements as if they were a self-evident and indisputable fact, but without providing any names. Further, they offer a frightening picture of how these Chinese enclaves will demand autonomy before attempting a "reunification" with China. In 1996, Konstantin Sorokin noted as an evident and unquestionable fact the "growth of uncontrolled 'creeping' migration of Chinese into Russia (there are about 2 million of them in our country), the formation, especially in the Russian Far East, of 'Chinatowns' not subject to Russian laws, the massive purchase of real estate by Chinese entrepreneurs east of the Urals, facilitated by the passivity of local and central authorities" (1996: 107). In 2005, Alexander Khramchikhin was no less adamant:

> [The] East of Russia (in the best case scenario, the space to the east of Lake Baikal, possibly up to the east of the Yenisei River, and at worst, to the east of the Urals) will become, in the space of a couple of decades, a giant 'Kosovo'... It will be settled by Chinese and will become part of China economically, financially, administratively and politically. Formally, it will be considered Russian (until such time when a president in the Kremlin finally cedes de jure what has been already lost de facto) and the few citizens of Russia still living there will reside in ghettos. China understands very well that Russia

will cede her own East, despite living from its resources. China is well aware that it will not survive without the appropriation of surrounding territories. China wants to live and therefore follows the only possible path ensuring its survival (2005: 61–64).

As in the nineteenth and early twentieth centuries, contemporary thinking about Chinese immigration conforms to common ideas that migrants will inevitably and automatically make claim to the resources of the host society. What this implies is that the volume of resources remains essentially the same, thus the emergence of new people will automatically take them away from the existing population. A few common clichés about Chinese migrants are widespread:

- they take jobs away from Russians;
- they take away/steal Russian forests, metals and other natural resources; and
- they divert capital away from Russia.

Intimately linked to the overall set of migration myths is the belief in the absolute and inherent criminality of Chinese migrants (Vitkovskaya and Panarin 2000: 267–38). Specific to this particular discourse is the existence of China's ominous "triads".

From "Yellow Peril" to "China threat": from "enemy" to "opponent"

Although the idea of the "China threat" carries similar connotation to "Yellow Peril", it still indicates a shift in thinking between centuries. It is not merely, if at all, a question of differentiated treatment in the relationship to "Yellows" – and it is unlikely that anyone today would regard the Chinese, Japanese and Mongols as a single community with common interests merely on the basis of race. The fear of the "Yellow Peril" was based on the idea that "Yellows" represented an enemy with inhuman, alien logic and motivations for their actions.[7] The "stranger"

---

7   A typical example is that of the Norwegian polar explorer and social activist Fridtjof Nansen, who demonstrated his humanitarian nature in a giant-scale assistance to refugees and displaced persons in a famine relief effort in the Volga region following World War I. Nansen organically and completely naturally thought in terms of racial differences, confrontation and inevitable battle between "races" for a mutual annihilation (Nansen 1915).

appears not in the guise of a concrete enemy with very real interests and constituting a serious, possibly lethal, threat. He becomes the personification of "absolute evil", the embodiment of utter foreignness and fundamental incompatibility. He's the equivalent of the Devil. With him, any kind of negotiation, bargain or compromise is impossible. His logic simply cannot be understood. Conflict with him involves total confrontation, a mortal war that can only end with the annihilation of one of the parties. Gudkov argues:

> The issue is not about specific nuisances or individual actors – an antagonist, an opponent, a socially dangerous individual, i.e. about actions that are predictable and understandable through their own specific reasons. To ensure an actor becomes an "enemy", he must have a number of general characteristics: uncertainty and unpredictability, asocial force, ignorance of all regulatory or conventional constraints. With the emergence of the "enemy", conventional systems of positive reward and incentives for cooperation do not work, or take second place… From the enemy emerges a storm, a mortal danger to the very existence of the group (2005: 12).

The limits and lethalness of the threat follows from the fact that its vector is an individual of a fundamentally different world, an intelligent, reasoning creature that is not a human being.

With the disappearance of the epithet "yellow", racial discourse becomes peripheral in the analysis of social relations and problems. Racism, of course, remains, and racial differences continue to inform and reflect the nature of human connections and relationships, but the widespread notions of an unbridgeable gulf between races, and the vision of other races as aliens, has generally gone. The object of fear does not merely become concrete, it also becomes more rational. The "enemy" is becoming the "opponent", and the imagined "war of the worlds" is transforming into a conflict between states and peoples. The horrifying vision of a collision between civiliations gives way to fears about Chinese expansionism, about an influx of migrants. The conception of "threats" translates onto a rational plane.

This shift could have far-reaching consequences. As a phobia becomes rationalised and as its mystical and transcendental component becomes peripheral, its mobilisation force is significantly reduced. Very indicative in this sense are the dynamics of anti-Chinese sentiments among the population of Siberia and the Russian Far East; peaking in 1990, they drastically decrease later with the intensification of economic and human contact with China and the Chinese. Moreover, recent studies show that migrants come to be regarded as an important resource which then requires protection

(Blyakher and Pegin 2010: 485–501). This may become a guarantee, if only with respect to a rational immigration policy by the authorities. By using xenophobic sentiments as an instrument of power, occasionally contributing to their formulation and dissemination, the ruling elite are not immune to a boomerang effect. Sometimes they themselves become infected by the completely irrational fears created partly by them, thus leading them to irrational actions and decisions – often with disastrous consequences.

One of these consequences is clearly stated in the title of the book by David Shimmelpennink van der Oye (2009): *Towards the Rising Sun: How Imperial Myth-making Led Russia Into War with Japan*. It was precisely the syndrome of "Yellow Peril" that led to the catastrophe of the Russian-Japanese war. Similarly, Officer of the Imperial Russian Army Baron Roman Ungern von Sternberg attempted to organise a "new Mongol invasion" against a "rotten Europe" (Jozefovich 2010). This farcical, but nonetheless bloody, episode in the Civil War waged in Siberia came about partly out of the sincere belief of its instigator that a "yellow invasion" was inevitable and that it may be instrumentalised.

A complex combination of arrogant beliefs in the superiority of the "white man" and powerful latent fears about an all-sweeping and devastating "yellow wave" gave rise in 1900, at the time of the Boxer Rebellion in China, to an extraordinarily intense panic in the vicinity of Blagoveshchensk. The panic of the population and the confusion of the authorities led to a pogrom in the course of which thousands of Chinese residing in the city were drowned in the waters of the Amur river (Dyatlov 2003: 123–4). Against this background of fear in the face of immigration, the completely irrational decision made by contemporary Russian authorities to prohibit foreigners from trading on open markets appears fairly innocuous and does not have such fatal consequences.

Thus the unique situation of two distinct waves of Chinese economic migration to Russia, waves separated by the deep chasm of the Soviet era, shows that the migrant phobia can find overlapping but ultimately different forms of expression. Indeed, very different fears and prejudices can be concealed behind a historically formed concept such as the "Yellow Peril", and the profound cultural differences setting apart the Chinese migrants and the Russian host society can possibly give rise to a "war of the worlds". This has far-reaching consequences. If migrant phobia is undergirded by a conflict of interest, rather than fears predicated on ethnic survival, then the emergence of peaceful coexistence and cooperation is a perfectly realistic outcome.

6. The Case of the Amur as a Cross-Border Zone of Illegality

Natalia Ryzhova

This chapter concerns poaching and other illegal fishing activities in the Amur, the border river separating Russia and China. Both Russian and Chinese citizens take part in these activities, which have greatly reduced the number of fish in the river.[1] Other factors have also significantly contributed to a reduction of fish stocks, such as industrial development on areas adjacent to the river, outdated technology, deforestation and generally poor environmental conditions. However, reports issued by Russian officials and media sources lead readers to believe that Chinese poachers have a particularly negative impact on the river and other natural resources.

The aim of this study is not to allocate blame but rather to reflect on what can be done in response to environmental degradation. Water resources are a classic example of natural "resources of general use" (common pool resources). It is precisely through the example of the catastrophic depletion of river resources that the so-called "tragedy of accessibility"

1   Some ideas for this article were drawn by the author in the course of a discussion of the project "Property Rights in Extralegal Extraction of Natural Resources: Enforcement and Social Norms (study of cases in Russia, Kyrgyzstan, Tajikistan and Mongolia)". I wish to thank Prof. A. Oleynik (Memorial University, Canada), Prof. F. Thoumi (United Nations International Narcotics Control Board), Sh. Abrorov (Tajik National University, Tajikistan), Dr. A. Dooranov (Kyrgyz National University, Kyrgyzstan), Dr. E. Lee (Institute of Economic Research, Far Eastern Department of the Russian Academy of Science, Russia), Dr. E. Nevzorova (Baikal State University, Russia), and O. Shagdarsüren (National University of Mongolia, Mongolia).

          DOI: 10.11647/OBP.0026.06

(Hardin 1968) is usually discussed. In essence, it considers that if a river is common, its resources will be drawn up until they are completely degraded. This involves factories discharging waste, farmers cultivating the soil and using agricultural chemicals, power stations modifying river outflows and fishermen eliminating first the most valuable fish then other breeds. Each "member of the community" (i.e. user) can, by increasing his burden on the river, increase his own income, and the resources of the river will be reduced slightly. However, if all users do the same, the impact on the resources of the river will be significantly higher. If a user reduces his consumption, the resources of the river will improve slightly, however his personal gain from it will be far lower than the amount of lost revenues. Studies for solutions to the "tragedy of accessibility" are being conducted in the social sphere, with the creation of incentives for the social unacceptability of predatory use of natural resources. Research by Nobel Prize winner Elinor Ostrom (1990) and her synthesis of other projects' empirical results demonstrate that communities themselves, without government interference, find effective strategies that prevent the "tragedy" from occurring.

But what happens when shared resources are crosscut by state boundaries? What kind of incentive can the state create against predatory practices, when it sees the task of maintaining the border's impassability as its first priority? In response to these questions, the chapter examines: the formal rules regulating fishing activities and the legal mechanisms ensuring effectiveness of these rules in the Russian Federation; informal fishing practices (i.e. those that violate applicable laws); and social enforcement (i.e. social norms ensuring the effectiveness of formal rules).

Enforcement of property rights to natural resources and informal practices

According to Douglass C. North (2003), institutions make up formal rules, informal constraints and means of enforcement, i.e. procedures for ensuring the effectiveness of these restrictions. Studies conducted in countries with transition economies show that changes in formal rules and attempts to introduce institutions determining the economic life of society, radical changes in accepted social norms, and a transformation of former illegal practices into legally acceptable and recognised economic activity, have led to the prevalence of an informal economy in these countries.

Russia and China have not been spared these "side effects" of the transition to market economy, and an informal activity is developing not only in the sphere that is traditionally most "suitable" for this, such as in trade, public catering and the service sector, but in the sphere of nature management as well.[2] Of course, the informal use of natural resources is not an exceptional practice occurring only in China (or in the border regions of Russia). In varying degrees, it is common in both developed and developing countries, as well as in countries with transition economies. Research studies have described poaching practices in the context of Canada (Bodiguel 2002) and illegal gold and diamond mining and timber smuggling practices in Africa (International Labour Office 1999). The reasons for the prevalence of informal nature management are often understood by researchers to be found in ineffective legislation or the inefficient application of that legislation (Acheson 2006).

However, the quality of legislation and of legal enforcement (i.e. enforced through the courts or fines) is not wholly determined, not even to a significant extent, by the resolution of the problem of informal nature management. Aside from the legal support of formal rights, "informal" mechanisms exist that operate through social norms, civil society institutions, etc. North, as well as other researchers (Posner and Rasmusen 1999; Sobel 2006), have pointed out that formal, including market, institutions require the existence of special enforcement norms (and not associated only with written law) rooted in traditions, customs and religion, i.e. in social and moral norms. Contrasting the role of formal rules (such as their fluidity in the process of market transition) and social norms (e.g. survival rate of imported legal rights) in terms of their impact on the development of the informal economy, the authors agree that social norms take precedence.

The fact that social norms take precedence over legal enforcement is clear from everyday examples. It makes sense to expect that massive annual poaching of spawning fish will be more likely to occur in a society where the practice of poaching is morally acceptable and rests upon traditional economic norms than in a society where poaching nets constitute an historically forgotten and socially excluded anomaly.

---

2   For example, the number of amateur "grey" companies exploiting various natural resources in China had reached 250 thousand tonnes by the twenty-first century, a quantity dozens of times higher than any country in the world for a similar index (International Labour Office 1999).

As transpires from academic and expert publications (Hentschel, Hruschka and Priester 2002), informal nature management is to a large extent characteristic of developing countries rather than developed nations. There are numerous reasons for this, such as poverty, technological archaism and weakness of political institutions. Other mechanisms of social enforcement are carried out through the media. On the one hand, newspapers and television provide a framework for discussions of social life and constitute a guide that takes up, disseminates and creates stereotypes, including the admissibility or inadmissibility of certain commercial practices. On the other hand, as a resolution to voters' lack of information, the media can exert a significant influence on political institutions and decisions, including in the field of environmental protection. A number of papers link the media (or more precisely the media's (in)corruptibility and freedom of speech) to political institutions and effective resolutions for the protection of the natural environment (Suphachalasai 2005).

The causes for the prevalence of the informal use of natural resources are frequently examined through the concepts of property rights theory, which are less well-defined in developing countries and in countries with a transition economy. Ronald H. Coase (1960) was one of the first to draw attention to the economic significance of ownership rights with a well-known "theorem". According to this theorem, externalities (the discrepancies between costs and benefits) occur only when property rights are poorly defined. Lack of clarity in property rights gives rise to conflicts between recipients of benefits and costs: in the case of air polluted by plant emissions, for example, costs are borne by the people living in the vicinity while benefits are drawn by the owners of the plant. According to Coase and his followers, a way to overcome externalities lies in the pre-definition of property rights. Yet if property rights are divided between various actors, who will prevent all owners from adopting opportunistic behaviour? It is after all reasonable to try and obtain additional benefits rather than to relinquish them.

The necessity to resolve this social dilemma is far more pressing when it comes to resources of common use (such as water resources from seas and rivers, common pastures, national parks, etc.). Common pool resources (CPR) may be available either for all or for only a limited number of individuals. The first alternative is referred to as CPR with open access (water in a river, air in a city), the second is CPR with restricted access (national parks). The situation in which a few individuals acting independently and rationally in the pursuit of their own interests, ultimately destroying the limited common resources, is known in the scientific literature as the "tragedy of the commons/common accessibility". This pessimistic view of CPR was first described in Garrett Hardin's work (1968). He pointed out that ownership of public resources may take place if: a) the right to ownership was never established; b) the State has legalised it; c) there are no effective controls in place; and d) it is virtually impossible to implement it.

In the theoretical frameworks aimed at a resolution of the CPR dilemma, a key question has long remained: "Why do people choose (or should choose) a rule that will constrain or restrict their choice?" (Buchanan and Yon 1999). A large number of cases has accumulated, demonstrating that the resolution of this social dilemma takes place in the negotiation process, provided the community has the opportunity and time to organise itself. The outcome will be different if the resolution of the issue is attempted through coercion – by state intervention, for instance, and the nationalisation of resources (Ostrom, 1990). An overview of theoretical works suggests that the resolution of the problem of informal practices in the use of common pool resources is achievable through the resolution of the social issue of harmonisation between individual and common interests.

Characteristics of the empirical basis

Given that the focus of this paper's research interests are the institutional provision mechanisms (both legal and social) guaranteeing the implementation of standards in nature management, and that the media constitute one of the mechanisms to ensure this, empirical data will essentially be based on media materials.

This empirical basis will include:

a. A *normative* basis (the Russian Constitution, the Water Code (*Vodny Codex*), federal laws relating to fishing and the state border, various regulations and agreements).

b. An *official* basis – publications of the Russian Federation's Federal Security Service (FSB) and the Federal Customs Service.[3] The choice to include these bases was informed by the fact that these

---

3   The selection of cases was made on official websites of the Federal Customs Service (http://www.customs.ru) and the Federal Security Service (http://www.fsb.ru) with the keywords "China" and "resources" (for the period 2001–2010). From this sample were selected those texts in which border violations in the field of fish resources were reported – the total number of these cases was 18.

services are officially responsible for the ongoing representation in Russia of the fight against smuggling. This representation is limited by many objective and subjective factors, such as internal (customs management) or external (i.e. originating from the federal centre) policies concerning the frequency and nature of links to the public. However, these same constraints can be interpreted as advantages, given that formal regulations are supported not only by concrete strong actions, but also by congruent discursive practices. Accordingly, a change in the frequency of official reports about sanctions, or indications within those reports of an increase in the severity of penalties can be viewed as signals directed to adjust informal practices.[4]

c. A *social* basis – authored publications in the media, posted on Internet sites, relating to violations of Russian fishing regulations by Chinese ("social China") and Russian ("social Russia") citizens.[5] If the bases of the FSB and the Federal Customs Service have been studied with a view to typifying and characterising informal practices, journalistic texts have been examined in order to study the characteristics of social enforcement. The number of authored newspaper pieces in each basis equals the number of statements in the official basis, totalling 36 texts.

d. A *Chinese* basis – publications of the Chinese news agencies Xinhua and Renmin Ribao.[6] The idea to refer to these texts was to compare Chinese and Russian mass media from the point of view of social enforcement in respect to the resources of "common rivers". Unfortunately, due to the small number of these texts, formal quantitative comparison is impossible and only a few qualitative conclusions have been drawn.

---

4   "Lu Guisan was sentenced to 2 years imprisonment to be served in a penal colony. Note that this was *the first time* a sentence was passed for the smuggling of biological resources [emphasis added]. As a rule, criminals get off with fines or suspended sentence" (FCS 2006).

5   Media outlets include NTV (http://www.ntv.ru); RIA-novosti (http://dv.rian.ru); *Nezavisimaya gazeta* (http://www.ng.ru/ngregions); *Komsomolskaya Pravda* (www.kp.ru/daily); *Amurskaya Pravda* (www.amurpravda.ru); *Zolotoy rog* (www.zrpress.ru); *Teleport* (http://www.teleport2001.ru).

6   The search engines of the agencies Xinhuanews (http://russian.news.cn) and Peoples Daily Online (http://russian.people.com.cn) returned only five articles with the key words "fish", "fishermen" and "Amur".

e. *Scientific* (Lyapustin, Pervushina and Fomenko 2010; Sherbina 2008; Vaisman and Fomenko 2006; Simonov and Dahmer 2008) – used for the typification of informal practices in the fishing industry. They are partly used for the qualitative characteristics of social enforcement, since scientific texts may also impact on the guarantee of regulation effectiveness.

Research methods have included a quantitative and qualitative content analysis using the software QDA Miner v.2.0.8 with the module WordStat v.5.1.12 developed by Provalis Research (Montreal).[7]

Formal regulations and legal enforcement

Russian legislation includes a definition of the "right to common use of natural resources": guaranteed by Article 42 of the Constitution of the Russian Federation is the freedom to use, in all liberty and without charge, the atmosphere, water resources, etc. Starting in 2004, Russian legislation on fisheries and water resources in general have improved and become stricter. Russian Federation's Water Code of 03.06.2006 No. 74-FZ defines the right of citizens to common water resources (Article 88) as follows: "citizens are entitled to free use of water resources for personal and domestic needs (including movement and sojourn on strips of land in the vicinity of bodies of water to engage in amateur and sport fishing, and to moor marine equipment)".

Also in existence is a law relating to *special use of natural resources*, which defines the possibility to use certain portions of natural resources in accordance with their intended purpose. Obtaining this right is subject to a fee. In addition to this code, these activities are regulated by Federal Law of 20 December 2004 No. 166-FZ "On fishery and conservation of marine biology resources", as well as other legal acts (in particular, regulating industrial quotas and authorisations, zonal delimitations, etc.). In addition, legislative acts have also been developed and adopted, aiming

---

7   In this study, a correlational dictionary was used. For example, to the one category "fishermen, to fish", derivative words such as fisherman, fishermen, fish, fishing were also linked. When counting the number of cases of that category, it was calculated in how many texts the category occurred: for example, the category "poacher" was found in 11 (61%) of the 18 official texts in and 12 (67%) of the 18 informal texts. When counting the number of mentions, it was calculated how many times each category was found in the total number of words of the given base. For example, the category "Chinese" was found 50 times in the "official" base, which contains 2034 words.

at strengthening accountability with respect to poaching. Thus, the Federal Law "On the introduction of amendments to the Code of the Russian Federation concerning administrative violations" has increased sanctions for violations of fishing regulations.

In principle, amateur and sport fishing is free, but each angler must have the appropriate ticket, as well as the right to operate motor boats (if used). In recent years, this type of activity has become much more regulated. Thus, for instance, the Federal Fisheries Agency may (and should): impose bans on fishing in certain areas for certain species of fish, and even certain categories of citizens (fishing being allowed for example for children under 16 years of age or pensioners older than 70); close off some areas for certain periods (e.g. during spawning); limit the minimum/maximum dimensions and weight of fish caught; determine the types, quantities, designs and mesh sizes of authorised instruments and catching methods, including the types of vessels and times of use. To catch certain species of fish within the context of recreational fishing, a licence (special permit) may be required, and will be subject to a fee. Violation of these restrictions may incur administrative and criminal liability. Article 256 of the Criminal Code "Illegal fishing of aquatic animals and plants" allows for fines ranging from 100 to 500 thousand roubles, or imprisonment for up to two years; Part 2 of Article 8.37 of the Administrative Code of the Russian Federation, "Violation of the rules regulating the use of wildlife", introduces a penalty of one to two thousand roubles and confiscation of the vessel and other fishing equipment.

Industrial fishing (fisheries) involves the commercial harvesting (catching) of marine biological resources through the use of special means of quality control, processing, handling, transportation and storage of catches and their by-products. The right to use aquatic biological resources is based on the authorisation to harvest (catch) aquatic biological resources and agreement on the use of fishing sites. Some contradictions exist between amateur and commercial fishing. On the one hand, licensees frequently engage in uncontrolled and predatory fishing, thereby restricting access of amateur fishermen to water sites, and, in some cases, leaseholders demand illegal additional fees for fishing at water sites allocated to commercial usage. On the other hand, commercial fishermen point out that amateur fishermen frequently engage in poaching and pollute waterways and river banks.

To return to the issue of fishing in the border river, it should also be noted that active legislation has banned the harvesting of aquatic biological resources by foreign individuals. Of course, Chinese citizens engaging in poaching activities in Russian waters violate the legislation for the provision of the integrity and sovereignty of Russia's state borders. An agreement "On cooperation in the field of conservation, management and reproduction of living aquatic resources in the Amur and Ussuri border rivers", was signed on 27 May 1994 between the governments of Russia and China. According to this document, the conservation and reproduction of fish stocks and the regulation of fishing activities with regards to the protection of biological resources take place within the framework of the protection of national borders. In order to implement this document, an operation called "Fishing-season-Amur", previously known as "East" and "Frontier", is carried out every year.

The main actor implementing legal enforcement in the sphere of fishing activities is the state inspector for fish conservation. If we are talking about informal fishing activities in the border river, then the provision of formal regulations is also guaranteed by border and other services of the FSB, and, for contraband fishing production, by the customs authorities. Additionally, in the course of special campaigns aiming to curb smuggling, the Ministry of the Interior, the Ministry for the Environment, the Ministry for Agriculture and other departments and agencies are also involved.

Chinese legislation, in contrast to Russian legislation, includes stricter sanctions (including the death penalty for the smuggling of tigers, pandas and wild Asian elephants) in respect to violations of environmental legislation. At the same time it allows for criminal, administrative and disciplinary sanctions not only within the law, like the Russian Criminal Code and Administrative Code, but also directly in the legislative acts governing customs and the use and protection of natural resources (Lyapustin, Pervushina and Fomenko 2010: 53). In China, the State Council's acting Committee for wildlife plays an active role and public security bodies are actively involved in the control of implementation of legislation relating to environment protection (ibid.: 47).

China and Russia regularly hold meetings and engage in joint campaigns aimed at reducing the number of cases of poaching and smuggling of fish resources from Russia to China. However, despite attempts to harmonise legal enforcement, and regardless of the tightening of applicable sanctions, poaching remains widespread, and every year the situation is only getting worse:

> The ubiquitous and widespread nature of poaching, whose aim is frequently to prepare production for subsequent contraband, has been highlighted by the results of activities carried out within the environmental framework of the Ministry for the Environment, the Ministry for

Agriculture and the Federal Agency for Fishing. Information originating from all stakeholders in the Far Eastern federal district, demonstrates the massive amount of illicit acts. According to data by the administration of the Primorye region, in 2008 over 700 raids were carried out to curb poaching, in the course of which around 600 violations of the legislation relating to environmental protection were found, including poaching. As a result of the activities undertaken, over 50 species of illegally caught animals were confiscated. In 2009, following weekly anti-poaching raids in the Primorye, 981 offences were found. In the region of Khabarovsk, in 2008, 686 crimes were identified, just in the area of illicit traffic of aquatic biological resources (they numbered 618 in 2007) (Lyapustin, Pervushina and Fomenko 2010: 23).

Concrete methods exist to legally enforce formal rules (analysis of publications of the "official" base): in five out of eighteen of the cases analysed, the FSB declared the launch of a criminal investigation. Criminal cases, recorded in the database, mostly involved violations of the state border and the smuggling of large quantities of fish, but did not include poaching. Russian legislation does not allow for criminal prosecution for illegal trafficking in fish, only for its illegal production. Therefore, all poachers (Russian or Chinese), who do not have nets in their boats, can claim that they "found" the fish, "decided to look after it", "were surprised to find the fish in the boat when they returned from dinner", etc.

The main sanction for Chinese citizens is the confiscation of their equipment, and, in some cases, boats, as well as short-term detention and subsequent transfer to the Chinese authorities. In only one case out of eighteen, the FSB announced a sentence, which, incidentally, was also relatively mild:

> "The tribunal of the Amur region sentenced to three months' detention two citizens of China for violating Russia's state borders… The court sentenced the perpetrators to a period of three months' imprisonment, to be served in a penal colony. Given that they were detained during preliminary investigations, the sentence has already been served by the prisoners. They were therefore released and left Russia's territory" (FSS 2004b).

The changes in the legislation and mechanisms for its enforcement implemented in Russia and China and resulting from negotiation processes, do not lead to a decrease in cases of poaching and appear in fact to merely exacerbate the social dilemma of differences between individual and public interests.

Informal practices in fishing activities

The analysis of the "official" basis of the FSB and Federal Customs Service shows that, as indicated by official documents regarding the poaching and smuggling of fish resources, up to 25% of all violations occur on the Russian-Chinese border (followed in second place by forests, then sea products, wildlife and flora, then finally minerals). Nonetheless, official statistics indicate that forests are the main resource for which regulations are violated (Lyapustin and Fomenko 2003).

Of course, informal fishing on the Amur border river has a long history (Lyapustin 2006). Given that informal economic activities aim at avoiding the costs linked to compliance with laws and administrative regulations, we can say that informal fishing on the border river began with the creation, in the Russian Empire, of formal rules regarding the use of natural resources in the Far East. At the turn of the twentieth century, there were illegal (i.e., in violation of the law) cross-boundary practices: in particular in relation to fishing by Chinese nationals of the most valuable fish species in inland Russian waters and exploitation of the indigenous population for this purpose. However, until 1 January 1913, i.e. until the abolition of the 50-verst free-trade strip, fishing in the Amur River had a more *extralegal* character (i.e. unregulated by applicable legislation): the Chinese harvested, bought and exported without duties resources such as fish (Lyapustin and Fomenko 2003).

Changes in the existing rules, as well as the socio-economic and political turmoil in the pre-revolutionary, Soviet and post-Soviet periods, did not inhibit access to fishing resources in the Amur River by Chinese citizens, although an extremely strict enforcement in the 1960s-1980s did reduce illegal (from the point of view of Russian legislation) Chinese activities along the Russian bank, which due to particularities of the riverbed, is richer than the Chinese side.

It would be nonetheless naïve to imagine that Soviet citizens were not involved in informal fishing practices. They did not have any economic stimulus to fish on the Chinese side. They had, however, numerous reasons to engage in illegal fishing practices on their "own shore". Moreover, prohibitions introduced in the Soviet period and at other times frequently contribute directly to the creation of informal rules:

> On 'average', in the 70's and 80's, the catching of [mandarin fish] was probably a sporadic occurrence... [sometimes] up to a quarter of the fish caught with

floating nets were mandarin fish. However, because of the ban on catching them, the mandarin fish caught by fishermen for personal consumption and through commercial fishing was not included in statistics... In our assessment, the effectiveness of all these prohibitions is very low... when there were indeed very few (until the mid 1990's), fishermen did not release the *zheltoschyok* [*Elopichthys bambusa*] they caught (it seemed silly to release fish that was dead or half-dead). In addition, it is impossible to follow every single fisherman, and *zheltoschyok* is considered a delicacy by many residents of the Amur. Since during the Soviet period it was difficult to sell 'red book species' officially, the *zheltoschyok* caught by fishing companies ended up in the homes of fishermen (Novomodnyi, Zolotukhin and Sharov 2004: 19).

"Pilfering" was just one form of the informal economy of Soviet times. Fish brought home (as well as any other commodity) became the subject of monetary and non-monetary forms of exchange. However, emerging informal practices became fixed over time, and changes in formal rules (e.g. transition to the market) just created a terrain for its transformation. Indeed, during the economic collapse, when Far Eastern fishermen as well as other workers did not receive their salaries for several months, a survival mechanism emerged on its own. As a result of this and other reasons, various informal and illegal practices consolidated, were becoming a tradition.

The Amur fish resources were dealt with in a "traditional" manner, i.e. they were exploited highly intensively both on the Russian and Chinese territories. As a result of official and unofficial fishing, stocks showed continual decline and by 1970, no longer reached 2000 tons (see Fig. 1).

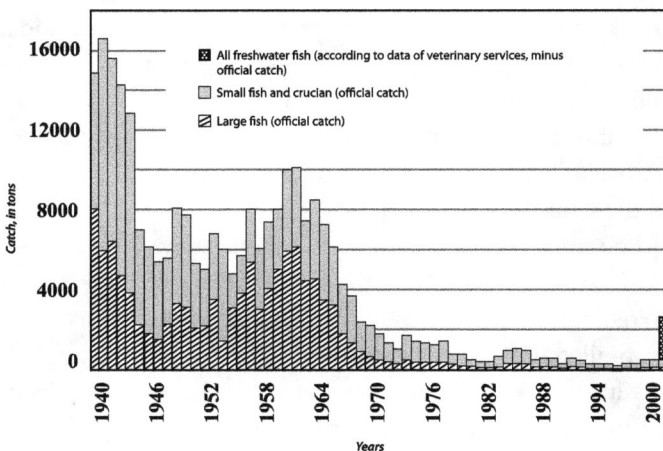

Fig. 1 Evolution of Amur fish caught through nets (source: Novomodnyi, Zolotukhin and Sharov 2004: 8)

Here, the consensus among researchers is that China has consistently used rivers' biological resources more actively than Russia, due to the vast population living on Chinese territories:

> As is well-known, in China's Heilongjiang Province, in areas adjacent to the Amur, fishing and fish farming constitute some of the key industries. Further, in the second half of the 20th century, and especially in the past two decades, the province's population has grown significantly. Under the impact of intensive fishing and environmental changes, sturgeon, salmon and several other species of fish have gradually disappeared from the Songhua River. The number of sturgeons in the upper and middle Amur have also decreased significantly. In the mid-1960s, a strategy was adopted in the province to expand the fish farming sector as an alternative to fishing, and by 2002 the fishing industry already represented just 12% of the total fish production in the region (over 400 thousand tons) (Novomodnyi, Zolotukhin and Sharov 2004: 28).

Despite the greater activity of Chinese fishermen, their activities on their bank of the river are, as a rule, mostly circumscribed to the realm of formal regulations. Levels of poaching in China are significantly lower than in Russia. (Lyapustin, Pervushina and Fomenko 2010). In Russia, illegal catches exceed official ones, and the volume of poaching, particularly the illegal fishing of sturgeon, is constantly on the increase. Research on the informal economy is always confronted with the task of evaluating its volume in absolute and/or relative terms. According to Amurrybvod's data, poaching in the Amur River exceeds legal activities by a factor of two-three (Khabarovskyi krai 2009). These estimates are probably inaccurate. The official catch of chum salmon in the Amur was less than a thousand tonnes in 1999, but according to the methodically justified estimates of Pacific Scientific Research Fisheries Centre (PSRFC) specialists (Novomodnyi, Zolotukhin and Sharov 2004) the consumptive catch of autumnal salmon in the area of the Amur, a length of 1,200 km, amounted to about nine tonnes in 1990. In other words, the discrepancy is already nine times wider, but to this must be added the illegal trafficking of sturgeon, including caviar, as well as other fish (mandarin fish, *zheltoschyok*, catfish, etc.). According to PSRFC's conservative estimates, the illegal catch, just for sturgeon and only in the main part of the river, was not less than 750 tonnes in 1990. Thus, the excess of informal trafficking of fish over formal activities is to be multiplied by at least ten.

Extralegal fishing practices along the Russian riverbank include:
- fishing without documentation for personal consumption, including prohibited species, through prohibited means, etc.;

- use and appropriation of unlimited fishing rights for industrial aims by representatives of indigenous and minority peoples;
- small-enterprise catch by unregistered groups;
- bribery of people in charge, procuring extralegal fishing;
- non-observance of the border regime, creation of networks in Russian waters; and
- reciprocal exchanges with regulatory officials (inspectors and individuals responsible for legal enforcement can trade the fish themselves and, through personal agreements, establish "acceptable" and "unacceptable" forms of violations; such informal contracts being reinforced by reciprocal links – you scratch my back and I'll scratch yours – beyond monetary exchanges).

Practices ensuring extralegal trade include:

- purchase of fish obtained by extralegal means, "legalisation" through use of forged documents, and export to China;
- smuggling of caviar, including live and fertilised, for consumption and breeding purposes;
- smuggling of fish products, including fish prohibited by Convention on International Trade in Endangered Species of Wild Flora and Fauna (CITES);
- extralegal delivery of fish products to points of sale;
- processing of fish, sea products and caviar for small-enterprise purposes (cutting, salting, packaging), without issue of the documentation appropriate to conducting such business;
- creation of enterprises carrying out illegal traffic in fish products, including businesses registered to figureheads; and
- trade without documents or with forged documents (including under the guise of products confiscated by conservation organisations).

Many practices are to some extent connected with cross-border exchanges – fish caught illegally are sent to China using false documents:

"In the course of search operations, it was revealed that the CEO of one of Vladivostok firms, had acquired for profit more than 127 tonnes of frozen salmon and about 65 tonnes of salt without any documents and had signed a contract with a Chinese firm for the supply of this fish. To obtain the necessary documents for export, three certificates of quality issued by another firm were presented to the Primorye office for Rossel'khoznadzor [Russian Agricultural Council]. On the basis of these documents, veterinary certificates were obtained. To make it look as described in the accompanying papers, on the order of the CEO, the entire fish production was packed into bags tagged with the name of the company listed in the fake quality documentation. After that, the dishonest dealers registered the cargo as export, and part of the cargo was sent to China. But when they attempted to send another batch of vehicles with the fish products, they were detained simultaneously in three places by the Far Eastern Customs Service: in Ussuriysk, in Vladivostok and in the Khasan area…" (FCS 2010).

The FSB and the Federal Customs Service reported informal fishing practices in Russian waters by Chinese citizens, and in particular concerning: Chinese fishermen obstructing the Amur with their nets and not complying with the border regime; buying of illegally obtained fish for export to China, smuggling of fish products; organisation of informal small-enterprise teams on both sides of the river; and the creation of enterprises involved in illegal fishing and/or fish export, including businesses registered to figureheads.

Fishing on the opposite (Russian) coast is the most common practices of the *private* (i.e. non-commercial) use of cross-border natural resources by citizens of the PRC. The aspiration of Chinese to catch fish on Russian territory is due to the fact that, in China, former fishing grounds are significantly regulated by dams, are degraded by industrial pollution, and wild fish populations have been legally and extensively fished for many years, for both commercial and domestic purposes. As a result, many species of fish have disappeared. On the Russian side legal fishing has always been limited, and industrial and agricultural pollution has been lower.

Every year, jointly agreed periods of total fishing ban are set with the aim of preserving fish stocks' reproduction. During these periods, operations are carried out by the Russian border guards in conjunction with other services to halt these types of activities (commonly known as the Fishing-season-Amur special campaign). The majority of the reports in the analysed basis were made precisely during that campaign: from 11 June to 15 July 2003, more than 70 boats with Chinese citizens were detained (FSS 2006); in 2001, over the same period, 40 charges were made (FSS 2001); in 2006, in one day, about 500 fishermen went fishing on 180 boats (FSS 2006b).

Both "amateurs" and "professional teams" are involved in informal fishing activities. Even when they hold an official licence, "professional" fishing teams often do not respect the periods and locations specified on the licence, evade fiscal payments and also fail to respect employment requirements for their employees. The seasonal work of paid fisherman is extremely difficult, requiring great physical and moral strength (every evening and early morning the fishermen place and remove the nets and all day gut and salt the fish), and in case of sickness or other *force majeure* they are not remunerated. Sometimes, Chinese are hired to carry out such work:

"In the Far Eastern region, on the Amur River, in the area of Smidovichesky in the Jewish Autonomous Region, border guards foiled an attempt by a group of poachers consisting in five Chinese and three Russians to fish salmon... As it turned out, a local entrepreneur had organised an international group of poachers. He had hired some Chinese who had come to Russia on a visa but did not have the right to be in the border area and had promised them a solid reward if the plan to fish salmon was successful. The detained poachers were transferred to law enforcement authorities for trial" (FSS 2004a).

Prior to the recent changes in legislation differentiating between amateur and commercial fishermen, a clear "dividing line" existed, and it never occurred to those who engaged in commercial production to call themselves "amateurs". Following changes in legislation, it became beneficial to informal traders to be registered as amateurs. The head of Federal Agency for Fishing declared: "a sub-category of fishermen has now emerged who catches dozens or hundreds of kilos of fish. When our service for the conservation of fish detains them, they say – we are amateur fishermen, we have the right... one hundred, two hundred, three hundred kilos of fish" (Newsland 2010).

In terms of legislation, the Chinese fishermen who are active on Russian territory can not in any case be classified as "amateurs". It would be interesting nonetheless to find out to what extent this activity is commercial or private. Out of the eighteen cases, the FSB pointed out in fourteen of them that they had caught a group of people. However, it is far from clear in these cases whether these violations constitute an individual strategy or whether they represent a particular operation through a business scheme. For example, the following quote mentions a specific "Chinese citizen", however the volume and price of the exports points to a commercial nature of the operation:

"Employees of the office of the FSB for the Jewish Autonomous Region foiled an attempt yesterday to smuggle a large cargo of Amur sturgeons and kalugas into China. In a private house in Birobidzhan 1,300 kilos of fish were discovered. According to the owner of the house, the fish was hidden by a Chinese citizen who had promised to take the goods to China this week. FSB Public relations officer Sergey Dorofeev said that the value of the fish which the Chinese had, in all likelihood, purchased from poachers, is estimated at 130 thousand roubles. In China, its value is considerably higher" (FSS 2002).

On the other hand, if it is reported that a group of offenders has been caught, it does not necessarily indicate affiliation to a commercial entity:

"Two citizens of China were sentenced to three months imprisonment by a court in the Amur region for a violation of Russia's state borders. The regional office of the FSB reported that in June the Chinese were detained by border guards in the Svobodnensky area in the upper Amur, 118 kilometres downstream, near the Russian coast as they were poaching fish. A wooden rowing boat and fishing equipment were confiscated from the perpetrators. The court sentenced them to a period of imprisonment of three months to be served in a penal colony. Given that they were detained during preliminary investigations, the sentence has already been served by the prisoners. They were therefore released and have left Russia's territory" (FSS 2004b).

Judging from the temporal dynamics of communications, an illegal commercial activity was recently actualised for the purpose of export to China. This conclusion is confirmed by a study by Sergey N. Lyapustin (2006). The informal export of fish is based on the use of forged documents. Both Russian and Chinese firms can act as exporters:

"At once, 5 criminal cases were filed by Sakhalin customs regarding the procurement of fish products. In the course of a few years, more than 1500 tonnes of frozen humpback salmon, squid and plaice have been delivered to China and the Republic of Korea through fraudulent documents. The total amount of smuggled sea products amounted to more than 34 million roubles…" (FCS 2009).

The following is a schematic diagram illustrating how extralegal practices are coordinated from the date of purchase (procurement) of fish until it is exported (Fig. 2). In the first stage, in order to avoid penalties, extralegal actors (members of indigenous communities, individuals, small groups) bribe inspectors. As a result, fish is not confiscated and can be traded. The fish production is then bought by firms specialising in export. The purchased illegal goods need to be legalised. To this end, the firm can use documents registered to other companies. The presence of registered documents can also be explained through ties to organisations issuing veterinary certificates, quality control certificates, etc. As a result, exporting firms are able to submit documents to customs for export of fish products, for instance to China. The registration of the paperwork at the customs may also be accompanied by bribes – for example, to accelerate the completion of procedures. Finally, the "properly" registered fish is supplied to consumers in another country. In this scheme, the key role is played by the "exporting firm", which is "registered" in the name of a Russian citizen. However that citizen may simply be a figurehead while the actual owner is a Chinese (or other) importing firm. Of course, this scheme is not unique, either in terms of interaction or its key players.

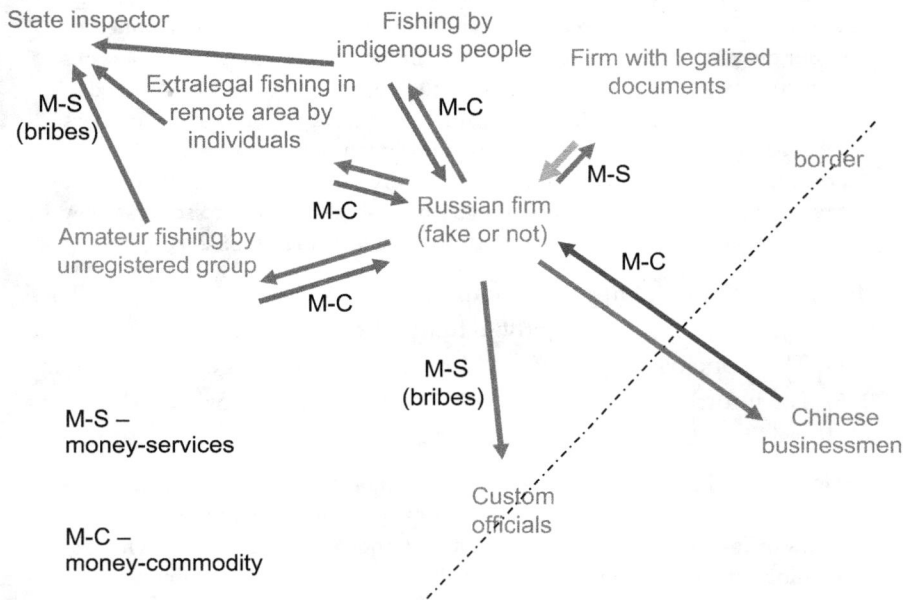

Fig. 2 Illustration of the coordination of extralegal fish traffic

A comparison of informal practices of Chinese and Russian fishing activities shows that both sides are actively involved in the predatory use of fishing resources in the river across the border. Informal fishing practices are based on traditions and historical continuity and, consequently, social norms exist that provide legitimacy (recognition) of informal rules. Tightening of legal enforcement does not affect practices, something which can be explained if we accept the fact that the main reason for the existence of the illegal economy is the desire of market participants to overcome state pressure. So what is the solution?

Social enforcement

Following Ostrom's (1990) theoretical concepts for solving the problems of collective action, a solution may be found by coordinating private and public interests given that "societies" (or stakeholder groups) have in this case very different motivations. The most significant conflict of river interests is between Chinese and Russian communities. China strives to maintain fishing activities in the border zone with Russia, stressing that representatives of ethnic groups should not be banned from fishing. Russia seeks to restrict Chinese fishing because the fish generally passes by the Russian bank. It is necessary for China to guarantee work to its population, but it does not have the possibility to invest in environmental projects – thus the greater part of Chinese industry does not have treatment plants. And Russia wants to protect water resources from harmful Chinese emissions.

Let us consider for a moment how the difference between these interests is reflected in the mass-media, which, as I pointed out in the theoretical review, can constitute one of the very mechanisms of social enforcement. A quantitative content analysis of the "official" and "social China" basis revealed a similarity between them in respect to the criterion of word frequency. In official reports, the most common categories encountered are: China, Russia, detain, poacher, frontier, FSB, fish, Amur, border and boat. In newspaper publications about Chinese poachers, the categories are: Amur, Russia, fish, China, poacher, border authorities, fishermen, river, border and violation. Of the 45 categories most frequently encountered in official publications, about 35 (or 80%) are also found in the "informal" basis. Conversely, of the 45 categories most commonly encountered in newspaper publications, 32 (or 88%) of them occur in the "official" basis.

The prevalence of all usage categories reaches a level of statistical significance here, i.e. the revealed similarity takes on a systematic character. But if such a selection of categories for official publications is logical (after all, the publications of the FSB and Federal Customs Service report discovered violations), their unusual consistency with unofficial publications points in all likelihood to the adoption of official stock phrases by journalists. Does this constitute simply an extension of legal enforcement or does it reflect the journalists' weak interest in covering this topic? Or could it point to a lack of freedom [of speech], both in the selection of topics and their coverage? If the latter is correct, then one may surmise that the media unduly contribute to social enforcement. To answer these questions more research is evidently required.

Interesting conclusions can be drawn by analysing the context of the categories emphasised in the texts. Official publications do not have an emotional colour, they point dryly to the Chinese fishermen's violation of Russia's territorial borders and attempts to export resources to China: "prevention of export of large cargoes to **China**"; "were taken to **China** in the space of a few years"; "part of the shipment was exported to **China**"; "served their sentence in **Russia**"; "Chinese **fishermen** showed fierce opposition"; "the **fishermen** violated the national border"; and "the **fishermen** who violated the border defended themselves".

Newspaper articles reporting on the same facts, but using such phrases, paint a far more pessimistic, and sometimes disastrous picture: "Chinese **fishermen** ignore the border"; "investigations lead to some organisation in **China** aiming to take over"; "for that kind of crime in **China** they get their heads chopped off..."; "some restrictions were introduced for the Amur sturgeon at least, but in **China** fishing of king-fish is allowed in any quantity"; "sentences that are passed in **China** for border violations are very strict"; "by contrast **Russia** has no laws to protect goldfish"; and "to take over the waters still belonging to **Russia**...".

Linguistic devices inciting phobia in order to maintain the unacceptability of Chinese poaching are common. "Factual" evidence is also employed for these aims, provoking widespread, often negative, discussion of the transfer of islands to China:

> "The fact is that Chinese fishermen, even before the demarcation of the area of Tarabarov and Bolshoi Ussurii islands, began to take over the waters still belonging to Russia. Border guards claim that poachers in the area began to violently resist arrest, arguing that they were catching 'their own fish in their own territory'" (Sergeev 2005).

The media discusses negatively not only the poaching carried out in Russian waters, but more generally any fishing activities in the Amur by the Chinese, including those carried out in their own waters:

> "Khabarovsk residents have heard that our Chinese neighbours exploit the fish stocks of the Amur far more actively than us... stating that the Chinese and us have different attitudes to the river – is not saying anything new, Sergey Denisovich argues" (Pimin 2000).

Interestingly, certain scientific texts (which because of their paucity were not analysed quantitatively) include similar rhetoric:

> "Poaching by Chinese fishermen is the scourge of the Middle Amur. Uncoordinated with the Russian side, the construction of dams on the Chinese coast will lead to an intensification of the erosion of our coast. In fact, China will certainly play a leading role in the ecological destabilisation of the Amur basin and of the river itself. If Russia and China do not take action, the additional human impacts on the larger ecosystem of the Amur basin may lead to a regional environmental crisis even without any dams on the main riverbed" (Podolskyi and Gotvinskyi 2007).

The social basis of texts that discuss or mention Russian poaching on the Amur River differs significantly in terms of words most frequently used and include the following categories: fish, roubles, thousands, poacher, Amur, Russia, market, goods and the past. Overall, these texts show much more diversity in both form and content and deal with characteristic stocks, the consumer market and its security problems and market competition with China: "this year red **fish** is increasingly directed towards Beijing"; "but even the increase in domestic prices in **Russia** in comparison to **China** does not bring more humpback salmon to native stalls"; "but Russians do not see it on their shelves or tables"; and "**Chinese** businesses quickly pay for goods delivered and, if necessary, in cash, unlike **Russian** companies". They also note that poachers only play a secondary role: "The number of **poachers** in the lower reaches of the Amur River has decreased significantly"; "200 fishing enterprises and national communities, let alone **poachers**, fish in the lower reaches of the Amur"; and "half are caught by **poachers** and by the unemployed population."

It is interesting that a few texts about fishing activities on the Amur border river published on the Russian-speaking Chinese sites give a sense of "acknowledgement" by their neighbours of their guilt. Contextual use of categories most frequently encountered underscore the social significance of fishing for local populations (ethnic groups, descendants of fishermen), and of the ongoing efforts to increase fish stocks which were previously destroyed in a predatory manner: "The **border** line between **China** and **Russia** had been fully settled"; "**Chinese fishing** industries foster the protection of rare types of **fish** that live in the Heilongjiang"; "this is the third release of **young fish** organised by the **Chinese** government"; "more than 20 tons of quality **young fish** are found in this river"; "**Fish from the river** represents the main source of income for local residents"; "her father is a **fisherman**, a husband – a veteran"; "**fisherman** Guan Sanchen, a member of the Xibo ethnic group"; "there, as before, the population engages in **fishing** activities"; "**Russia** and **China** are world powers"; "**China** and **Russia** act jointly"; and "on both sides of the border one find **Russian** and **Chinese** houses".

In general, when comparing the basis of publications on Chinese and Russian poaching, the conclusion can be reached that Chinese poaching is considerably more widespread than Russian (though WWF analytical reports indicate the opposite). Both official and unofficial texts aim at reinforcing the strict social unacceptability of the Chinese poaching in Russian waters, but not against Russian poaching in the border river. Never was there a direct indication that the numerous violations of prohibitions by Russian fishermen have an impact on resource conditions in the common border river. On the contrary, informal communications suggest that Russians "have a right" to the resources of the border river, and that the Chinese have already lost this right on account of their "behaviour". However, such rhetoric constitutes a direct path to the realisation of the full "tragedy of the commons", i.e. to the final exhaustion of limited resources.

Conclusion

Of the eight principles articulated by Ostrom (1990) relating to increasing the likelihood of success in solving dilemmas of coordination between individual and social interests, none are met in the case of the cross-border Amur river. However, three in particular are critically infringed. First of all, according to Ostrom, the rules should be worked out by the players themselves: both Russia and China are strongly centralised states, and all formal rules, common to all regions and communities, are produced at the top of the power hierarchy. Second, the rights of users of fish resources to self-organise and establish their own rules are not actually (or formally) recognised by local and central authorities to any extent. Therefore, any decision can be made only on the basis of unanimity, not only within the groups of Russian or Chinese fishermen, but also between them. However, to achieve such unanimity, enormous cost and time resources are required – a task insurmountable within reasonable timescales. Third, resource users are not able to appoint or select overseers accountable to them. On the contrary, the main controllers are the representatives of the centre (the State Security Service, for example).

Despite the fact that international practice and science are now identifying ways to overcome social dilemmas linked to the exhaustion of fish resources, for the Amur border river the answer to the question in the title is a resounding yes. Tragically, the present generation of children may grow up to see the waters of the former "Father Amur" devoid of any form of life.

7. Prostitution and the Transformation of the Chinese Trading Town of Ereen

Gaëlle Lacaze

Since the 1990s, a large part of the informal trade conducted by Mongols from China to Russia by way of Mongolia has followed the trans-Mongolian railway, in existence since 1956 as the main transit route for commercial exchanges between Beijing and Moscow. It was reopened in 1992 (*People's Daily Online* 2005). It then became the Mongolian "suitcase" traders' privileged path, compelling the Mongolian and Chinese governments to regulate the number of people crossing their common border. According to the people who were there during the 1990s, Ereen hot ("Ereen city") was then a very small city, with few asphalt streets, essentially limited to the current central square (see Fig. 1).[1] At that time, the city was permeated by a foul smell due to a lack of a sewer system.

The cross-border place of Erlian-Zamyn üüd was planned during the year 2000 along the railway as a Free Trade Zone by a Chinese-Mongolian bipartite contract; this contract implemented a system of permission for

---

I would like to thank all the members of the North Asian Borders Network, particularly the publishing team and Franck Billé for their editing work on my article.

1   *Erlian* is the Chinese name of the city and *Ereen* its Mongolian equivalent. In Mongolian, Ereen means "motley" and Zamyn üüd, "the road's door". In this article, I refer to the Chinese-Mongolian Free Trade Zone as "Erlian-Zamyn üüd" and to the Chinese city itself, which is part of this zone, by its Mongolian name "Ereen hot".

                                    DOI: 10.11647/OBP.0026.07

short stays in the trans-frontier zone. The Free Trade Zone of Erlian-Zamyn üüd later became for Mongols the main place of transit for Chinese industrial goods. In the 2000s, the city developed into an open market city and almost 70% of Mongolian commercial exchanges with China cross the border at this place (Ministry of Industry and Trade 2007). By 2010, urban infrastructures had been highly developed, with the bad smell of the city now but a distant memory. Overall, the Chinese government has invested almost 26,000,000 RMB [US$ 4.1 million] for the city's development (*People's Daily Online* 2005).

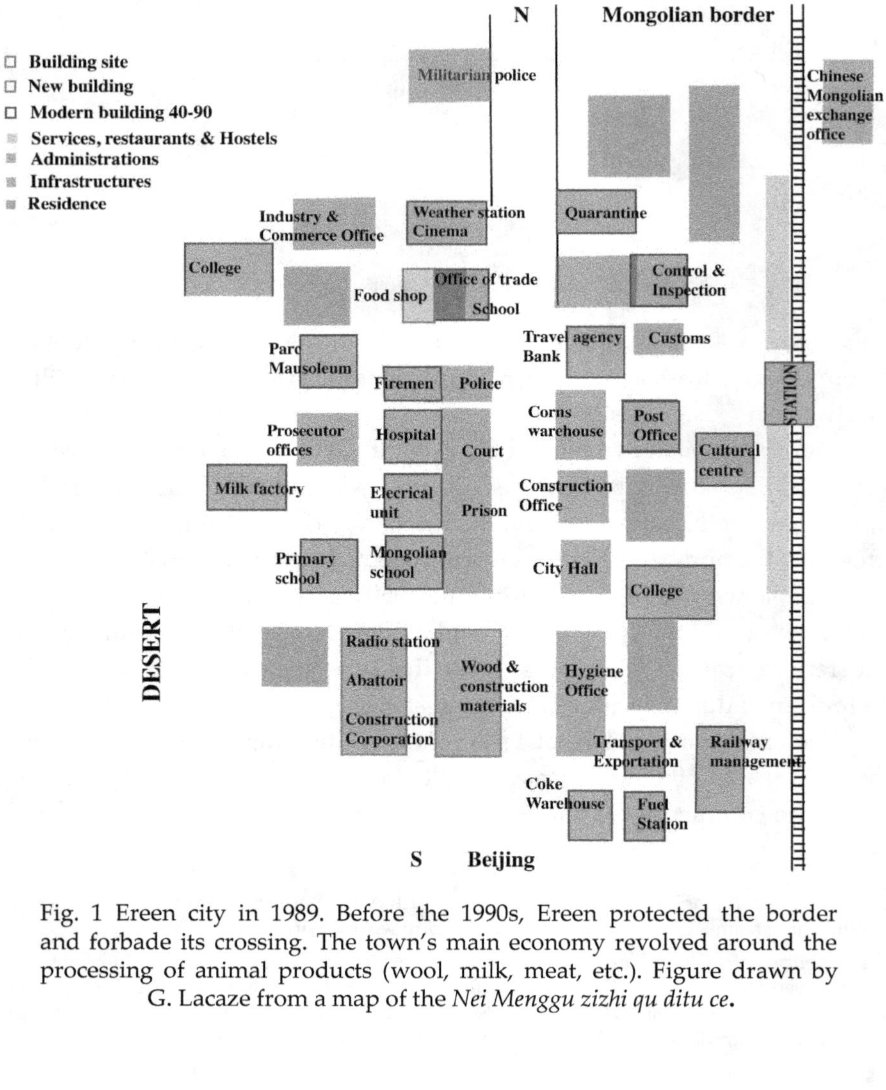

Fig. 1 Ereen city in 1989. Before the 1990s, Ereen protected the border and forbade its crossing. The town's main economy revolved around the processing of animal products (wool, milk, meat, etc.). Figure drawn by G. Lacaze from a map of the *Nei Menggu zizhi qu ditu ce*.

I have been conducting research on Mongols' activities in this Free Trade Zone since 2007. The first results of this research reveal the global organisation of the zone. Ereen acts as a big market-city while Zamyn üüd remains a transit place for people and goods. This chapter first examines the transformation of Ereen from 2007 to 2010. The main changes are the construction of "New Ereen" in the western section of the city; the opening in the south of two huge supermarkets, as large as an entire block, dedicated to construction materials; and the sculptures of dinosaurs, in the southwest, past the city gates on the road to Beijing. These changes are a good illustration of the local government's main political goals with regard to the city's development. I then examine how the appropriation of the city by Mongolian migrants underlines differential postures in terms of gender, social status and economic power. It sheds light on a new kind of nomadic activity developed by Mongols who have appropriated for themselves the political management of the city. I conclude with an analysis of the daily life of several Mongolian prostitutes. The type of sex work found in the city of Ereen reveals the contemporary strategies of some Mongolian women.

The context

While Ereen is a large open market, Zamyn üüd resembles some modern caravanserai (see Lacaze 2010). Both places attract many manual workers since the numerous commercial exchanges lead to new jobs and work opportunities such as, for instance, carrying goods, loading and unloading trucks or wagons, etc. Every day, numerous Mongols cross the border at Zamyn üüd and Ereen and their numbers increase year after year. They are "itinerant traders", wholesalers (*chanjuud*) as well as retailers (*naimaachin*), or "temporary-permanent migrants" such as drivers (*jolooch*) and prostitutes (*yanhan*). Because Mongolian citizens have the right to stay in China for thirty days without registration, some have been working and living in Ereen for several years without a visa, simply returning to Mongolia once a month. These monthly trips across the Mongolian-Chinese border enable them to permanently remain "temporary migrants" in China. I am referring to them here as "temporary-permanent migrants".

During the summer, Ereen also welcomes many Mongolian tourists. Indeed, the Mongolian "new rich" travel there to purchase furniture, school equipment or construction materials at a lower price than they would at home. These shoppers also like to travel to Ereen because they have free time to spend in the bars, restaurants, nightclubs and brothels the city has to offer.[2] In the month of July in particular, a large funfair stands on the city's central square and numerous tourist attractions sprout all over during the hot season.

The temporary-permanent workers facilitate the itinerant traders' activities. The *chanjuud* and the *yanhan* stay longer in Ereen than the *naimaachin* and the *jolooch*, who carry out multiple trips between Zamyn üüd and Ereen, between Mongolia and China. The *chanjuud* and *jolooch* are mostly men, while the *naimaachin* and *yanhan* are mostly women. Thus, the appropriation of the Free Trade Zone of Erlian-Zamyn üüd by Mongols illustrates the transformations that take place in the social organisation and gender relationships of contemporary Mongolian societies, both in Mongolia and China.

In Ereen, prostitution is mainly "voluntary".[3] While this means that women are not forced to work as prostitutes, it does not mean that their work is entirely free of coercion either. Prostitution in Ereen is well organised and occurs through *ger* (brothels) that are officially registered as commercial establishments. They are concentrated in red light districts like in many other cities in China (Pan 2004). The increase of Ereen brothels between 2007 and 2010 reflects the global expansion of the city where the *chanjuud*'s activities have grown rapidly in comparison with the *naimaachin*'s. The several life stories I have gathered from prostitutes during summer 2010 underline the strategies developed by Mongolian women confronted with poverty, temporary economic difficulties or unfavourable relations of domination.

---

2   Ereen brothels are known as *geting*, which has no meaning in Mongolian. This term is likely to be borrowed from the Chinese *gedeng* ("suspended lantern").

3   I am purposely avoiding the controversial debate of "forced" versus "free" prostitution, for two reasons. Firstly, the issue of choice is quite ambiguous. Choosing prostitution is heavily determined by numerous factors such as the incapacity of meeting financial duties because of poverty, low position in power relationships, or clashes in social status and situations – as in the case of women who have to remain subservient to their husbands while supporting their family and extended family. Moreover, on their first trip, women are not fully aware of their future working conditions; thus, one cannot argue that they have a clear idea about this work. Secondly, the issue was hotly debated in 2005 in France (Handman and Mossuz-Lavau 2005), in the context of the new regulation relating to "passive soliciting". Abolition (of prostitution), fastidiousness (regarding its regulation) and liberalism (for the abolition of regulations relating to prostitution) were the main positions expressed in this debate. None of these positions fits the Chinese situation.

Fig. 2 Satellite pictures of "the free trade zone or Erlian-Zamyn Üüd".

Methodology

I have used different ethnographic methods in the course of these periods of fieldwork. In 2007, I followed several *naimaachin* in their trips on the railway and across the border, as well as in Ereen, Zamyn-üüd and Ulaanbaatar. I drew the *naimaachin*'s "walking figures" (de Certeau 1991) and shed light on the traders' significant places (see Lacaze 2010). For the second period of fieldwork, in 2010, following Lilian Matthieu (2000: 99–116), I focused my research on "one place": *ger* No. 51 in a street called Jin Cho in Ereen.[4] Compared to the collection of life stories or to the study of politics related to prostitution, this method allows the analysis of individuals' strategies in a marginal context while avoiding the stigmatising dynamics of marginality and shame associated with prostitution.

Over twenty days I established relationships with a dozen Mongolian women selling sex both inside and outside the brothel. I spent time with them in the afternoons, teaching them English before clients started coming to Jin Cho. During this fieldwork, I made the

---

4   Jin Cho is likely to be the Mongolian rendering of the Chinese *Jincheng* ("Golden palace").

conscious decision to avoid the point of view of customers and officials. I focused this ethnographic research on women from Mongolia because of the specific administrative processes managing the migrations of Chinese people.

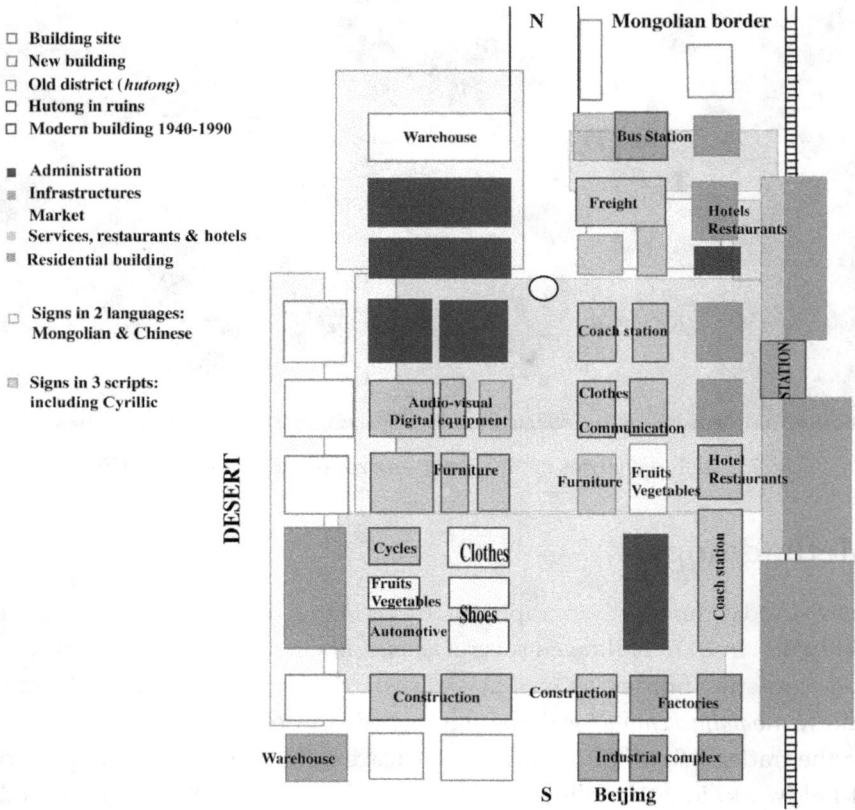

Fig. 3 Ereen in 2007. The town is organised around Mongolian traders' activities. Figure drawn by G. Lacaze.

I initially investigated processes of transformation of spaces in places, according to Michel de Certeau's theory (1991), and later sought to understand the life, emotions and sentiments of Mongolian migrants settled in Ereen. During both periods of fieldwork I met Mongolian drivers who organise the crossing of the Sino-Mongolian border. Except for the *naimaachin*, I did not formally collect biographies. Even if people were willing to share their life stories with me, they would only offer some pieces, underscoring defining moments and avoiding others. Little by little, all the people I worked with shared some pieces of their life with me. Later, I tried to organise the various elements of these individual life stories. Indeed, I conducted some formal and classical fieldwork with *naimaachin* while, at the same time, collecting informal information with prostitutes. If these two phases of gathering ethnographic data are different, they also share some similarities, allowing for a comparison of the results emerging from both.

These ethnographic methods allow a comparison that underlines the city's development from 2007 to 2010. The analysis of the changes that have taken place in the organisation of the city illustrates its appropriation by Mongolian wholesalers and, in addition, the increase in temporary-permanent Mongolian migrants in Ereen. Ereen plays an important role for Mongols. By contrast, it is not as important for Chinese people even if many Chinese migrants come to the city, attracted by its "wilder" and warmer environment and somewhat less stressful life. In my study of Ereen I thus focused my research on Mongolian activities and representations.

Development of Ereen

The period between 2007 and 2010 saw vast development in the infrastructure of Ereen, and the appearance of several markets specialising in construction materials. The city's expansion is encouraged by the political agenda of both the Chinese and Mongolian governments, and by the industrial and economic interests of its Chinese residents.

In 2007, Ereen was composed of different districts of various sizes, each of them specialised in a particular activity: residential areas, shops, markets, warehouses, etc. The city was comprised of almost ten districts, mainly located west of the railway (see Fig. 3).[5] At the centre of the city, the "new market" (*shine zah*) and the "old market" (*huuchin zah*), as well as the "window shop" (*shilen/shiliin delgüür*) and the "circular shop" (*buduun delgüür*) were the main places for buying small manufactured products. In other words, they were places dedicated to Mongolian

---

5   I drew this map while walking through the city. The map scale is quite approximate as it is mean as a tool to identify people' appropriation of places, the specialisation of the various town quarters, and the location of each activity.

retailers – *naimaachin*, who buy mostly shoes, clothes, furniture, mobile phones and other small digital devices. At the periphery of the city, surrounding these central places, many shops offered products intended for Mongolian wholesalers (*chanjuud*), such as construction materials, warehouses or freight infrastructures. Near these places for wholesalers were several residential buildings. Scattered all over Ereen were places for the Mongolian itinerant traders' daily life, such as hotels, bars, restaurants and public baths, as well as places for their entertainment (bars, nightclubs, gaming houses or brothels).

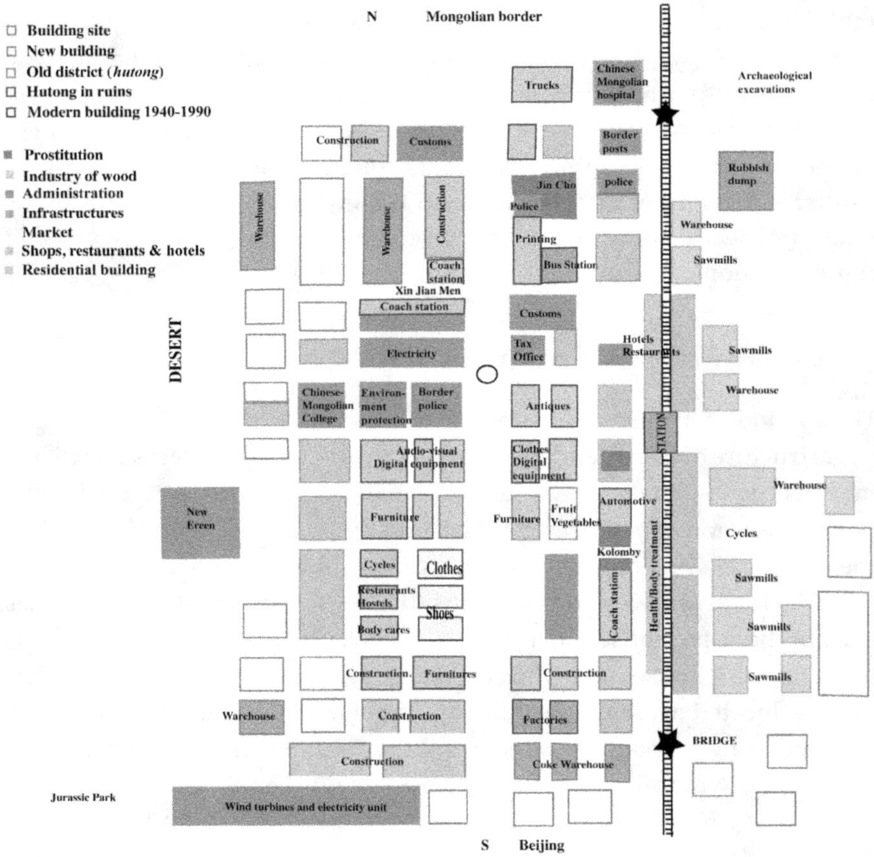

Fig. 4 Ereen in 2010. The map highlights the dramatic expansion of open markets dedicated to construction materials. Figure drawn by G. Lacaze.

Fig. 5 Satellite photo of Ereen.

Fig. 6 Satellite photo of Zamyn Üüd.

By 2010, Ereen had changed considerably (see Ereen map, Figs. 4 and 5).[6] With the exception of the central markets and shops, it had been totally reorganised. Even the centre of the city had been transformed through the ubiquitous emergence of numerous beauty institutes, hairdressers, bars, restaurants, internet cafés and sex shops. The former red light district had also been transformed, as will be illustrated in the third part of this chapter. New districts had been added to the original city: two in the north, three housing blocks in the west, two in the south and several housing blocks in the east, on the other side of the railway. Except in the east, all the newly-developed parts of the city included residential buildings, educational infrastructures (i.e. kindergartens), hospitals and free health centres, and, in the town centre, a Mongolian Arts academy and a Mongolian traditional sports complex. Several new districts are still under construction at the city's periphery, indicating that the development of Ereen has not yet come to an end (Fig. 7).

Fig. 7 Hostel built for wholesalers coming from Beijing. New buildings at the south-west of the city built between 2010 and 2012 (Ereen city, August 2010). Photo: G. Lacaze.

Today the northern part of the city is devoted to the administrations in charge of organising freight, like customs offices and warehouses. Its western part is now called "New Ereen", on account of the new city square, the Dinosaur Museum, the new primary schools and the Chinese-Mongolian College located there. The architecture of these new builds is characterised by a hypermodern style. Their overall shape and external materials are similar to the buildings erected in Beijing for the 2008 Olympic Games (Fig. 8), even if the large windows are hardly appropriate to Ereen's climate in the middle

---

6   I would like to thank the taxi driver who showed me, in detail, the city's new developments.

of the Gobi Desert. South of Ereen, two newly built districts are dedicated to construction materials (Figs. 9a and 9b). They are open markets enclosed by buildings, including several roads. These market areas are like small "specialised cities" within the larger city. They are completely dedicated to Mongolian wholesalers. East of Ereen, on the other side of the railway, is an area dedicated to sawmills and timber warehouses. This part of the city is the centre of commercial exchanges between China, Russia and Mongolia.

Fig. 8 The new Dinosaur Museum and the new city hall (Ereen city, August 2010). Photo: G. Lacaze.

Figs. 9a [previous page], 9b, 9c. New districts dominated by construction materials outlets (Ereen city, August 2010). Photo: G. Lacaze.

Fig. 10 Wind turbines and the town's electric power station (Ereen city, August 2010). Photo: G. Lacaze.

In the southwest, the city's government has set up wind turbines and an electric power station (Fig. 10).[7] A little further to the west, along the road to Beijing, in the middle of the Gobi Desert, a section as wide as a plateau has been totally covered with sculptures of dinosaurs. This "Jurassic Park" illustrates the new status of the city, consecrated in August 2007 as the "Dinosaur Capital" in recognition of the many dinosaur remains discovered in the area.[8] But despite the eagerness of the local government to transform the image of Ereen, the city remains a large "trade palace", facing a caravanserai to which nomadic people flock in their thousands for various commercial purposes (see Figs. 2, 5 and 6).

Appropriation of the city by Mongols

The global map of the city reveals its appropriation by both Mongolian itinerant traders (*naimaachin* and *chanjuud*) and by temporary permanent migrants. Its development betrays a strong increase in construction materials, which mostly concern the wholesale sector. This increase induces the multiplication of infrastructures dedicated to accommodating Mongolian wholesalers, who stay several days in Ereen in order to manage the stock of products and its freight, or wait for customs clearance and Mongolian import permits, etc. Moreover, places catering for the itinerant traders' daily needs (hotels, bars, restaurants, public baths) and their entertainment (nightclubs, gaming houses, brothels) have multiplied all over the city (Fig. 11).

Mongolian and Chinese citizens belong to different categories of migrants, undertaking different kinds of activity. They include businessmen, manual workers, moneychangers, cross-border drivers, prostitutes and other sex workers. There are also Mongolian wives of Han industrialists, businessmen or managers, needed for exchanges with traders coming from Mongolia. The latter are less numerous than the former; indeed, marriages between citizens of Mongolia and China are always perceived negatively in Mongolia. It is judged preferable for Mongols to marry Inner Mongols than Hans. In a similar way, only a few Inner Mongols are married to Hans. Inner Mongols are usually poorly educated and therefore Hans find them

---

7   Every day, the electricity supply is interrupted between 4 am and 6 am, except in areas with private generators.
8   The inaugurating ceremony of the "Dinosaur Capital" was retransmitted on several Mongolian television channels.

less attractive than the exotic "Other" from Mongolia.[9] Except for this kind of multi-ethnic "sexual-economical exchange" (Tabet 2005), migrants generally develop their activities inside their own "group".

Fig. 11 The "Mongol bar" (Ereen city, August 2010). Photo: G. Lacaze

Migrants are either Mongols or Han from China, or Mongols from Mongolia. They tend to privilege people of their own group, lineage or family. This process induces the development of ethnic niches and specialises each family or domestic group in one single economic sector.[10] For example, Mongols from Mongolia and Chinese people prefer to employ persons from their own province or family. Most Horchin Mongols living in Ereen specialise in prostitution. This Inner Mongolian eastern group was deeply involved in the Chinese Communist Party and belongs nowadays to a social network – within police or juridical institutions – which allows them to develop the role of "pimps".

---

9   I prefer to neutralise the gender of this "Other" because some Mongolian men live with Han Chinese women. However, the majority of multi-ethnic couples living in Ereen involve Mongolian women and Chinese men.

10   One could compare this organisation to the former guilds, which were very powerful in pre-communist China (Lagrange 2008).

Moneychangers are also quite numerous in Ereen as only one desk at the Bank of China is allowed to exchange foreign currencies such as the Mongolian *tögrög*, the euro or the dollar. Moreover, all hotel owners have to declare their customers each day. The administrative permit for a short stay in Ereen compels every itinerant person to surrender their passport to the owner of their hotel, so itinerants are not able to change money at the official bank and need informal moneychangers. The moneychangers are mostly Inner Mongolian women from the Borjigin or Harchin groups.

Among Mongolian temporary-permanent migrants, privileged relationships are less reliant on genealogical links. Less numerous and not as used to living in China as Inner Mongols, migrants from Mongolia are included in smaller kinship groups and relational networks. They are involved in less diversified activities and, as a result, their employment opportunities are more restricted. Some regional affinities therefore emerge among migrants from Mongolia because of the intermediaries or middlemen needed for various kinds of activity in Ereen.

For any commercial activity running in Ereen, a Mongolian speaker is required. Established Chinese businessmen generally employ Inner Mongols to work as intermediaries with traders coming from Mongolia. Smaller Chinese retailers – for instance those working in small shops in the two Ereen markets, the "old" and "new" markets (*shine* and *huuchin zah*) – have invented a kind of commercial dialect, a Mongolian *pidgin*. Mongolian prostitutes, for their part, have to be introduced to a pimp through a mandated intermediary who receives money for her mediation. The prostitute has to work, usually for a few days, to reimburse the pimp's investment, her introductive debt.

The need for commercial intermediaries accounts for the rapid growth of Mongolian or Inner Mongolian temporary-permanent migrants.[11] Among these temporary-permanent migrants, Chinese citizens are more settled and fixed than Mongolian citizens, who regularly move across the border. Chinese citizens participate in "pendulum migrations", returning seasonally or at regular intervals to their homeland, while, as mentioned earlier, Mongolian migrants have to cross the border once a month in order to renew their right of residence in China. Among the migrants, taxi drivers (both cars and bikes) and truck drivers, mostly men, are more mobile than other people. Some of them work together with a family member, usually a husband,

---

11   Commercial intermediaries play a similar role to the former *compradors,* who organised the Guild's foreign commercial relation in pre-communist China (Lagrange 2008).

wife, mother or son. Taxi drivers within the city tend to be Chinese citizens, either Han or ethnic Mongols, while cross-border taxi drivers are Mongolian citizens. The Chinese citizens drive small cars or taxi-bikes (with or without an engine) through several official companies, while the Mongolians drive 4x4 Russian army jeeps, the so-called "sixty-nine" (*Jaran yos*), or second hand Japanese or Korean jeeps (Fig. 12).

Fig. 12 4x4 Russian Army Jeep "Sixty-nine" driven by Mongolian cross-border taxi drivers (Ereen city, August 2010). Photo: G. Lacaze.

The taxi drivers

During the summer of 2010, I spent a few days with several cross-border drivers, who used to stop their jeeps on the square in front of my hotel. I had already met some of them in the course of my previous fieldwork in 2007. Cross-border drivers come to Ereen after the morning train, full of Mongolian traders, and they return to Zamyn üüd with the other traders before the border closes.[12] Their movements are linked to those of the

---

12   In Erlian-Zamyn üüd, the Chinese Mongolian border is open seven days a week, from 8 am to 6 pm or 7 pm. It is closed on Mongolian and Chinese public holidays.

itinerant traders, themselves governed by the arrivals and departures of Mongolian trains. According to the railway timetable for summer 2010, two trains arrived daily to Zamyn üüd from Ulaanbaatar, a regular train at 7.10 am and an express train at 8 am. Every day, two other trains leave Zamyn üüd for Ulaanbaatar at 5.45 pm and 9.20 pm. Every night, at 3 am or 4 am, a bus arrives in Ereen from Beijing. Its customers are usually *naimaachin* and *chanjuud* returning to Mongolia.

Cross-border drivers usually reside in Zamyn üüd and only a few of them have elected residence in Ereen. Occasionally drivers residing in Zamyn üüd spend the night in Ereen, in a hotel. Then, with other Mongolian drivers, they drink and gamble late into the night. On various occasions, I noticed that only a few of the drivers who stayed in front of my hotel ever walked into the funfair on the central square, located just behind them on the other side of the avenue (see Fig. 13). In July, the city's central square welcomes several fairground stalls and Chinese open-air dances are organised on weekend nights in nearby parks and squares. One evening, as the cross-border drivers were playing cards, they did not hear the Chinese army's concert playing on the central square facing them. They spend little money and do not fully participate in the city's life and economy. They are like ghosts, haunting the city during the day, looking for customers to drive across the border or for goods to transport for Mongolian businessmen based in Ulaanbaatar. Cross-border drivers exist almost in an inter-world of itinerant trade.

Since 2000, when cross-border relationships were officially and administratively organised (see Lacaze 2010), the number of cross-border drivers has been increasing every year. They numbered 400 in 2007 and 600 in 2010,[13] and originated mostly from the southern *aimag* ("provinces") of Mongolia (Dundgov', Dornogov', Ömnögov' and Bayanhongor), which are close to the border or in the vicinity of the railway line.[14] Mongolian cross-border drivers own their jeeps. They earn on average 1,500,000 Tg [$1,150] per month, for a 6 am to 6 pm work day, seven days a week, usually without any day off, except when the Chinese or Mongolian section of

---

13   This information was given to me by the drivers themselves as well as by other Ereen residents. It is not readily available in official sources but is nevertheless included in "internal" reports of the Mongolian diplomatic or customs services, as well as in the documents of a few bilateral administrations. These reports are not easily available but all Ereen residents know their content.

14   The drivers hold special passports allowing them to cross the border several times a day.

the border is closed.[15] Drivers decide for themselves whether to work or not, and will regularly take a break for a few days. In 2010, among the Mongolian people living in Ereen, cross-border drivers were the largest category of migrants, paralleling the number of Mongolian women working as prostitutes.

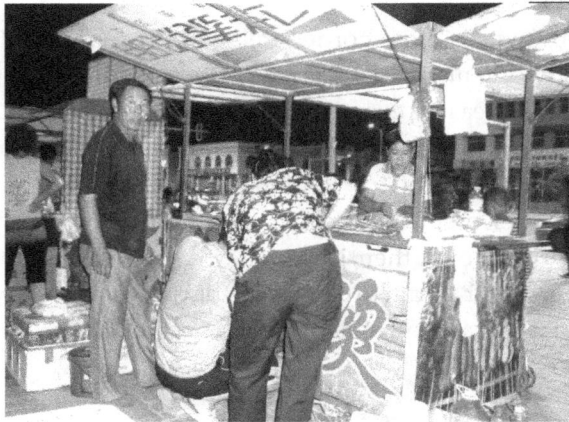

Fig. 13 The Summer funfair in the city centre (Ereen city, August 2010).
Photo: G. Lacaze

---

15   In Mongolia, the standard salary for manual work is approximately 300,000 Tg [$230].

Of their own free will?

One of the main visible transformations of Ereen has been the growth of activities related to "body care" and the sex industry. Indeed, these activities concern, in particular, beauty institutes, hairdressers, massage parlours and sex shops. These places are specifically devoted to people who work in the sex industry and need special body care daily. The city's sex industry includes people working as striptease artists, call girls, hostesses or prostitutes. The majority of them are women although, since 2007, a few Chinese men have started to work as transsexual prostitutes in the city's bars and nightclubs.

On the city map of Ereen in 2007, a few brothels were grouped within three enclosed quarters: the streets called Kolomby ("Colombia") and Shin Tian Men, and at the back of the "circular shop" (*buduun delgüür*).[16] Many prostitutes also worked in several hotels with special public baths (usually saunas) and in the massage parlours disseminated throughout the city. At that time, no sex shop existed and condoms were sold in pharmacies. According to several Chinese and Mongolian Ereen residents, in 2007 around 300 Mongolian women worked officially as prostitutes in Ereen. The same sources claim that Mongolian women numbered 600 in 2010. In addition, 150 Chinese women and 100 Inner Mongolian women also worked in the city. The number of prostitutes who have emigrated from Mongolia has doubled over the last three years. Its growth corresponds to an increase in sexual demand, coming predominantly from Chinese citizens, industrialists or managers, and from Mongolian citizens, mostly drivers and wholesalers who are alone and with cash to spend when they stay in Ereen.

In Ereen, sex industry customers belong to different "sexual cultures" – Russified Mongols, Sinicised Mongols and Chinese – that consider prostitution as a "normal" phenomenon or "usual" service for men seeking sexual satisfaction. Prostitution fully partakes in the Chinese "sexual culture": besides concubines, prostitutes play an important role in Chinese masculine sociality (Micollier 2007). It does not have the same place in Mongolian or Russian culture, even if they both largely accept extramarital sexual relationships.

In 2010, Shin Tian Men disappeared from the Ereen map. The several brothels that were located at the beginning of that street moved to

---

16   Shin Tian Men is likely to be a Mongolian rendering of the Chinese Xinjiang Men ("Xinjiang door").

another street, built in 2008, called Jin Cho. The number of brothels then increased rapidly. By 2010, Jin Cho was a cul-de-sac with around sixty brothels, all numbered, one next to the other. In each "red light house" or brothel, five to fifteen Mongolian women work as prostitutes. Jin Cho specialises in the higher scale of prostitution activities: the women who work there are under thirty and conform to the local standards of beauty, meaning they are thin, elegant and have white skin (Fig. 14).

Fig. 14 Mongolian woman working in Jincho (Ereen city, August 2010).
Photo: G. Lacaze.

The prostitution organisation

The Jin Cho cul-de-sac opens onto the main avenue of Ereen, through a visible arcade standing two gates away from the central police station, and it is enormously popular.[17] Although prostitution is forbidden in China (Attané 2005), the Jin Cho brothels are duly licensed, officially

---

17   The first night I walked on the main avenue, there were so many cabs in front of the Jin Cho arcade that I thought for a moment that it was the new depot for the city's taxis.

recorded as commercial establishments – usually hairdressing salons – and their owners regularly pay taxes. According to the residents' points of view, the Jin Cho brothels are considered to provide around 20% of the city budget. Thus, the status of the brothels is quite ambiguous: they host forbidden activities but are officially licensed. At the same time, Mongolian prostitutes are officially recorded as individuals engaging in illegalities; they are routinely arrested by the Chinese police and frequently fined.

Since 2009, the Mongolian frontier-police have been allowed to control people in the Chinese part of Ereen's Free Trade Zone. The owner of *ger* No. 51 and many prostitutes in Jin Cho told me that this new allowance given to Mongolian border guards results in increased pressure on Mongolian temporary-permanent migrants, especially on prostitutes. When crossing the border once a month, Mongolian prostitutes used to bribe border guards in order to avoid the affixing of the "black stamp", which then forbids them from travelling abroad for five years. The new bipartite regulation means that prostitutes now also have to bribe the Mongolian border guards who arrest them in Ereen.

Usually prostitutes and pimps share the payment of the penalty equally, while the profits from sexual services are 30% for the pimp and 70% for the prostitute. Every month, women earn an average of 2,000,000 Tg [$1,500]. They regularly send money home or bring it with them when they go back. They can also borrow money from their pimp at a 50% interest rate; they have to work for a few days in order to reimburse the loan. Therefore they can take more money home than they have already earned. In this case, they will need to ask another woman in the same "house" to act as guarantor for them. If the woman who has borrowed the money fails to come back, the woman acting as guarantor will need to work to reimburse this credit. Some pimps use this credit system in order to compel "their girls" to stay longer. During the twenty days I spent in *ger* No. 51, Lisa went to Mongolia for ten days when her mother was hospitalised, and later came back.[18] Emmanuelle left Ereen for good, after having worked there for around two months. Betty came back after a break of several weeks and Lola went home for a while.

Given their strong reliance on each other and the routine sharing of knowledge and secrets, the women develop very close relationships.

18   All names have been changed for the purpose of this article.

During working periods, prostitutes are also allowed to purchase their individual free time, in order to spend time together or with a close friend. When a woman needs to take some time off, she needs to inform her pimp if this falls during a period of rest, and at other times she will pay him his usual share of the profits. Anna told me she felt as if she were in a "free jail" (*chölööt shoroon*). Indeed, if Mongolian women come in their hundreds "of their own free will", working conditions for prostitutes generally remain coercive.

In Jin Cho, pimps are mostly Inner Mongolian men, Horchin Mongols. Prostitutes, by contrast, are women from Mongolia. Each actor within the prostitution activities has his/her specific duties. The pimp officially registers women working in his *ger* as temporary residents. It means that he bribes the Ereen police and pays the official licence. The pimp's duties also entail providing a room for work activities (single tricks) and sleeping, giving condoms, and protecting the women when necessary. The *ger* regulations require prostitutes to be "at home" at 8 am when they have spent a night out with a customer, and to be ready to work at 6 pm, after their daily preparation (public bath, shopping, hairdresser, make up), except if they are already with a customer. After 3 am, when there are no more customers, they are allowed to sleep.

The duties of the prostitutes are to bring the pimp consequent benefits, to be hard-working and to adopt "correct behaviour", which means to avoid becoming involved in scandals, drawing public attention to themselves or being drunk. Transgression of these rules results in penalties or, with stricter pimps, in beatings with a billiard cue. A wide credit system allows the pimps to tie down prostitutes and restrict their movement. Available data testify to the absence of "forced" prostitution in Ereen and the National AIDS Foundation Review mentions that women who work as prostitutes in Ereen mainly come of their own free will (2007). Nevertheless, the Ereen city brothels' indebting process of "voluntary" prostitution appears to provide a gateway to sexual slavery. In addition, Mongolian women forced into prostitution have to pass through Ereen on their way to the south of China.

Daily life in an Ereen brothel

I spent twenty days and nights with twelve women who work at *ger* No. 51. These women felt they were lucky on account of their pimp's kindness. They called him *aav* ("daddy"), while pimps are usually called *ah* ("elder brother, uncle") in the other *gers* of Jin Cho. In each *ger*, prostitutes rank in a hierarchy depending on their age, education, seniority, look, behaviour, etc. Nevertheless, they constitute a close-knit community that lives together and shares duties, a private room and bed, some clothes and make-up, money and guarantees, clients, information, as well as mobile phones, condoms and food. I never saw anyone eating a takeaway meal alone: at around 3 pm, one by one, women ordered a meal from one of the restaurants located on Jin Cho and always shared their food with someone. This commensality alludes to a consubstantiation process linking together the prostitutes of the same *ger*. The very character of the women who prostitute themselves completely dissolves into the community associated with the place of prostitution: they are enmeshed in a "community of destiny" (Mathieu 2007). It looks as if they share a common body, the prostitute's body, constructed as a sexual object.

The individual personalities of the prostitutes are erased by their persona; such transformation underlines the "light" of the atmosphere of the "house" (Pan 2004). This character of the prostitute, individually and collectively acted out by all the women living together in the common scene of the *ger*, induces a kind of dissociation process inside each of them. In their daily life, women appear to be enacting a role, as if they are playing a character in a play. For four to six hours every afternoon, all the women prepare their body in order to intensify their power of seduction. They require several hours to seek the character that best fits their personality and particular mood.[19] This role acting is reinforced by the fact that Mongolian women use a pseudonym with their customers.[20] They become someone else through a kind of metamorphosis.

The transformation process symbolically protects the prostitutes against the shame related to their activity. All the women I met in *ger* No. 51 hide the true nature of their job from their relatives, friends or acquaintances left behind in Mongolia, explaining that they work in hotels or restaurants

---

19 Women working as prostitutes in France explain that they "act in a play", "are like in a game", "elaborate their prostitute's character" (Handman and Mossuz-Lavau 2005).

20 Women who work as prostitutes in France usually use condoms, in part to "take some distance" symbolically (ibid.). Mongolian women are supposed to always use condoms, but in reality this is not systematic. In comparison with French prostitutes, Mongolian prostitutes develop a less symbolic process to effect distance and to build self protection. They kiss customers for instance, while French prostitutes exclude kisses from their sexual repertoire. This may explain why the character's artifice seems so theatrical in the case of Mongolian women who need to over-invest in their role in order to make up for a lack in symbolic and bodily protection.

in China. Women who come only during the summer to work in Jin Cho tell friends and relatives that they work in Mongolian tourist camps. This activity is somewhat schizophrenic. All the prostitutes I met insist on the psychological dangers related to this dissociative process. For the prostitute, the danger is to lose her sense of "self", her real personality, and become just a prostitute in her eyes and in the eyes of others. Besides, the fact that the "character" of the prostitute lives at night, a temporal disconnection also occurs in the "real" individuals, ordinary people who live by day. This dissociation allows these women to live more or less psychologically safely with the "prostitute stigma" (Pheterson 1996).

At the end of the night, many of the women furtively leave their customers' hotels and meet in another place in order to drink alcohol together. This is seen by other prostitutes as the behaviour of "bad workers", as they may potentially cause a drunken public scene as often fights ensue between prostitutes. Such behaviour seems to underscore the violence and shame of the "prostitute stigma". Some of the women are alcoholics. In the space of twenty days, the doctor made three visits to *ger* No. 51, twice for excessive consumption of alcohol and once for pregnancy. Alcohol potentially gives women the strength to work, and it is also felt to purify tainted bodies at the end of the night. It allows the reconstitution of the "full individual", the associative process of a torn personality. But dissociation results in symbolic and affective violence, which may then lead to violent behaviour.

Mongolian women working as prostitutes also experience some positive emotions. They sometimes feel pleasure when having sexual intercourse with some of their customers – usually Mongolian men who speak the same language as them. For instance, Marilyn fell in love with a customer and ran away for six months before finally leaving him. She had just recently returned to Jin Cho when I met her. For poverty-stricken Mongolian women, prostitution represents one possibility to obtain sexual and economic autonomy as well as liberty of movement. Through prostitution, women try to improve their present and future life and, in this sense, Ereen acts as a privileged destination.

Conclusion

Officially, the Erlian-Zamyn üüd free trade zone is about ten years old. It was constructed through the Chinese and Mongolian governments' political will as well as the financial interests of the traders, industrialists or investors of both states. The development of Ereen is all the more surprising when compared to the situation in Zamyn üüd. Initially, Ereen targeted Mongolian retailers, the *naimaachin* and, following the establishment of free trade zone, became focused on the wholesalers, the *chanjuud*. Mongolian cross-border drivers now organise the freight going through the border. Strong networks have been elaborated in order to manage the freight and trade between Ereen and Ulaanbaatar through Zamyn üüd. Intermediaries, such as cross-border drivers, have found a much needed role in the exportation channels from China to Mongolia. This later transformation confirms the status of Ereen as a major trading place.

The subsequent increase in the importance of wholesale, paralleled by a relative decline in retail, has transformed the nature of the dominant trade in the Free Trade Zone. It has resulted in an increase in the number of temporary-permanent migrants who facilitate the long stays of Mongolian wholesalers and of the Chinese industrialists who supply their demand. This process is particularly evident in the increase in the number of temporary-permanent migrant women who come from Mongolia to work as prostitutes. Indeed, in Chinese sexual culture, any contract concluded between businessmen/partners has to be consecrated through entertainment, which usually includes dinner, alcohol and the services of a prostitute. Compared to the number of cross-border drivers, the number of Mongolian prostitutes is increasing more rapidly. This suggests that the growth in commercial relationships is speedier than the growth in the number of people crossing the border. Further, it may also underscore the degradation of the socio-economic situation of women in Mongolia.

It remains to be seen whether these trends are indicative of a transitional or permanent orientation. Many elements suggest that the city's dedication to wholesale trade will probably endure, despite the city government's goals to promote a new official image for Ereen as the Dinosaur Capital. Nevertheless, this image reinforces another specialisation of Ereen; for several years now, Ereen has been welcoming many "shoppers" who come for holidays to engage in gambling, prostitution and drinking in this "city of pleasures". On an economic and political plane, wholesale trade and tourism offer the most "interesting" vector for a rapid development and permanent enrichment of Ereen.

8. Ritual, Memory and the Buriad Diaspora Notion of Home

Sayana Namsaraeva

Nayan-Nava – a horse flew
Nayan-Nava – a nomad sang:
"Wherever I unsaddle my horse
There will be my home and my homeland..."
– Bair Dugarov, contemporary Buriad poet[1]

In recent years there has been a rapid growth in the number of studies exploring transnational, transborder and diasporic lives, some of which reflect on trans-state processes after the collapse of the Soviet Union. The emphasis is on the increase in trans-border mobility and especially on cross-border contacts between different segments of one ethnic people, those living outside the homeland in diasporas and those who constitute what I call the "the kin-majority" in the historical or national homeland (Diener 2003; Safran 2004; Kosmarskaya 2006; Markowitz 2004; Shami 2007; Sanders forthcoming). With the dramatic political and economic changes in post-socialist countries, it has become clear that new socio-spatial entities have emerged, where ethnic space functions beyond the territorial boundaries of nation states.

---

1   http://www.sibogni.ru/archive/37/420 (accessed 15.6.2011). All translations of quotations from Russian, Khalkh Mongol and Buriad languages are mine, unless otherwise indicated.

                    DOI: 10.11647/OBP.0026.08

This chapter is an effort to advance our understanding of recent developments in the region of North Asia shared between Russia, China and Mongolia by examining the trans-border dimension of Buriad[2] social space. Being an ethnic minority in all these countries, the Buriads can be described using anthropological theories of diaspora. Those Buriads who moved away from Russian colonisation in Eastern Siberia almost a century ago will be referred to as "diaspora" groups or "kin minorities"; they consist of 42,000 people living in Mongolia and around 7,000 living in Inner Mongolia. Those who stayed behind at their home villages in the Transbaikal region (Russia) are referred to as the "kin majority" and they comprise 445,000 people. Meanwhile, the neighboring Mongol speaking territories just across the border to which the newcomers moved (Hulun Buir in Inner Mongolia, China, and the eastern provinces *aimags* in Mongolia) are called "host societies", or sometimes "host countries" if there is need to stress the public policies toward the newcomers.

Relations with "home" and with the "host" society continue to be distinguishing features of diasporas. Robin Cohen (1996) and William Safran (2004) both stress the role of the host country (with its public policies toward the newcomers) and a "homeland orientation" as being among the major elements distinguishing diasporas from ordinary immigrant expatriate communities. Therefore, a key issue regarding the Buriads who moved to Mongolia and China and have now already lived there for several generations is to define what is "home" in their understanding; we need to ask whether or not they still have a homeland orientation after generational changes, and if so, where they locate it. If we take various historical cases of migration, it could easily be imagined that "movers" scattered away outside the homeland and formed diaspora groups, while "stayers" continued to live at the homeland. However, I am wary about using the term homeland in this way in the Buriad context, because, as I will show later, there is confusion and ambivalence in defining what is "homeland" (*nutag*), not only from diasporic perspectives but also from the majority Buriad point of view. This being the case, I shall pursue the goal

2   Throughout this article, I use the spelling "Buriad" rather than the alternative "Buriat", the Russian spelling "Buryat" or Chinese spelling "Bu-li-ya-te". This is because: (1) this is the Buriad official spelling based on Cyrillic according to the Buriad–Orod dictionary (Cheremisov 1973), and (2) only in the Buriad Republic (Russia) does the Buriad language have the status of being one of the official languages, unlike in either Mongolia or Inner Mongolia (China). The Khori dialect was taken as the point of reference for Buriad literary language.

of ascertaining not only the different notions of the Buriad homeland and what they might mean to people in diasporas, but also the idea of having several homelands in a much broader context – from the perspectives of different generations, and at different geographical and historical points.

The choice to concentrate my field research in particular Buriad diaspora communities – in Bayan-Uul, Dadal and Dashbalbar in Eastern Mongolia, and in Hulun Buir in Inner Mongolia – was determined mostly by the migration routes of some Aga Buriad[3] families (who were close kin relations of my grandparents' families in the villages Uzon and Suduntui in the Aga steppe – nowadays the Aginskii district in Zabaikal'ski krai, Russia). The intended final destination for many such refugees was Hulun Buir in Inner Mongolia, but only some of them succeeded in reaching it, because the long march through Eastern Mongolia was exhausting for families with young children and for the cattle. Many families decided to slow down at thinly populated and convenient places with enough space for grazing along the Ulzii gol river in Eastern Mongolia, where they ended up establishing several permanent communities. Thus many families "on the move" were segmented into smaller parts and re-dispersed in the areas around the settlements along the migration route (see map in Appendix II highlighting Buriad emigration in the 1910s and 1920s). The devastating political persecutions of Buriads in the 1930s and forced relocations during military actions in Eastern and Inner Mongolia during the Second World War caused renewed chaos, and people were again separated from their kin. Many were unable to find each other for decades.

Before addressing the main topic, I want to add some self-reflective notes on research ethics. One may see me as of a native anthropologist: born in a Buriad family in Aginskoye (Russia). However, I began research on Buriad diasporic groups only recently. Distanced from this natal society due to many factors, I think of myself as neither an insider nor an indigenous researcher, and I do not claim an "authentic" point of view to the anthropological community. Kirin Narayan, who herself has a complicated family background, critiqued almost twenty years ago the traditional view that polarised "real" and "native" anthropologists and the sharp divide between "insiders"

---

3 Aga Buriads mostly consist of eleven *Khori* Buriad clans and constitute the main group of the Eastern Buriads. An estimated one third of the Aga Buriads fled to neighboring Mongolian territories mostly in the period between the 1910s until the end of the 1920s. More on lineage composition of Buriads in Tsydendambaev 1972 [2001].

and "outsiders" (1993). Nowadays, ethnographic writings are richer, and draw attention to personal experience, self-reflection and autobiographical accounts that bring more subjectivity and dynamics into academic writing. Moreover, there is a growing tendency to treat personal experience also as ethnographic data, especially by those who do "anthropology at home"; they more often position themselves somewhere between being an ethnographer and an informant, trying to maintain a double vision that combines both (Collins and Gallinat 2010). Accordingly, I will use my own recollections (including from times before my professional training) and personal experiences of family reunions. I will also include personal impressions of witnessing difficult moments of family reunion, when people who had been separated by state boundaries, catastrophically changing politics and personal anxiety, finally succeeded in finding one another.

The significant geographical distance between my natal home in Russia and my fieldwork sites in Mongolia and China did not allow me to feel "at home". Deploying my grandparents' kinship ties with people whom I had never met (in most cases) also presented me with a number of challenges, even if we speak the same dialect. So, my experience in the field was not dramatically different from that of other "outsider" colleagues, despite having more emotional involvement and personal responsibility. Being familiar with Buriad culture did not grant me insider status either. On the contrary, I felt as though I was being examined on how "authentic" I was; it seemed that, by looking at me, the diaspora could make judgments about Buriads in Russia in general, whether or not they were still bearers of Buriad customs and identity or have already become entirely Russified. Perhaps some of them saw me as the right person to talk to not only about their family, but about all matters concerning Buriads. Those I spoke to touched upon broad topics including how Buriads live in Russia; in which ways Orosiin (Russian) Buriads – or *khoit nutgiin Buriaduud* (Buriads from northern homeland) – are different from *Mongoliin Buriaduud* (Mongolian Buriads); and popular issues like "how we Buriads live in three countries" and "in which country do Buriads live better?'. They often compared their own experience to that of their kin who live in Chinese Hulun Buir and call themselves Shenehen Buriads.

On hearing these conversations about different places and different people I could not help but see them all as reflections on the notion of the "Buriad homeland", and the expression of personalized concerns about kinship and places that are called *nutag* (homeland). In the following section I highlight the range of historical and cultural senses of the term *nutag* in order to link it with migratory Buriad consciousness, and I investigate how the changing discursive landscape of *nutag* evolved finally into diasporic reflections on community and individuals.

The "homeland" lexicon in the Mongolian language

The Mongol language (including its Buriad dialect) has developed a rich vocabulary to express the socio-spatial characteristics of the notion of homeland. Many meanings can be expressed by the term *nutag,* which is used in various grammatical forms as a noun, adjective and verb in numerous word-combinations. Traditionally *nutag* refers to the area of seasonal migration, for example, *gazar nutag* (land territory) and *nutag belcher* (grazing space); it also suggests that many criteria must be met for good grazing land. Thus *nutagluushtai* is an adjective qualifying places with good potential for grazing livestock. In the historical and anthropological literature we can find references to the variety of its uses. For example, Bat-Ochir Bold (2001) shows that part of the *nutag*-related lexicon was created during the Manchu period following changes in jurisdiction over land in Mongolia. The term was used to express a shift in rights to use or possess land. For example, pastures could be measured and divided (*nutgiin deeslekh*), confiscated *(nutag khuraakh)* and granted to a different owner (*nutag evdekh*). Furthermore, people could be expelled from their land (*nutag khüükh*).

Uradyn Bulag (1998) also explains various meanings of the term *nutag* but focuses more on everyday conceptions that reinforce its "territorial" meaning. There is a traditional view that a specific land is possessed by ancestral spirits, and is thus confined to a particular people. Usually the main inhabited area and the boundary of the *nutag* is marked by *oboos* (ritual cairns), which embody the local spirits and are places of communal worship. The *oboo* were associated with obligations to make offerings to ancestral and local spirits (*gazariin ezen*), which are considered to have control of nature and living creatures. Offerings, either during the large collective ceremonies (once a year) or during individual visits to homeland *oboos* (*nutagee oboo takhikh*), were aimed to obtain the protection of spirits and thus to legitimise people's rights to use the *nutag*. It is believed that favorably inclined local spirits (or "masters of the land") would sustain the fertility and vitality of the places with rich pastures and clean water sources, enabling people to increase their herds and have numerous children.

Nutag can be located at different levels, from a larger space to a local one, and can vary in scale depending on whether it refers to the group or to the individual. Expressions such as *törsön nutag* or *turel nutag* can be translated as "birthplace homeland" or "natal land" and do not signify strict territorial limits, while another term *toonto nutag* "placenta homeland" points to the particular site where the parental encampment (*ger* or *yurt*) was situated at the moment of the child's birth. A special ritual, at which the child's afterbirth was buried under the *yurt* (*toomtolkho* or *toonto khadagalkha*) establishes an intimate and magical relation between the person and the birth place. Interestingly, another meaning of *toonto* is a special type of knot, while the verb form *toontodokho* means to "tie-up". This seems to indicate that the person is understood to be "tied-up" and attached to the place where his/her placenta is kept and remains connected to it throughout life. People believe in the special power of the *toonto nutag* over the individual fate and spiritual strength. Strong attachment to *nutag* in general evokes deep emotional feelings and sentiments, and becomes a source for constant inspiration of nostalgic lyrics and poetical longings. The obligation to attend it and execute life protecting worshipping practices (*toonto taikha*)[4] at the individual birthplace involves specific connotations and additional complexities of the "homeland" concept for Buriads.

The phenomenon of the *toonto nutag* also represents a personal feeling of aging; ties with the *toonto nutag* change over the life-cycle and generate repeated "return" practices with the course of time. Ideally, a person should return to the place where his or her life started to signify the symbolical

---

4   Folk worshiping practices at the toonto (*toonto murgekhe*): a person should offer butter and put it on a stone marking the birth place at the old location of the ger (*toonto taihan tohotei chulun*); the same person should walk around the place (*toonto goroolkho*) and roll around naked on the ground (*toontodoo khölvörkhö*) in order to "embrace the earth" and absorb strength body from the "source" in the ground containing personal vitality and life force. Nowadays people prefer a rather simplified version of the worshiping ritual: instead of rolling around naked on the ground as tradition required, people just lie down on the ground with their clothes on. Sometimes it is enough to scatter the soil of *toonto nutag* on one's hands and neck, to drink water from the local water source and wash one's face and other exposed parts of the body. Offerings of rice, biscuits, tea or milk are also made. Nowadays, when long distance migration (both within the national states and across the border) has become a common phenomenon, elders recommend that those who live far away should take with them a piece of stone from *toonto*, so that they can still feel in touch with the homeland.

accomplishment of the life cycle, when one's death also symbolises transition to the next rebirth. Maurice Bloch noticed that in many cultures death is represented as a part of a repetitive cyclical order, and "good" death is that which occurs in the home, the place of the ancestors with living descendants to maintain the continuity of the lineage. "Bad" death, on the other hand, occurs at the wrong place, away from ancestoral shrines and thus represents the loss of regenerative potential (Bloch, 1999). Similarly, Bulag writes that "Mongol tradition held that one should be buried in one's natal land or homeland (*törsön nutag*) after death." (Bulag 1998: 75).

That is why, especially in the diaspora perception, to pass away in a foreign land was perceived as a karmic punishment and a serious obstacle for a better rebirth. Strictly sealed off state borders with Soviet Russia (especially between the 1930s and the end of the 1980s) denied migrant Buriads not only the opportunity to go back, but also the possibility of making a short visit to their *toonto nutag* and parental villages, which, in many cases, were just across the Russian border. As some families remarked, "Our *nutag* was the distance of a dog barking". Members of the second and the third diaspora generation recounting their family histories remember their parents facing their homeland to the north while telling their praying beads, showing their desire to return to their *nutag* before they died. After their tragic lives and death in exile they wished to access the lost homeland if not in this life then in the next rebirth and prayed to be "reborn again at homeland" (*nutagtaa khoito türelöö olokho*).

This strong desire also likely influenced diasporic funeral practices. Reports of several researchers who visited the diaspora in Shenehen show burned corpses, as it was believed that bones should not be buried in foreign land, while the smoke of fires would take the souls of the dead back to the homeland (Sanzhieva 2006). Some informants also said that their parents on their deathbeds asked their children to visit their *toonto nutag* when the Russian state "opens the pass" (*khargei nekhe*) through the border, thus symbolically bringing their souls back to *toonto nutag*.

Surprisingly, the term *nutag* is also used for the binary opposing concept to "homeland": "foreign land". For instance, the expression *khari nutag* can be translated as "unknown" or "foreign" land, an "alien" and "outside" terrain. The way diasporic people now speak about their host society (which was a foreign land for their parents when they arrived) helped me to understand that the dual meaning of *nutag* was an effort to transform the "foreign" land into "homeland". Different verbal forms of the term *nutag* emphasise the different stages and emotional tension of this inversion.

As a Shenehen elder said about their diaspora community, *"Ishe erheer maanad nayad jil nutaglaja bainabdi"* (Since we came here more than eighty years ago, we have been [living here and] making it [our] home). As people have to learn to adapt themselves and their livestock to a new place they can express this through complex grammatical constructions in the causative and passive voices, such as *nutagjuulkha* or *nutagjuulagdakha,* to indicate that the unfamiliar conditions of new place would be transferred with the course of time into a familiar homeland.

Techniques of creating homeland in exile

Anthropologists writing about Mongolia have been intrigued by the different engagement of pastoralists with land and space, and they interpret the Mongolian concept of the landscape as an interactive field of engagement, where cyclical movement between different seasonal encampments can be viewed as passage from one kind of space to another, each time requiring an engagement in relations with the spiritual powers of the locality (Tserenhand 1993; Humphrey and Onon 1996; Bulag 1998; Sodnompilova 2005, and others). They argue that pastures are traditionally not held as private property, since people associate land with spiritual and temporal agencies who are considered to be the "owners", "masters", or "stewards" of the land from which people live. Regular seasonal movement within a familiar landscape requires reestablishing relations with the "owners" of a locality each time upon arrival at summer or winter pastures, because after people leave a place (a year ago or even longer) it becomes to a certain extent "alienated". People should remind the spirits about themselves and renew their ties with this segment of homeland by holding certain "home making" rituals.

Detailed descriptions of these rituals are found in the writings of the Mongolian ethnographer G. Tserenhand (1993) and the Russian ethnographer of Buriad origin, Klara Basaeva (1998). They explain that movement from the winter encampment to summer pasture was highly ritualised. It included several "blocks" of rituals. These are enacted at the moments of departure, arrival at the new place, marking a "chosen" place as already reserved (*geriin on avakh*), rituals of worshiping and symbolic "payment" to local spirits (*ejen,* masters of the land) for the right to use their territory, rituals of "feeding" the master of the fire place in the newly erected *ger,* etc. Actually, moving away and separating from one encampment means homecoming to another encampment.

In the cyclic seasonal movement between at least two homes – summer encampment *zuhalan* and winter encampment *übeljöön*[5] – the latter was perceived as the main and more "fixed" one. Severe winter conditions required herders to locate winter encampments at secure places: less windy with low snow cover and pastures for different types of domestic livestock. Standing wooden fences (*khashaar*) to keep cattle warm and secure from wind and wolves, the wooden winter *ger*[6] and horse tethering pole (*serge*) all marked the territory as someone's permanent place of residence, even if the family left it temporarily for summer camp(s). Winter encampments with permanent constructions stand closer to one another and are more compact, organising a group of kin families into a small settlement (*ail*).

In general, the orbital trajectory could be widened and narrowed depending on environmental conditions (draught, plague, etc.) and other circumstances, such as war, land disputes between pasture claimants, or when the expanded clan divided into several lineages. In these cases, the trajectory could be changed. People searching for new pastures (or a more peaceful place) could move to another orbit, where a foreign landscape could be again "domesticated" and transformed into a new homeland using these rituals. An additional set of rituals was used for settling if the family arrived at a completely new place. This ritual was a sort of "transplanting" of the homeland to the new settlement. In Buriad folk practice the separating group carried with them some stones from their natal *oboo* at the parental *nutag* and put them into the foundation of the worshiping site at the new location.

Ethnographic literature provides some descriptions of this practice among different groups of Buriads. For example, Taras Mikhailov (2004) writes that groups of Ekhirit Buriads that have moved to a new place would take stones from the *oboo* on Baitog mountain, where, as people believe, a powerful local spirit resides. At their new settlement, they would erect a cairn using the stones, thus creating a substitute of Baitog *oboo* at the new place and keeping lineage succession (Mikhailov 2004). Buriad refugee-migrants followed the same traditional practice when they arrived. As I was told in Dashbalbar, migrants brought with them stones from their

---

5   Interesting comparison between pastoral herding and sailing activities have been made (Chabros 1988; Pedersen 2007). It is suggested that movement between pastures is not perceived as movement; even though there is a change in the surrounding landscape as *ger* and its contents remain the same.

6   Buriads used to build winter wooden *ger* a shape of seven/eight wall yurt or Russian style wooden houses. Felt yurt in which family lived during the summer was built inside the wooden carcass of *ger*, thus making it much warmer in winter.

nutag and put them into the base of the Buddhist temple that the newcomers erected near their settlement at River Jarakhei. Another example from Shenehen tells us that newcomers "adopted" a local *oboo* which had been worshiped by local Evenkis before the Buriads arrived. They put some stones, brought from the homeland, into the existing construction of the *oboo* at Bain Khaanei mountain.

Nevertheless, individual practice could differ from group practice. One family history from Bayan-Uul in Mongolia tells how a Buriad son accomplished his father's last will – to return a little piece of gray stone back to the *oboo* at Budalan mountain at his father's *nutag* on the Russian side. The son, who is today a famous Mongolian poet and representative of the diaspora's second generation, was only able to visit his father's natal village, Suduntui, at the end of the 1990s, when he himself was 70 years old. He found his relatives in the village and told them the amazing story of his father who, just before he escaped, had grabbed at a gallop a piece of stone from the local *oboo* and fled. He carried it on his body when he was hiding for two years in the forest from Mongolian soldiers, who, on Soviet Russia's order, were hunting for "counter-revolutionaries" who had escaped from Russian territory. He kept it with him after he was caught, sentenced to prison, and sent to dig fortification ditches on the Mongolian border with Manchukuo in the 1930s, when he was wounded during the Japanese Kwantung army air attack on the frontier, and when he was released from the prison after Stalin's death in the mid 1950s and returned to his wife in Bayan-Uul. Probably it was his individual choice that he did not want to be "rooted" in exile, because he kept this piece of stone hoping that one day he would go back to his *nutag*. Perhaps he kept it with him as a sacred object, as a "piece of home", as a protective symbol that tied him to his homeland. By bringing this piece of stone back to his father's homeland, the son symbolically completed his father's life trajectory, returning him to the place where he was born.

Engagement with local spirits upon arrival to a new place required a ritual donation to local masters (*gazarai ejen*). Before building a new house (*buusa*), a vessel (*bumba*) was filled with precious and valuable things (silver coins, pieces of coral, etc.) depending on the wealth of the family, and buried. This symbolically bought the permission of the masters to reside at this place. After this moment the site was considered occupied and it belonged to the family, with the right to pass it on down the patrilineal line. One of our family legends concerns the maternal grandfather of my father, who was a skillful *darkhan* (blacksmith). When the family prepared to move, he took with him only his instruments. He stored pieces of gold and silver somewhere at his *buusa*, thinking that one day he would be back, but he never returned. In 2006, his son, now at an advanced age, travelled to his father's *buusa* from Dashbalbar, to where the family had migrated. He was impressed to see how spacious the old *buusa*, now covered by nettle bushes, must have been. When I visited my uncle a couple of years ago, he joked that during severe economic crises in Mongolia in the 1990s, he often dreamed of finding the family's legendary "hidden treasure" and becoming rich. Yet when he journeyed to his father *buusa*, he took nothing. When I asked him why, he said that taking things away from the *buusa* now, when they had been stored for so many years, could make the *gazarai ejen* angry: he didn't want to disturb them.

Buriad migrants in exile used traditional technique of "creating" home at the new place, a technique based on long existing pastoralist tradition and practice of regular migrations between seasonal pastures. One could even suggest that for Buriads migration to Mongolia was not exile, that it was just an extension of their orbital trajectory, especially since Aga Buriads previously used to move within large tracks of land in extensive nomadic pastoralism. Indeed, some of them living near the border with Mongolia used to cross it and temporarily camp on the other side at summer pastures, but they were always free to return for winter residence. The tragedy of Buriad migration and what actually constitutes this group as a diaspora, to my mind, appears to be in people's emotions and feelings about the sudden traumatic separation from their families and close kin, when strictly sealed state borders extinguished the hope of returning to *nutag*, *toonto nutag* and other worshiping places on the other side of the border. Political upheavals in the region and Soviet-style campaigns of persecuting "counter-revolutionary elements" both in Russia and in the host countries (China, Mongolia) made this group of people feel unwelcome everywhere. The people in the diaspora attempt to explain the sense of catastrophic deprivation by saying "Losing the homeland, we lost everything" (*nutaga aldaad bükhiigöö aldabdi*).

The feeling that they had "crossed the borderline" of normal life and have to survive in a strange apocalyptical world was formulated in a self-reflective explanation: life in exile in *khari nutag* was not a real life. Rather, it was a strange existence in an inverted world where, as in a cracked mirror, everything went in the wrong way and all engagements with the world and objects were not correct. In diaspora tales, life in exile is described as life on the "wrong side" (*buruu tala*) and done in a "wrong way" (*buruu*): as if they milk cows from the "wrong side" or saddle and mount horses also from the "wrong side".

Through decades and lines of separation: practice of legal, illegal and imagined border crossing

Techniques of border crossing mean not only going away but also coming back, like the "nomadising" that used to be practiced in the frontier area. Despite state policies to divide and to control land and people, local inhabitants – especially if they belong to an ethnic group separated by state borders – generate local knowledge and cultural practices of how to keep borders "open" and how to go through this "slightly complicated door". In this section I will describe how Buriad migrants challenged strictly sealed Russian-Chinese and Russian–Mongolian border to visit their kin on other side. It is mostly based on oral histories of separated families, and it shows how they see acts of border crossing both as it was done *physically* (legally or illegally from the point of view of official border crossing regime) and *in an imaginary way,* via occasional messengers who could bring oral messages, short letters, pictures, little gifts and even spiritual messages received through special shamanic rituals.

Oral histories present different stories of migration, depending on the time, locality and other circumstances of the flight. Some groups of families prepared their migration well. Firstly they sent rangers (*türüüchul*) to search for suitable and under-populated pastures across the border. They managed to take the livestock bit by bit and to send some men of the family to prepare encampments for arrival of the rest of the family, elders, children and other belongings. Other families fled in a hurry, saving their lives from mass red-terror execution and not able to take anything with them. One elder describes her childhood memories, how she and her parents passed by the emptied neighboring village of Tokchin:

> Everything was disemboweled (*zadarkhai*), empty houses, unfastened doors and gates, wooden chests (*khanza*) thrown away empty (*angarkhai*), family belongings thrown everywhere and cattle unattended. It was very frightening (*aya güi*) to be there (Dolgor, 95 years, Uzon, Russia, 2008).

Groups of mobile armed horsemen were able to cross border regularly, hiding from the border patrols, whose service was disorganised during the civil war in the 1920s. When border control tightened in the 1930s, open crossing became impossible, but still "courageous people" (*berkheshuul*) continued to cross the border through secret mountain and forest passes at night to visit their families. Some locals in Suduntui used to joke that the wife of their neighbor, who fled to Mongolia during the civil war, continued to give birth to children until the moment her husband was caught and killed by a border patrol. Families were separated in different ways. Manlai explained an episode of separation from her husband's family,

> My father-in-law was a rich man from Borzya. After he moved to Shenehen he came back several times to carry his family over the border. But I was the only daughter of my parents and refused to move away following my in-laws (*khadam*). Who could take care of my parents if I left them? Father-in-law came at night and cursed me loudly because I again refused to join him. Later I heard that he was caught by the GPU[7] and died in prison. I was also locked in prison because they thought that I kept contacts with my in-laws and other *bodkhul* (those who resisted and fled) people. But I was from a poor family, and our neighbor Dugar, who worked for Communists, helped me to escape the punishment. Soon I got married again. In the 1980s I went to Shenehen to visit my other relatives and saw there my former in-laws. They still blame me for the death of their father…(Manlai, 99 years old, Suduntui, Russia, 2009)

Almost all Buriad families along both sides of the border experienced human tragedies. Numa was left with her grandparents when she was only two years old. Her parents settled in Bayan-Uul and later wanted to bring her there, but she was a sickly child and the grandparents preferred to keep her with them. Once, when Numa became dangerously sick, the shaman explained that the child's spirit regularly flies away to see her mother, who missed her so much that the spirit might leave Numa's exhausted body to be reborn again in the parents' family. As Numa explains the situation now, the shaman turned into an animal (*amitan*) and ran over the border to pass her mother a message that she should not miss her daughter so much, and that other children would be born to their family soon. Numa remembers that from time to time her parents sent her occasional gifts, like pieces of pressed sugar cane, with messengers:

> These pieces were all dark from sack dust, and when I ate it, it had the flavor of tobacco (*makhorka*). Who knows, who risked their life to bring it to me from so far? Now I have more relatives in Bayan-Uul than here. My parents had six children there, they all live well, have their own families with many children.

---

7   GPU was a special department of NKVD, the Soviet secret police from 1922 until 1934.

Now they have dispersed all over Mongolia. At first I received message from them in the 1960s, when our *Voroshilov kolhoz* was allowed to send working brigades to cut hay across the border on the Mongolian side. People found each other there and sent me letters. Now when I go to visit them, they treat me with respect (*hööl bolodog*). "Our Mongols" (*manai Mongolchuud*) [this is how she calls her siblings and their children] came here in the 1990s and we went to the *toonto nutag* of our parents. (Numa, 85 years old, Uzon, Russia, 2008)

Although separated by state boundaries people still felt an obligation to visit and to support their parents and elders across the border, especially during celebration of Sagaalgan (lunar New Year) or other communal celebrations. If the border was closed and snow cover would reveal their footprints, people invented special tricks to avoid detection by the border patrol. Some attached deer hooves to their snow shows, while others fitted their shoe soles backwards, so that the patrol would start hunting in the wrong direction.

Illegal border crossing was a "cat-and-mouse" game that was deadly dangerous. Yet people responded to the oppressive situation with irony and sarcasm. One "humorous" story tells how a young husband decided, together with other young people, to visit elder kin during Sagaalgan, according to tradition. The wife collected presents for the parents into a sack, and the husband went away. The group was caught at the border and sentenced to prison. Only twenty years later did the husband return to his wife; he had survived in a *gulag* camp somewhere in northern Kazakhstan, was released during the "years of Khruschev's Thaw" and went back to his parental village on the Russian side in the mid 1950s. He again illegally crossed the border, this time to see his wife on the Mongolian side. At the moment when he opened the door, his wife was busy cooking something. When she saw him at the entrance she said, "Are you back? You've been celebrating New Year holidays (*sagaalgakh*) with your relatives for a long time…" The attraction of this story is its special way of making tragic events into an object of comedy. It plays around wife-husband relations, about relations between parents-in-law and daughter-in-law, and evokes classical fables of a wandering hero and his adventures. It also reveals the true technologies people used to cross the border. The story has the underlying context that people in fact crossed the border when they needed to, and this is just a story about one man who was unfortunate.

The pain of separation found an outlet for suppressed emotions in Buriad lyrics. The song "*Ütakhan Ononei erie deeguur*" (Beside the long Onon River) recalls a woman dreaming of flying as a bird to cross the Onon river, an allegorical symbol of separation, to meet her beloved. In Soviet official discourse, this song was considered to be a longing song about Buriad soldiers who had been sent to fight against the fascists during World War II far away to the west. But women sang the song much earlier, before the war started, and they sang about men who departed to the south, not to the west. Many women continued to wait for decades for their husbands and sons to return home.

One story from my maternal grandmother (*nagasa-eji*) Dari-Tsyren and her mother Balma represents the human tragedies of many separated families. As many Buriad Cossacks were involved in the anti-Bolshevik movement in Eastern Siberia, people from Uzon village crossed the Mongolian border in early spring of 1922 to join troops of the warlord Ataman Semenov in Hulun Buir. As my great-grandmother's caravan crossed the Onon river near Ul'hun border pass, there was the sound of a machine gun firing, and part of the caravan turned back in panic to hide in the forest. Balma, who was pregnant with Dari-Tsyren, was separated from her husband, who was at the head of the caravan. Her husband's part of the caravan, which safely crossed the border, settled in Mongolian Bayin-Uul not far from the border, while her part being cut off from the head of the caravan had to return to Uzon on the Russian side. As she grew up, Dari-Tsyren never talked about her father and even denied his existence, claiming that she was the daughter of a single mother. She even registered herself as "Balmaeva" – a surname derived from her mother's name.

Dari-Tsyren's personal response to family disaster was to be silent about her lost father and his relatives. For her, having witnessed decades of political repressions against so called "counter-revolutionaries" and members of their families, it was the only way to survive. She revealed some information about her father only recently under pressure of shamans, who requested this information from her in order to "improve" the life of her children and grandchildren. As *nagasa-eji* told us, her mother Balma never saw her husband again, but every evening she rode a horse to the road to wait and see whether a man would appear on the horizon. She waited for him for the rest of her life and did not marry again[8].

Other families tried to relieve the pain of separation by imagining symbolical meetings with kin; it was believed that staring at the full moon would allow communication between relatives. As the daughters of Erdem-Belig remember, when they saw their father for the last time at the end of the

---

8   Several years ago we found that Dari-Tsyren's father finally had reached Hulun Buir. A few elders in Buriad community in Hulun Buir still remembered him; according to them he suddenly disappeared in the mid 1930s. Some GPU files now open to the public reveal the role of informants within Buriad exile community in helping GPU agents to "kidnap" Dari-Tsyren's father from Hailar. He was later killed in a Soviet prison for his "counter-revolutionary" activities.

1920s, he told them, "Look at the full moon every fifteenth day of the month and think as if we see and talk to each other" (quoted from Balzhinimaeva 2012: 8). At that time there was no postal service and no telephone calls. The official atmosphere of paranoia about "foreign spies" created a situation of general suspicion. The fact that someone had relatives abroad was already a crime, and the family would fall into the social category of "untrustworthy". Photographs and letters occasionally received from abroad would be destroyed and the names of relatives there could not even be whispered aloud. In public discourse people in exile were more dead than alive. All of these acts can be seen as violations of memory on an individual level.

Neighbours often informed on each other because of some personal antipathy, jealousy or desire for revenge. It was not so much having relatives abroad (almost everybody had then) but keeping contacts with them that was seen as a reason for informing and accusations. One family told me that their father, having been frightened by regular visits of the KGB secret service in the 1960s and 1970s, burned letters from his brother, who had moved to Inner Mongolian Shenehen. When his wife asked him, "Why don't you read them first?", his answer was "There's no need (*khereg ügi*) to know; it can be dangerous for us". This man felt that he was not even safe holding the information inside his head. The paranoia of the state produced a general atmosphere of fear, and this man seemed to have lost confidence in his ability to maintain a barrier between the inside and outside worlds. A sense of his own permeability, and total state control over his private life, made him feel afraid. The act of publicly burning letters, with his wife and son as witnesses, was done to reassure himself that not only he but also his family members would be more secure without knowing this information.

Other families had a different attitude and preserved their private narratives, letters and pictures hidden "at the bottom of the chest"[9]:

> Around the 1960s I received a letter from my elder sister from Shenehen. She sent me a picture of my mother and my sister's daughter Tuya (Fig. 1) who was born there. But I could not read it, because it was written in old Mongolian script. In Soyuz [the Soviet Union] we learned Cyril writing [Cyrillic script].

---

9   In Mongolian nomadic culture a chest (*khanza*) was a piece of transportable furniture provided with a length of adult dress (*degel*), where family keep all seasonal cloth and other valuable belongings. In this type of usage of the chest acquired an additional allegorical character linked with chronology and layers of memory. Upper layers contain everyday objects which are more often in use. Deeper strata often hide more precious and personally valuable things.

I heard that one repressed lama returned from *gulag* prison back to Tsogto-Khangil [a neighbouring village about 20 km away]. Only he could read my letter, because other people couldn't read old Mongolian script. So one evening I rode my horse to his house. He read it to me, but also said not to show this letter to anybody and to burn it. I did not burn it and kept it at the bottom of my chest (*khanza*). I also kept some other letters that I received through "people's hands" from time to time, but I was afraid to show them to anyone. Even if I couldn't read them, anyway I was happy, that they remembered me, that they were alive and in good condition. I embraced the letter, cried, stroked the pages with my hand, and dreamed as if we were all together again, as if I went to see her over the border to Shenehen, as if she came to see me. When my sister came to *nutag* from China in the 1980s for the first time after 60 years to visit me (Fig. 2), with her daughter Tuya, I opened my chest, took out her letters and asked her to read all of them, that she had written to me in the last twenty years (Sanjit, 87 years old, Aginskoye, Russia, 2008).

Fig. 1 Photographic evidence sent by Sanjit's relatives to inform her that they are alive in exile. Hailar (Inner Mongolia, China), 1960s.

Fig. 2 Family reunion. Sanjit and her elder sister from Shenehen.
(Aginskoye, Russia, end of 1980s).

The border-crossing regime in the late Soviet period, especially the Soviet-Mongolian part of the border, was relaxed compared to the Soviet-Chinese border, which remained strictly sealed until the end of the 1980s. Some people were allowed to cross the border, but not everyone. There were a number of special Soviet-Mongolian border regulations, which infiltrated categories of people who could cross into the frame of the official Soviet-Mongolian friendship treaties. Alexei Yurchak (2006) raises the question: what was the nature of the late Soviet system and way of life that had this paradox at its core? Exploring the period between mid-1950s and the mid-1980s, he criticises the prevailing binary characterisation of Soviet life produced in the west and later in the former Soviet Union and responds to the earlier argument of Susan Gal and Gail Kligman (2000), that in these societies, "... *[r]ather than any clear-cut 'us' versus 'them' or 'private' versus 'public', there was a ubiquitous self-embedding or interweaving of these categories*". But he also comments on their underlying assumption that socialism was based on a complex web of immoralities: "[Gal and Kligman] claim that '... everyone to some extent [was]complicit in the system of patronage, lying, theft, hedging and duplicity of thought which the system operated', and that often even 'intimates, family members and friends informed on each other'" (Yurchak 2006: 24). Caroline Humphrey (1994) pointed out that the state and state institutions in socialism were not defined as separate from the people or the public sphere, but incorporated everyone, top to bottom, through complex, multiple, and shifting "nesting" hierarchies consecutively embedded like Russian dolls. The following stories present vivid examples of what kind of "immoralities" people had to face if they wanted to visit a homeland across the border, and how relations based on ethnicity and kinship needed to be hidden and concealed.

It was a common practice in the Soviet block states to set up "brother capitals", "brother towns" and even "brother state farms". Uzon village, officially named *kolhoz Voroshilova*,[10] was considered to be one of the best and most "progressive" (Rus. *peredovoi*) collective farms in the Chita region. The Mongolian village across the border, Bayan-Uul, became a "brother collective farm". In this official partnership the Mongolian village was the "mentee" (Rus. *podshefnyi*) while the village from the Soviet side acted as the "mentor" patronising partner (Rus. *shefskii*) in the official discourse of Soviet-Mongolian relations. Ironically, Bayan-Uul, a hundred kilometers away from Uzon, had been established by Buriad emigrants who had fled from Uzon and the neighboring villages Tokchin and Alhanai. In official discourse, these "brother state farms" were local symbols of Soviet-Mongolian friendship, and examples of how Soviets provided economic and social help to Mongols. But in private and individual discourse "Mongols" from the Mongolian side and "Soviets" from the Russian side were all connected within a net of related kin groups. To illustrate how official, private and individual categories were mixed at the local level, I use the story of a retired Communist Party functionary, Lodoi, who was the Chairman of the Uzon collective farm during the 1970–80s:

> Visits from Bayan-Uul, our Mongol *podshefnii kolhoz* were arranged and controlled by the *okruzhnoi partkom* [district Communist party committee in Aginskoye distric center]. They gave me instructions on how to make a good reception for Mongolian guests. We, a group of *parthozaktive noyod* [Rus. *parthozactiv* local party and administration activists; Bur. *noyod* bosses] usually went to meet the Mongol delegation at the nearest Russian border pass not far from here, at Ul'hun. But you know, the Head of Bayan-Uul Somon in Mongolia at that time was my cousin Jamso. We knew that we were *brother-relatives* (*akha-duu*). He was one of the sons of my father's elder brother Ausha. I found Ausha in 1961. At that time our *kolhoz* was allowed

---

10   Kliment Voroshilov was one of Stalin's comrade-in-arms.

to send work brigades to Mongolia to cut hay in the frontier area according to the Soviet-Mongolian Border Cooperation Agreement. Buriads there one by one contacted us and asked about their relatives. They all were from our *nutag* (*manai nutagei zon*). I asked them about my uncle Ausha, they told me that he lives in *Eren*, not far from them. I went to *Eren* and found him. He cried and wailed [Bur. *uyeraa-baria*] that all his life he hid the fact that he had relatives in Soyus [Soviet Union]. Only later he told his sons about us. So, you see Jamso was a son of my uncle Ausha. Usually Jamso came as a member of Mongolian delegations, also with some important Khalkh Mongols from the Aimag center. We greeted each other, but Jamso spoke only Khalkh Mongol like the whole Mongol delegation or Russian with other Russians from Chita [the regional capital city]. What a time! We did not dare even to talk to each other [with Jamso] openly in Buriad language. As Chairman of the kolkhoz I had a 'state Volga' car.[11] Once after an official meeting I invited Jamso with Mongolian guests to the riverside to have an unofficial party there. While others were busy drinking and eating, I briefly asked Jamso about Ausha-*ahai* and other family related things. It was really strange time (*jigte sag*)! But I also denied that I had relatives abroad in all official papers and forms. I also denied that I was 'kulak spawn' [Rus. *kulatskoe otrodie* or Bur. *muu zonei ulegdel*], even if the whole *kolhoz* knew that my parents were repressed and other relatives lived in Mongolian Bayan-Uul (Lodoi, 78 years old, Uzon, Russia, 2008).

Even if Lodoi expresses his surprise at the conditions of the time, as a local functionary he understood very well how to combine his individual needs with official tasks. He used official visits to go to Mongolia and found time for his personal wish to find his relatives there. As an official functionary he lied and denied that he had relatives abroad. As an individual, he kept memories of his family and tried to maintain relations with them. He also understood why his relatives did not dare to openly reveal that they were his kin or speak Buriad among accompanying Khalkh Mongols, because Buryats in Mongolia were still the object of latent ethnic discrimination from the Khalkh majority. Lodoi also understands why Russian language was the only language of official communication during meetings with Mongols, because it was the language of transmitting the official Soviet ideology and the language of the Soviet ruling elite. In his story he calls them *obkome orod* (Russians from the regional party committee). His story is an interesting example of attempts to keep up individual family relationships under an official pressure to cut these ties.

---

11   "State Volgas" were government-owned cars usually used by party functionaries. These cars were seen as luxury means of transportation and owing a personal "Volga" (light vehicle produced at the Volga car plant VAZ) signified success and a privileged official position.

Oral history tends to reveal the underside of political and social changes in neighboring countries. People's stories show that so many things in their lives at individual and collective levels were dependent on international politics, relations between neighboring countries and internal politics. Retired Chinese Communist Party (CCP) functionary Namdak, remembers that he came to Aginskoye for the first time in 1986 as a member of the first official Chinese delegation from neighboring Hulun Buir. By that time the Soviet Union and China had signed an agreement to develop Soviet-Chinese Border Cooperation, and for the first time a Chinese delegation came to Chita region. Namdak had been *darga* (boss) of Baruun Somon (Hulun Buir, Inner Mongolia) for fifteen years, and his *somon* was one of the leading districts in Inner Mongolia for agricultural production and cattle breeding. The Soviet partners invited the Chinese delegation to visit one of the best collective farms, *kolkhoz* "Pobeda" (Victory), which was in the Aginskoye district. The head of this Buriad *kolkhoz* at that time was someone named Majeev. Surrounded by Chinese and Russian officials and translators, Namdak and Majeev had a very formal conversation about agricultural productivity, comparing how much grain they obtained from one hectare of land, herd average milk yield, etc. Only on the third day of the official visit, when they were away from the Chinese and Russian officials, Namdak confided to Majeev that he was also a Buriad and started speaking Buriad language with him. He said that his relative's *nutag* was not far away in a village named Borzya. As Namdak remembers, Majeev's first reaction was very contained: he just gave a sign to wait and called someone. Obviously he needed to organise a time and place to meet and speak freely without Russian and Chinese attendants. Majeev organised a private meeting with Namdak on the pretext of an official visit to a sheep herder's farm, and put his people to check the road so that no one could come close to the farm during their semi-secret meeting. Because it was the time of an alcohol prohibition campaign in Russia (*sukhoi zakon* or "dry law"), as Namdak remembers, Majeev showed him how to drink pure alcohol by pouring some water on top, and "…we cheered our meeting and spent all night drinking and singing Buriad songs." (Namdak, 76 years old, Manzhouli, China, 2008).

The end of the Soviet era again brought new complexities for the Buriad diaspora – starting from the 1990s, an open border crossing regime between China, Russian and Mongolia gave new "transnational" opportunities for the children of Buriad immigrants. Their ties with the ancestral homeland *nutag* and parental *toonto nutag* across the border were regenerated and also revised (see Chapter 10 in this volume). Frequent border crossing is increasingly linking the kin-majority and kin-minority, constituting them nowadays as a single cross border transnational ethnic group. The common social phenomenon of ethnic revival in post-Soviet space challenged all groups of Buriads, both those living at home (in Russian Eastern Siberia) and those in diasporas, with decisions about re-identifying their relations with the Mongol world, or their ethnic origin with the Buriad lineages, and this again raises the controversial and confusing question: what and where is the Buriad *nutag*?

Movement across the border as movement between homelands

Children of immigrant parents constitute a diaspora's second generation, and their life in the receiving society, as recent research on transnational communities has shown (Levitt and Waters 2002), cannot be adequately understood without reference to their ancestral background. The general observation is that only a small proportion of the second and third generations is involved in transnational activities and keeps social contacts with the homeland. In the Buriad case these generations face an interesting paradox in that the ancestral *nutag* is now accessible, and border crossing is no longer illegal. However, only a small part of such diaspora communities have decided to return to their parental *nutag*.[12]

If the idea of the homeland return was the main consolidating ideology of the generation of their parents, the next generation already feels rooted in the host society. Most of them see it as their new homeland and another *nutag*. Nevertheless, Buriads "anchored" at a different *nutag* (in Mongolia or in Inner Mongolia) still feel strong attachment to the parental homeland. The first homeland trip of the second generation in the descriptions of my informants is filled with overwhelming emotional stress and pain concerning the fate of their parents as people who "suffered greatly"

---

12   Statistics shows that starting from the 1990s around five hundred Buriads repatriated from China and only hundred from Mongolia: www.infpol.ru/news/670/66574.php?sphrase_id=206191 (accessed 31.5.2011). Personally I have observed that only a five-members family from Mongolian Bayan-Uul returned to their parental village Uzon. The pattern of movement across the border is more complicated in the case of Buriads from China. Many families after repatriating to Russia in the 1990s, returned to China in the 2000s due to the many factors connected with the tightening of citizenship rules in Russia and with growing economic opportunities in China.

(*zobohon zon*). They realise that the narratives of their parents, the stories about their childhood and beautiful homeland are all true. The process of learning about their family history and reestablishing ties with their kin at the ancestral *nutag* in fact brings into existence dual lives; it changes the life trajectories of all groups of kin on both sides of the border.

Many families have been separated not only by the Russian-Chinese or Russian-Mongolian border, but also by the Chinese-Mongolian border: that is why quite often the second generation expands their quest for family members into three countries. The life story of Gulgon is an interesting illustration of this phenomenon. Gulgon's father was a child when his family moved from Suduntui in Russia through eastern Mongolia to Shenehen in Inner Mongolia. The child became seriously ill during the long journey and his parents left him in Mongolia with a childless Khalkha family not far from the *Altan Emel* border pass between Mongolia and China. When Gulgon's father grew up he moved to the Buriad settlement of Dashbalbar (Mongolia) and brought his adoptive Khalkha parents with him. In 1990, the first Chinese border traders came to Dashbalbar and one of them, a woman from Inner Mongolia, started asking people about Gulgon's father. Gulgon contacted her and found out that she was his cousin – the granddaughter of his grandparents who had moved to Shenehen. Around that time relatives of Gulgon's wife Dimid came to Dashbalbar from Aginskoe in Russia searching for their kin in Mongolia. As Gulgon jokes now, suddenly he and his wife Dimid became "rich in relatives" (*türel bayin*), both in Soyuz and in China.

Now Gulgon and his wife are busy traveling regularly between different *nutags* (Fig. 3): the *nutag* of their parents in Buryatia (Russia) and the *nutag* of his relatives in China. Wedding ceremonies and jubilees happen frequently among extended family members across the borders of three countries. Gulgon's children also joined the "transnational field" by choosing to study at a Chinese university in Hohhot under the supervision of his relatives there, while one son studies in Ulan-Ude (Russia) and lives with a family of Dimid's relatives there. Her relatives from Aginskoe decided to send their children to study in Ulaanbaatar (Mongolia), arguing that the future of their children should be secured by living among Mongols who have "their own independent state" (*ööriin güren*). In their opinion, all Buriads came to Russian territory from Mongolia several centuries ago, and Mongolia is the real homeland of all Buriad-Mongols. They say, "… in earlier times Buriads came to their present *nutag* from the south, travelling northwards following the Onon river (*Onon goloo dakhaad*)". This widespread folk notion can be related to Bulag's research into the common identity of all Mongol peoples.

Fig. 3 Gulgon and his wife Dimid (both in Mongol dress) during one of the homeland visits to Buryatia accompanied with their kin (Ivolginski Buddhist temple near Ulan-Ude, Russia, spring 2010)

The notion that Mongolia is the ancient and present homeland for Buriads was discussed among Buriads not only during the 1990s, in the first flourishing of Buriad ethnic revival after the fall of the Soviet system, but also more recently, from 2005 onwards. Recent political processes in

Russia – in which the two ethnically defined Buriad autonomous districts (the *okrugs* of Ust'-Orda in Irkutsk region and Aginskii in Chita region) were dissolved into (or "unified") into the larger territories surrounding them in 2008 – were emotionally distressing for all groups of Buriads living in Russia and abroad[13]. Discussions on popular Buriad websites (possible only on the Internet due to the total control of the public media in Russia) have raised the old issues of Russian colonialism and the tragic Buriad experience of colonial encroachment. Here I quote some comments made during the discussion, which show that the ethnic majority (or at least part of it) regard themselves as potential emigrants, ready to move away to join other Buriads if the next stage of Russia's "internal colonization" proves too hard to bear, just as Buryat migrants did almost a century ago: "Now Buriads from Irkutsk region are moving to Buryatia. If Buryatia merges with Irkutsk, where can we escape to – return to Mongolia?"; "*Again* to leave our native land in search for our survival?" and "Shall we look for Buriad stability *again* in the Mongol world?"[14].

The obvious parallels between the earlier colonial and present-day situations have aroused interest among the kin majority in the history of the Buriad emigration to Mongolia and China, and in life there at present. The mutual cultural rediscovery of the Buriad kin-majority and the diasporic kin-minority has produced discussions about where true "Buriatness" is better preserved, and about whether or not the kin-majority in Russia are still holders of Buriad traditions, even if they live at the main homeland. After trips to parental villages across the border, the second generation diaspora strongly criticise the kin-majority for losing and even betraying Buriad identity in favour of "Russification". This period of discussion coincided with my field work in diaspora communities in eastern Mongolia, and people there criticised their kin in the Buriad homeland for not being able to resist the political reorganisation. They were blamed for their lack of courage in standing up for their right to ethnic autonomy, for their "sheep-like" (*khonin shendi*) obedience to the Russians and the Russian state. In conversation with me (as one of the "kin-majority") they expressed sorrow about this situation, saying, "You also have lost your homeland (*nutagaa aldaat*), as happened with our parents before".

---

13   More about details of the dissolution of the Buriad Okrugs are available in the field report by K. Graber and J. Long (2009).

14   http://www.buryatia.org and http://www.erkhe.narod.ru (accessed on 13.4.2007). Emphasis added.

Personally, I had the impression that the second generation has a feeling of discontinuity between their imagined idealised homeland, which was cultivated by their parents, and the present day situation in Russia where their kin-majority lives. It seems that Buriad territories in Russia differ greatly from the homeland they imagined. This leads to the paradoxical situation that the diaspora second generation is rejecting their parental homeland. The Mongolian journalist Jambaliin Ganga, a native of the Dashbalbar Buriad community in Eastern Mongolia, describes his ambiguous feelings on visiting his parental homeland in Aginskoe when, as a member of a Mongolian delegation, he was invited to the official celebration in Aginskoe of the merger with Chita region:

> [You] feel the fear of [the Russian] Empire at every step. It looks like [local] Buriads consider Russians to be superior. [That is why Buriads want to] speak Russian better than Russians, drink more than Russians, and [they] deny their [Mongolian] origin, even if they have higher cheekbones than us Mongols. [In the presence of Russians] they wanted to demonstrate that they have nothing in common with Mongols.
>
> ...Finally, we are witnessing how the last Buriad has been wrapped in a big Russian patchwork blanket and disappeared underneath. There is no Aga anymore on the map. When we were driving back to the Mongolian border I heard someone starting to sing an old song of Buryat [migrants]: "The homeland (*nutag*) of Khori Buriads is covered by white fog, [we] cannot return from the foreign land (*khari nutag*) and [our] eyes are full of tears and misery" (*Khori buriadiin nutag duuran tsagan manantai, khari nutagiin busakhagui düüren düüren nulimaste*). A [border guard] Russian soldier with a Kalashnikov [gun] led us to the border pass, and the song was not heard anymore. Goodbye, my Khori Buriad [land] which became foreign (*khari*) to me! (*Bayartai, khari bolohon khori buriadamni*) (Zhambaliin Ganga, 2008).[15]

Conclusion

The modern nation state borders that strictly delineated the territories of China, Russia and Mongolia have influenced the fate of Buriads in many different ways. From one point of view, these territories formed Buriads into a distinctive ethnic group, which evolved over several centuries in Eastern Siberia, separate from the rest of the Mongol world. From another point of view, various border crossing practices during the twentieth century allowed

---

15   http://buryat-mongolia.info/?p=437 (accessed 17.6.2009).

Buriads to sustain kinship ties as one united group, despite political isolation and strictly sealed state borders. And finally, in the post-Soviet era, borders also constitute Buriads as differently positioned groups in relation to Mongol identity. It seems that the new transborder dimension reveals a contradictory situation: the Buriad kin minority which lives in Mongolia in reality belongs to the larger Mongol-majority, and this means that Mongolia not Buryatia is more likely to be considered as the "kin-state" for Buriads. In this situation "return homecoming" can mean not only the return of the kin-minority to Buriad parental villages on the Russian side, but also homecoming practices of Buriads from China and Russia to Mongolia, where their Buriad kin live in a Mongolian speaking and culturally Mongolian surrounding as distinct from the largely Russified Buryatia or Sinicised Inner Mongolia.

Recently increasing movement across the borders has been connected not only to homeland visits but also labor migration and various economic activities in border regions. Uncertainty about the different notions of a Buriad homeland *nutag* (whether historical, parental, or the actual place of birth) is not so important any more for the diaspora second generation. Transborder mobility is perceived more as movement between different segments of one large homeland, in which everyone is free to return to one's chosen "main" encampment. This situation recalls the way things were before borders went up, when *nutag* was not dissected by lines of separation.

9. Politicisation of Quasi-Indigenousness on the Russo-Chinese Frontier

Ivan Peshkov

For darkness restores what light cannot repair.

Joseph Brodsky

In the changing world of the Russian-Chinese borderland, the Argun River basin has been stable since 1689 when the Treaty of Nerchinsk created a modern institutional basis for Russo-Chinese relations. Unlike the "lost" border with Chinese Turkestan and the relatively modern section of the border in the Far East, the Argun River borderland has been a long-standing frontier of Russian cultural and economic expansion and the place where the Chinese and Russian civilizations clashed. Russian-Chinese relations before 1917 were based on Russia's demographic and military domination in the borderland area and its regular attempts to transform Chinese Inner Asia into "Outer Siberia".

After the collapse of Qing China and Romanov Russia, that section of the border system in Inner Asia (the USSR, Mongolia and China border triangle) functioned as the Sino-Soviet border management model for the area. This model was characterised by a closed-border policy, special attention by state authorities to the supervision of border communities (special rights,

DOI: 10.11647/OBP.0026.09

movement control, propagandist idea of the border as bastion, etc.), and a very strong connection between socialist modernisation and militarisation of the area (at an economic, cultural and social level). The members of the transborder quasi-indigenous Inner Asian communities (Russian Old-Settler communities) share very traumatic experiences of that time. They were subjected to forced separation from their family members, social stigmatisation in their own countries, demonisation as spies and bandits, and long periods of isolation from their place of birth and the members of communities in other countries.

Quasi-indigeneity is a descriptive term relating to cultural and identity forms taken on by the first settler community following colonial conquest and by their descendants. The ambiguous character of the category has provided a possibility for a simultaneous justification of cultural prestige of a given community (more white than indigenous) and contact with indigenous culture and territory. My usage of the category of quasi-indigeneity to describe the colonial experience of Eastern Siberia aims at integrating a set of theoretical, legal, descriptive and original names of communities which cohered as a result of biological metisation and cultural syncretism in Eastern Siberia: the popular ("Old Settlers" (*starozhily*), biological and cultural (mixed communities), administrative (local Russian) and academic (nativisation and creolisation). The term overcomes the limitations of these various overlapping categories. Quasi-indigeneity is formed when former migrant communities become inseparably connected (biologically and culturally) with the indigenous inhabitants of a region.

In the Tsarist time, the dominant cultural hierarchy described the origin and cultural status of these communities one-sidedly using two different frameworks: the first one saw new communities resulting from the orientalisation process of the ancestors of the first-wave of settlers in Siberia; the second was connected to the negative and emotional descriptions of Europeans' cultural and psychophysical degradation in Asia that were used by Tsarist officials and ethnographers. Today's literature concerning the region predominantly employs imported categories such as a "creole" ethnic group (Hancock 2003: 159), neutral ones such as "mixed communities", local terms used to describe a given community such as "old-settlers communities" (Vachtin, Golovko and Shvaitcer 2004: 14), or processual categories like "Siberian nativisation" or Russians "gone native" (Sunderland 1996: 807).

To my peers born in the USSR in the first half of the 1970s the first image of the interwar-period Sino-Soviet border area was shaped by the Soviet television series entitled *Gosudarstvennaya granitsa (State Border)*, which depicted the dramatic history of the Soviet border guard. In one of the episodes the plot moved to "Russian" Harbin which – thanks to the courage of the main characters – was transformed into a battlefield involving Soviet intelligence and a complicated network of enemies including Japanese secret service, Russian emigration officials and Transbaikal Cossack bands.[1] In this way, the writers of the series reinforced the image of the island of the Russian Émigrés in Northern China with the Soviet discourse of the border as a space of permanent defence against enemies of the "motherland of the proletariat".

While in the last years of the Soviet Union the image of "Russian" Harbin became intimate and well-liked, one semi-mythical Russian community from Manchuria was never accepted. They were Ataman Semenov's Cossacks – viewed as an eternal enemy of every Soviet citizen. During my childhood stories of that group appeared several times in the most unexpected contexts. Soviet specialists returning from Mongolia told stories about their meetings with Ataman Semenov's or Baron Ungern-Sternberg's Cossacks who retained their old way of life and far-reaching autonomy from the authorities of the Mongolian People's Republic and the Soviet contingent in Mongolia. My relatives from Transbaikalia used a mixed discourse in which Ataman Semenov's crimes mingled with admiration for him, semi-legendary intimacy with his family and the doubt about the communist version of the region's history. The variety of contexts, times and places created the illusion of social importance and immateriality of the phenomenon.

Growing up outside Transbaikalia I was not able to integrate these stories into a coherent whole and was treating them only as local folklore from the borderland areas. Many years later, when I began to conduct fieldwork in Transbaikalia, Mongolia and China, I realised they were completely fictitious. The local Russians in Mongolia in most cases did not have any links with the Cossacks, the Sino-Russians were a racially mixed group of anti-Cossack-oriented peasants, and the post-Soviet Transbaikalia hardly resembled the "Cossack Vendée".[2] Most communities associated with

---

1   This was the third episode of the series, "Eastern Frontier". The Cossack bands were described as the "border bands".

2   The term "Cossack Vendée" was used in the discourse of Russian emigration based on a sentence from the poem by Marina Tsvetayeva, "Lebedinyi stan", about the Don Cossack anti-communist uprising: "The last dream of the old world / Youth – glory – the Vendee – the Don". The translation of the sentence and the usage of the term can be found in *The Russian Civil War* (Mawdsley 2007: 85).

Semenov had no idea about the Ataman, barely remembered the Cossacks, and had at least moderate pro-Soviet attitudes. The Transbaikalian discourse regarding "Ataman Semenov's wild Cossacks" (the *semenovtsy*) was not only the ideological and emotional basis for decossackisation practices, but also the crucial lynchpin of Soviet mythology relating to the border as a place of symbolic and physical confrontation. This contribution of the legend to the symbolic instruments of the Soviet statecraft in the border areas was totally underestimated in the relevant literature.

Using the example of the Soviet (Russian) conceptualisations related to the two Siberian quasi-indigenous communities (the local Russians in Mongolia and the Three-River Delta Russians in China), this paper shows the links between the negative politicisation of quasi-indigenousness and the Soviet (Post-Soviet) conceptualisation of the "border as a bastion". The first group (Mongolian) was recruited from the Old-Settler peasants, Old Believers and local Buryats who had left their country because of the 1928 famine. In socialist Mongolia these people were discriminated against as a hostile group displaying a "non-Soviet lifestyle". The second group consisted of the Transbaikal Cossack immigrants to China, who wanted to avoid decossackisation practices. Most of them settled densely on the Derbul, Haul, and Gan river banks. This is from where the term "Three-River Delta" stems. In the 1950s the inhabitants of Cossack villages were resettled in large numbers in Kazakhstan and the Ural Mountains. Only in the 1990s did some of those people manage to come back from Kazakhstan to the town of Sen'kina Pad' in Chita Province.

Quasi-indigenousnes in Inner Asia in the twentieth century

The assumption of ethnic, confessional and political coherence of the borderland area has been crucial for the Russian (Tsarist) colonial experience in Asia, which was based on the agrarian use of nomadic frontier land and the forced expulsion of disloyal nomadic populations. This model of coherence included a special policy preventing frontier disloyalty based on reorientation of indigenous nomadic population towards Russia through control of transborder movement, separation of religious institutions from the authorities outside Russia, state support for migration and active militarisation of the indigenous population. In this context the "coherence" in the Siberian borderland area was understood as a Russia-oriented agro-nomadic world in which military institutions and cultural domination by Orthodox communities played an essential role. Before the beginning of the twentieth century an "ideal border settler" was conceptualised by the Russians as a member of the military (Cossack) or cultural (Orthodox peasant) colonial formations. The mixture of three strategic areas of state policy (concerning the land suitable for agriculture, railroads, and border management) provoked strong pressure towards denomadisation and acculturation of the indigenous peoples of Transbaikalia. As a result, the mixed population of Southern Siberia could reproduce the Eastern European peasant style of living, participate in Russian culture and demonstrate the Eastern European identity of Orthodox peasants (Peshkov 2011).

In the late Tsarist time the main problem with the Transbaikal border areas was seen to be the cultural ambivalence of the local population. Travellers and researchers interpreted the disappearance of racial and cultural boundaries between newcomers and the indigenous population as racial degradation and cultural weakness on the part of the local Russians. The founding father of Siberian separatism, Nikolai Yadrintsev, wrote in his monograph *Sibir' kak koloniia* (*Siberia as a Colony*):

> that the racial stability of Russians in the East is not so strong as it has been expected, that the Russians in many cases were rather likely to obey the "inorodtsy" than to rule them, and that they borrowed more from the "inorodtsy" than they could offer them (2000: 56).[3]

The controversies regarding the mixed population of the Transbaikal border areas resulted from the model of Russian colonisation of Transbaikalia and the formation of quasi-indigeneity. The Russian conquest of the Transbaikal region led to the development of new forms of ethnic and cultural identity based on cultural syncretism and mixed marriages between Russians and the inhabitants of the region. These mixed communities are referred to as the "Old Settlers" (*starozhily*). These groups included: the Old Believers, Gurans (*gurany*), Sakhalars, Karyms (*karymy*), and the people living near the Kolyma (*kolymchanye*), Anadyr (*anadyrshchiki* or *anadyrtsy*), Angara, and Lena rivers (*angarskiye* and *lenskiye*). Their mixed origin has been at the core of the Old Settlers' identity: a sharp dividing line exists between the Old Settlers and the natives on the one hand, and the Old Settlers and the Russian newcomers on the other. Such communities consist of members imaginarily related

---

3   *Inorodtsy* is a legal term used in the Russian Empire to describe its non-Slavic population.

to the first Russian migrants to Siberia (until the late eighteenth century) (Buraeva 2005).

The most numerous mixed group in Transbaikalia were the Transbaikal Gurans, an offshoot of Transbaikal Cossacks. Transbaikal Gurans is a proper name applied to Transbaikal Cossacks of mixed Russian, Evenki and Buryat descent. The group had a status that concealed its ethnically mixed nature and existed simultaneously on the border of the military-administrative and nomadic-agrarian worlds. It was characterised by a multipolar identity structure including unique ethnic, racial, social and political components. The specificity of the Gurans lied in the simultaneous occurrence of acculturation and socialisation processes in the framework of the Transbaikal Cossack military units. In that context Gurans were not Mongolian, Buryat, Evenki or Chinese, although they might have been of such origin, had the command of a particular language or may even have been Buddhists or Shamanists. The Cossack status integrated different groups of *mestizos*. The basic identity indicator of this group was the abandonment of the actual history of their ancestors' origin and the creation of a founding myth describing the role their ancestors had played in the conquest of Siberia. The Russianisation and Westernisation of the past did not collide with the strong oriental elements of their culture (Peshkov 2008).

After 1917 the Transbaikal quasi-indigenous groups dispersed as a result of red terror actions, showing an active resistance against Soviet authorities. The hostile attitude of the communist authorities to the Cossacks and the new socialist border regime led to devastating consequences for the everyday life of local communities. The first three decades of the new regime were particularly traumatic for these groups. Their mass migration into Mongolia and Manchuria began in 1918 and initially concerned only richer Cossacks escaping decossackisation practices. Over time, because of terror, starvation and persecution, they were joined by Old-Settler peasants, Old Believers and Evenki. The large numbers of Cossacks that comprised the first immigration wave established a long-surviving model for perceiving migrants to borderland territories (they were perceived according to their origin and political views). For many years Soviet propaganda defined both countries of exile as places of refuge of politically inactive (Mongolian) and active (Manchurian) White Cossack emigrants.

The first result of the decossackisation policy was the exclusion not only of the Cossacks, but of the cultural and racial hybridity of the area more generally. According to Slezkine's proposal to view the ethno-political structure of the USSR as a communal apartment with separate rooms for particular nations (Slezkine 2006), the project of the Soviet Transbaikalia was based on the Russians and Buryats staying separate. Mass migration completely transformed the region's ethnic situation. The local and indigenous inhabitants still played a nominal role in the symbolic and political life of the region, but generally most people had a migrant origin and very weak ties to the non-socialist period of the region's history and culture. In this context socialist modernisation turned out to be a powerful historical circumstance shaping adaptation in accordance with the socialist model of social relations and transforming the model of border management. The second result was the psychological consequences of the new bordering practices. The people living in the borderland areas demonstrated a particular level of political loyalty. According to the Soviet "hermeneutics of suspicion" political loyalty was viewed as a broad concept. Their origin, the participation of their relatives in the Civil War and the financial status of their parents had a significant impact on the selection processes of the border residents. The internalisation process of the Soviet propaganda patterns and the development of self-disciplining habits provoked radical changes in the normative Soviet personhood and standards of normality of the social life in the border areas. The third result included the remilitarisation of the area based on Red Army structures and long-term domination of military institutions. Groups with Cossack status were liquidated for the same reasons they had once been established (to form a military and economic complex on the Russian (Soviet)-Chinese borderline).

The quasi-indigenous groups were destroyed both in Mongolia and China. Emigration and mixed marriages led to the appearance of two new ex-Old-Settler communities: local Russians in the Mongolian People's Republic (MPR) and the Three-River Delta (TRD) Russians in China. Those communities differed from Russian immigrants in Inner Asia (i.e. the so-called Harbin Russians) with their village attachment, the local character of migration movements, the Old-Settler cultural background, and their erroneous perception as "Ataman Semenov's wild Cossacks". This situation provoked a negative politicisation of the groups as well as a tendency to perceive both the Soviet state and Soviet citizens as static objects.

The two groups had different historical experiences and socialisation paths in Soviet society. The TRD Russians experienced periods of cultural and economic domination in their area of inhabitancy (Lindgren 1938), the genocidal policy of Soviet military troops in 1929 and strong repressions after "liberation" in 1945. The immigrants were integrated but maintained their own models of self-organisation. At the time of the Japanese presence (1932–1945) the majority of the TRD Russians were citizens of the state hostile to the USSR and they started to realise all the consequences of that situation: serving in the army and participating in public and cultural life. From 1945 until 1956, this community was the object of the sovietisation policy of the institutions in the borderland territories. The USSR turned Russian private schools into Soviet state schools, organised access to Soviet propaganda movies, and encouraged people to return "home". The sovietisation policy and access to citizenship did not guarantee political and cultural rehabilitation in the USSR (Ablazhei 2007).

The TRD Russians were treated by the state with hostile distance. Those who returned to the USSR before 1953 (Stalin's death) were sent to prison or exile, and after destalinisation they were forced to settle in Central Asia (Northern Kazakhstan). Nowadays, the number of Cossack descendants in the region is quite low. After 1956, mass migration to the USSR and Australia began. Those who decided to stay in China were mostly of mixed origin (Chinese and Russian) or poor and without relatives in the USSR. 1966 marked the beginning of the "black decade" (the Cultural Revolution) in the life of the community, since all the Russian (Orthodox) people were accused of believing in superstition and of spying for the USSR. Aside from the physical extermination of many of its members, the group experienced strict bans on speaking or using Russian (even at home) and on practising its religion. As a result most of the group members born in the late 1960s have problems speaking Russian or do not speak the language at all (Basharov 2010). The situation of the group improved considerably after 1978 and nowadays there is a special socio-economic support policy of Chinese local authorities concerning this community.

In the case of the MPR the situation differed significantly. Most of the local Russians in Mongolia found themselves in the country because of the 1928 famine, which was not related to Cossack emigration. Before 1945 the community of refugees from the USSR to Mongolia was a small group of stateless peoples and Mongolian authorities were not interested in its situation. The second wave of Mongolia's sovietisation after 1945 complicated the lives of the local Russians. After 1971 those people had Soviet passports (but without the right to live in the USSR) and a generally Soviet identity (Mikhailev 2008), but were discriminated against as a hostile group displaying a "non-Soviet lifestyle". After 1991, mass emigration of local Russians began, mainly to East-Central Europe. The local Russians were viewed by the Soviets as the mythical *Semenovtsy* who had escaped to hide in Mongolia; they did not understand the significance of the name and started using it as a proper ethnonym.

The rhetoric of the black legend: the Soviet border as ritual

The main discursive pattern of the border conceptualisation in Transbaikalia was the black legend about the hostility of Ataman Semenov's wild Cossacks. The legend had a counter-factual, virtual and exclusive nature. We are dealing here with the case in which decossackisation applied to groups that had no Cossack status and often were even in conflict with the Cossacks. In the Soviet period, the memory of the Civil War was managed by the state in many forms. In the Soviet narrative of the Civil War special attention was paid to the practices aimed at demonising the participants of anti-communist resistance in Central Asia. The principal anti-heroes of the propaganda were the so-called *Basmachi* in Central Asia and the Cossacks from Inner Asia (*Semenovtsy*).[4] They were described as backward, aggressive people and instruments of foreign intelligence. In Stalin's time, terms such as *Basmachi* or *Semenovtsy* were used by the propaganda and functioned only in juridical context. After the 1950s, the *Semenovtsy* transformed into fully mythological characters, and was used as an exclusionary term by ordinary people.

The inhabitants of Siberia talked about the eternal Cossack communities of Inner Asia (Mongolia, China, Transbaikalia) with their old way of life and strong anti-Soviet attitudes. These communities were perhaps "invisible" – the *Semenovtsy* features having merged into the local mixed communities of Transbaikalia, Mongolia and Northern China. This otherwise marginal Siberian group attracted attention because of its cultural closeness; it was already familiar (the Soviets played the role of European observers of an orientalised Russian subculture). Soviet citizens were particularly provoked by the group's apparent readiness to treat them with violence. Moreover, the propaganda vision of the past was transferred into the present. The features attributed to the *Semenovtsy* combined political, racial and social aspects: anticommunism, mixed ethnicity and bilingualism, as well as aggression and aversion for the Soviet people. In the context of the black legend, the public

---

4   *Basmachi* is a pejorative Soviet term that stems from the Turkish verb *basmak* meaning "to oppress, to violate" (Ritter 1985).

consciousness of the late USSR conceptualised alternative and less prestigious models of Russian culture outside the Soviet Union and relations of ethnic and political solidarity. Ideas of ethnic hybridity and anti-communism and the existence of islands of pre-Soviet Russian life were seen as absolute evil. This pervasive stereotype was extremely difficult to counter.

The popularity and multi-dimensional impact of that legend were based on a rich rhetorical content, which significantly exceeded Russian self-orientalisation practices and the Soviet asymmetry between ethnic and political solidarity. The ability of Soviet propaganda to create a transborder phantom network of "Cossack resistance" is a fascinating example of a confrontation myth playing a founding role in Soviet identity in Siberian borderland areas. The mythology of Cossack resistance served a number of functions: it cautioned against an enemy, connected people emotionally with the events of the Civil War, presented the Soviet view on transborder areas as a place of confrontation and integrated the people of the Soviet frontier against their eternal enemies behind the borders.

The discourse-oriented approaches to Soviet society underline the dramatic effect of communist language innovations on social life (Halfin 2002, Halfin 2009, Humphrey 2009). The complex state-governed way in which people learned to "speak Bolshevik" (Kotkin 1997: 220) largely determined the pattern of collective and individual self-perceptions and memory. In that context "the Soviet language" was not only characterised by its overpoliticisation and sectarian attitudes towards the external world, but also had a tendency to make "performative utterances" about cultural, ethnic and social divisions (Fitzpatrick 2006). The specificity of the "political" in the USSR significantly broadened the boundaries of political action. From the perspective of Soviet discursive practices the collective ability to create common narratives generated completely new historical, temporal and eschatological perspectives. Historical events, the relationship between past and future, as well as the strong influence of assumptions about a communist future were conceptualised mainly from the political perspective of permanent confrontation. If, according to Sheila Fitzpatrick, we can use the term Stalinism as "a shorthand for the complex of institutions, structures and rituals that made up the habitat of Homo Sovieticus" (Fitzpatrick 2000: 3), the main role of the black legend was to support that ritual of permanent confrontation in the Soviet border areas.

The influence of military mobilisation aesthetics on socialist modernisation practices was very strong and is widely recognised in the literature (Fitzpatrick 1976, Skocpol 1988, Vishnevski 1998), but the connection of the socialist border to the outside world (non-socialist or with the wrong socialist country) provoked the "overmilitarisation" of social life in the borderland areas. In this context the socialist conceptualisation of the border (as a limitation of legal space and separation from the outside world) legitimised the military style of governance and the special policy of ritualising confrontation. The nature of this ritual is the legitimacy of an emergency by constantly referring to and recognising the enemy's presence and emphasising the necessity of defence. The mass production of virtual enemies in the Sino-Soviet border areas was based on complex exclusion discourses combining political, social and when possible – cultural (orientalisation) differences. Through this ritual the real quasi-indigenous communities became entangled with the virtual reality of the network of Cossack resistance, causing an "effect of realism" and the overlapping of myths, personal memories and the official version of the Civil War. From the perspective of the Soviet citizens it was an adaptation to the world of the Soviet propaganda and to the cultural and ethnic diversity of the border areas. From the perspective of the members of the stigmatised communities it was a Soviet collective madness having no basis in personal history. In that context, the mythology of Cossack resistance integrated the people of the Soviet frontier against their enemies and those from behind the Soviet border.

From the perspective of the ritual-supporting function of the black legend, the crucial element was the militarisation of the image of the stigmatised communities. The combination of Cossack features (the Soviet people described their contemporary *Semenovtsy* as the ones in the Cossack uniforms) and the expectation of physical aggression against the Soviets transformed the image of the quasi-indigenous communities into quasi-military formations. The transformation of the loyal Tsarist border guard into border bandits was conceptualised in that legend in the categories of Russian political mythology about the Cossacks' *volya* (freedom) as opposition to the legal state (Humphrey 2007: 6). The rule of the atamans (*Atamanshchina*) in Transbaikalia was described as criminal governance completely lacking international legitimacy. In the Soviet era, "Oriental cruelty" was the basic term used to describe the Transbaikal Cossack warlordism. Their crime was exaggerated and their "Oriental features" were emphasised. The authorities talked about them as Japanese collaborators, sadistic predators, separatists and political adventurists. The members of the stigmatised communities were viewed as representatives of the following political culture: the stereotypes about Cossacks were connected with stereotypes about "wild Mongols" and isolated Russian Old-Settlers. In this context, the discourse about the *Semenovtsy* had a rather complicated structure, the main purpose of which was a ritual transformation of the border areas into the space of unresolved fighting with the enemies of the Soviet people.

The strong symbol of continuity of anti-communist atamans' rule was the Three-River Delta, which was conceptualised as a space of extreme political hostility and reactionary models of living. Whereas the quasi-indigenous communities in Transbaikalia and the MPR were "silent" and masked, the TRD Russians were described as dangerous enemies awaiting an opportunity to attack the USSR. The negative mythology of the TRD gave the possibility to situate a part of the Cossack resistance network in a space beyond the control of the Soviet authorities, which in the Soviet view of the world automatically criminalised it. The key features of the Soviet description of that community were also transferred to Mongolia and Transbaikalia creating the permanent phantom presence of enemies along the borders. The mythological "Three-River Delta Russians", as a symbol of the reactionary past and anti-Soviet activity, played the necessary role of disciplining the inhabitants of Soviet Transbaikalia. That new virtual and unwanted frontier community was built in opposition to the ideal Soviet border community. The identities of the Soviet Transbaikalia and the Russian West Manchurians existed as mirror opposites (see Fig. 1).

Characteristics	Soviet Transbaikalia	Russian West Manchuria
Political orientation	communist	anti-communist
Dominated by	Non or Ex-Cossacks	Cossacks
Temporality	future-oriented present	past-oriented reactionary present
Frontier loyalty	loyal	disloyal bandits
Ethnic structure	Socialist nation (Russian, Buryat, Evenki)	Backward half-breeds
Characteristic feature:	Progressive	Reactionary

Fig. 1 Opposing features of Soviet Transbaikalia and Russian West Manchuria

In the virtual world of the legend a member of this semi-mystical community of *Semenovtsy* represented not only potential danger in the Soviet border areas, but also symbolised the limits of the Soviet state to control family life. From the perspective of this legend, the state proved completely powerless in the face of the modest resistance shown by the small rural Cossack population. This imaginary eternal Cossack community with its pre-revolutionary way of life represented the limit of the Soviet ability to enforce modernisation. From that perspective, the fear of the aggressive behaviour of the stigmatised communities only masked the deepest fear of facing what was perceived to be the opposite of "normal" Soviet personhood: a backward people intentionally avoiding the Soviet world.

Soviet society stemmed from the deep influence of socialist modernisation practices (their Stalinist version) in all spheres of the country's social and economic life (Starikov 1996). State interventions into people's family lives through politicisation of relationships between family members and forcing them to publicly deny their repressed relatives played a crucial role (Figes 2007), as did the family nuclearisation of urban Russians (Vishnevsky 1998). The preservation of traditional family values was perceived by Soviet Russians to be "Oriental" and therefore "backward". This cultural transition created the opportunity of perceiving non-Soviet village communities as examples of backward and half-Oriental subcultures. Alternative ideas of "Russianness" provoked aggression from the state and attempts were made to stigmatise these communities as politically hostile. The clear advantage of the Soviet version changed potential dialogue into hostile monologue and transformed "alternative Russianness" into a special feature characteristic of backward and antagonistic communities.

Practice of inclusion: the "silent enemy" and the group intentionally created for prosecution

The Three-River Delta Russians' repatriation to the USSR was similar to that of the Russians in Eastern Europe and the Balkans: a warm invitation to return was extended, followed by a difficult start in the new society. There was a lack of verifiable private history and basic social habits, as well as a lack of Soviet communicational skills. They had alternative views and the experience of an economy without starvation. This resulted in the treatment of the groups as hostile elements who should earn the right to return through hard work or imprisonment (Perminov 2008). This model of negative inclusion, called "the repentance way", created a new subculture displaying selective socialisation and adaptation to Soviet culture. Political terms were eliminated from the group vocabulary, but the old model of family life, religion and a strong social network remained and the community maintained some autonomy. The group did not accept the Soviet version of the region's past and avoided the names and terms used by the propaganda.

The situation of the local Russians in Mongolia was more problematic. The Soviet presence in Mongolia changed the group into hostages of Soviet memory. These local Russians exemplified a group intentionally created for persecution. Given the non-political (economic) causes of its immigration and its participation in World War II, the group expected acceptance from the Soviet state and their own gradual adaptation into Soviet society. This never happened. The Soviet colonial institution in Mongolia used the mixed policy of preventive segregation and partial inclusion: on the one hand, KGB units warned Soviet specialists against the hostile group of Ataman Semenov's wild Cossacks while, on the other, the members of the community were included in basic Soviet institutions in Mongolia (Soviet schools, kindergartens, special shops, etc.).

The Soviet people, influenced by propaganda, identified this group with the *Semenovtsy*, on the basis of a mythology tied to real and fictional features: ethnic hybridity, physical aggression and bilingualism. The combination of the term *Semenovtsy* with selective elements of Soviet stereotypes was a sufficient proof of their hostility. Based on the memories of local Russians and Soviet specialists it can be postulated that Soviet specialists never stopped thinking about the local Russians in terms of the Semenov myth. The discriminatory discourse concerned primarily men, with women being seen only as potentially sexual objects (they never had names and are only described as the "Semenov girls" – *Semenovki*). Males, by contrast, were depicted as aggressive men or boys attacking "Soviet children" at school. The nature of the conflict lay in the connection of the "norms" with the stereotype: ordinary Soviet people were confronted with *Semenovtsy*, "pure" Russians were faced with people of mixed origin, and educated people were dealing with villagers.

The degree of the conflict is puzzling considering that the set of behavioural features attributed to local Russians (Stepanova 2008) were not unfamiliar to Soviet people (excluding the strong Mongolian language skills). Mongolia was an ideal territory for integration with the society – it was isolated, dominated by Russians and had years of documented history. Nonetheless, the Soviet community continued its policy of rejection. The reasons for this hostility stemmed from a political neutrality perceived as a political stance (hence the accusation of a non-Soviet lifestyle). The community was seen as antipodal to Soviet society and a peaceful relationship with them was seen as impossible. Yet surprisingly, the local Russians were granted Soviet citizenship in 1971: a manifestation of a move to create Soviet citizens, even from a pariah group. However, this date has not appeared as a turning point either in the local Russians', nor in the Soviets' memories. They never noticed the change.

The TRD and local Russians had to conform both to their stigmatisation and to the inability to reconcile their version of history with the official one (shared by everyone else). This situation caused considerable adjustments in their collective memory and a selective Sovietisation of some private versions of the events. The two communities reacted to the political disciplinary discourse and to their rejection by other Soviet citizens in different ways. The TRD Russians stressed the fact that they were hard-working, and became distant and religious. By contrast, the local Russians in Mongolia became aggressive towards Soviet citizens, and developed an agricultural resourcefulness that led to profiteering in food production and other sectors. Their aggression towards Soviet specialists was a desperate reaction to their constant persecution, and their rejection by the MPR. New groups of negative identities appeared (the *Semenovtsy*) which were based on propaganda structures and had nothing in common with Civil War heroes. This new subjective Semenov-style subculture emerged from the Transbaikal Old Settlers' reaction to their marginalisation and to Soviet attitudes towards decossackisation. In this context, the negative inclusion of the non-Soviet constituted an element of transformation of the two groups into local Soviet subcultures which could be comprehended by Soviet society.

The black legend trapped in post-Soviet memory

The collapse of the Soviet Union and state propaganda machines radically transformed the political, emotional and economic condition of the region's life. Changes in state responsibilities caused the end of the "modernity era" in Transbaikalia and provoked "post-socialist backwardness" processes with uncontrolled mass migration to the western part of Russia and a long-term social crisis (Humphrey 2002a). This resulted in numerous attempts to idealise Soviet times and defend the legacy of the Soviet Transbaikal border areas. The power of the Soviet interpretation of the past has also been strengthened by academic writing and institutional continuity with the previous period. The Soviet version continued in the post-Soviet time in a more complex context of coexistence with discourses of Cossacks emigration and anti-communist historiography. Paradoxically, both the communist and anti-communist versions continued to involve the rhetoric of the black legend.

In today's Russian debates the main perception of the memory of the Civil War still has a Soviet origin. Ex-soldiers' internet sites in Russia are filled with memories of their confrontations with the Semenovtsy in the MPR and Transbaikalia during the Soviet era. Even today the Russian community in Ulaanbaatar is divided into ex-Soviets and local Russians. In 2008 an elderly lady in the Chita Historical Museum told me: "You look like a Semenovets from Manchuria". In the same year, Transbaikal Cossacks tried to organize an ethnographic expedition to the TDR, aiming at investigating Cossack culture in a completely decossackised area (Peshkov 2010a).[5] The stigmatised communities still remain in the shadow of the black legend and Soviet border rituals. From the post-Soviet perspective the stigmatised people remain members of enemy formations and the weakening of political discrimination is slowly being replaced by a "concern" about racial and religious purity of these communities.

These excluding practices have been so popular after the collapse of the USSR because of the temporal dualism in today's perception of the Russo-Chinese border. After 1991, the Soviet border model lost its former visibility but continues to have an influence on regional images of "bordering" and borderland. The experience of the new model of open border space coexists with the habits of the Soviet border regime. This invisible Soviet border has remained the basic social institution of the border areas, which defines what is "our own" and what is "other people's". This virtual institution also symbolises the meeting place with the semi-forbidden past of the border areas, still seen in Soviet terms (Peshkov 2010b). Thus, the collapse of the Soviet border regime and the lack of a political basis for discrimination changed the status of the stigmatised communities only to a limited extent. On their symbolic return to Russia they still face the Soviet border with the rituals of confrontation and the Soviet version of the region's past.

---

5   After the year 1956 most Russians in Inner Mongolia were regular peasants of no Cossack origin.

In contemporary Russia, there are two main discursive practices aimed at changing the status of the stigmatised communities. The common feature of these practices is the effort to partly rehabilitate these people without deconstructing the black legend. The first attempt is the depoliticisation of the stigmatised communities through cultural exoticisation. This community is recognised as the keeper of pre-revolutionary Transbaikal traditions and an instrument for justifying contacts with the "formerly forbidden history" of the region (Kurto 2009). The depoliticisation discourse has a special connection with the black legend, namely its emphasis on the Cossack legacy in the area and assumption about the unchanged cultural attributes of this community (Zenkova 2007). The second discourse concerns the frontier loyalty to the USSR on the part of the emigrants from the TRD. Historical fiction, memoirs and stories told by respondents from China reveal the tragic fate of Russian immigrants loyal to the Soviet state (Aprelkov 2009, Perminov 2008). In the context of the post-Soviet model of border perception this discourse has an enormous symbolic value and power. Frontier loyalty to Russia (the USSR) is the only way a stigmatised community can "cross the Soviet border".

Instead of an open dialogue about the past we have seen attempts to conceptualise the frontier zone as an area of difficult choice, in which the choice of the homeland (the USSR) is tragic, but the only one possible. Despite a certain moral ambiguity (the 1945 repressions against the inhabitants of the region were strongly based on intelligence data) this perspective ideally suited the modern perception of Russian history which, despite widespread sympathy with White Guards, assumes that after the Civil War the truth was on the Soviet side (Peshkov 2010b). In the situation of the Soviet-induced amnesia of regional history only the discourse of frontier loyalty will be able to start the process of integrating stigmatised communities into Russian society. From this perspective the black legend transformed from a propaganda phantom into a crucial part of the local mentality and an element of the Soviet border legacy in Transbaikalia.

10. People of the Border: The Destiny of the Shenehen Buryats

Marina Baldano

The border between Russia and China is far more than simply a geopolitical boundary, a barrier, or a line of interaction and contact between two powerful nations. Its formation and the dynamics of its status represent complex sets of human relationships, networks, control mechanisms and economic, social and cultural practices. The border is not merely a dividing line between two states – it epitomises the interrelations between individuals, groups of people and states while encapsulating what people think about the border, and how they conceptualise it. Essentially, the border is at the crossroad of institutions, contacts, conflicts and interests.

Mongolian cultural and historical space was at one time united but later divided by the Sino-Russian border. As a result of the division, particular groups of people have emerged, whose lives continue to be defined by this barrier. The ethnocultural group of the Shenehen Buryats, for example, formed as a result of cross-border migration. The border became a decisive factor in this community's emergence, existence and everyday life for most of the twentieth and early twenty-first centuries. The group emerged through the migration of several thousand Buryats into China, who were fleeing the horrors of the civil war and the Soviet government's rule in Russia. The group was consolidated when the Iron Curtain closed the border behind them. They maintained a powerful sense of nostalgia and attraction for their native land, where the majority of Buryats still lived.

   DOI: 10.11647/OBP.0026.10

The border became a site of conflict, as Soviet troops invaded in 1929 and in the 1930s and 1940s. The group also found itself the hostage of the Sino-Soviet conflict of 1960. When the border opened and became a site of contact, this further changed the make-up of the group and the economic strategies of its members. The border created this community, demarcated its main parameters and defined the direction of its destiny. The Shenehen Buryats may be called "people of the border", or a "border community", and their case sheds light on the shifting role played by borders in other areas of the globe.

To some extent, the story of the Shenehen Buryats began in the 1680s when, on the vast expanses of Central Asia, two empires met, thereby creating an international border line of enormous scale, of a total length of more than ten thousand kilometres. Its formation was a natural process of boundary demarcation between two large states, defined through claims and cessions of territorial expanses on which lived less numerous groups who, for reasons of expedience or through coercion, came to be included within these world powers. However, long before that, a Mongolian historical and cultural commonality existed. Despite its heterogeneity, it was unified through a similarity in language, common culture and memory of a great past. While the boundary disrupted this commonality, this was not evident for the nomads who had their own conception of the phenomenon of the border.

Here, pastoral nomadism was not simply an economic model, but also a way of life. Under the pressure of economic expediency, borders were mobile and shifted dynamically in the nomads' conceptualisations. Up to the 1920s, Buryats roamed with their cattle, frequently crossing Mongolian and Chinese borders when moving their encampments according to the seasons.

The 1910s saw the beginning of a process of national self-determination among the Mongols, leading to a change of status for certain territories that were included in the Qing Empire. This resulted in a change in the boundary line between China and Russia. The border was formed on adjacent territories (see Tsymburski 2000) inhabited by peoples "smaller in size and culturally lagging behind Russia and China" (2000: 56). This boundary, reflecting the strengthening of Russia and the weakening of China, has dramatically shifted to the south and west over the last 250 years, reducing the area under Chinese control. From the end of the 1920s, the boundary essentially stabilised. It did not change as a result of

Japanese aggression against China or of World War II. According to Yuri Galenovich, "in the 1920s our country was the only one to help China in its unification into one state. During World War II, our two countries were on the same side. In the 1950s the relations between the USSR and the PRC were officially relations between allies" (2001: 32).

The main movement of Buryats into China occurred between 1918–1922 and 1929–1931. Gasan Guseinov writes: "As internal axis and centre delineating the world and its periphery, the border is marked... in that region of personal experience that is most exposed to political changes" (2005: 11). Indeed, the causes that led the Buryats to seek refuge in neighbouring China were closely related to the policies pursued by the Soviet government against affluent segments of Buryat society and to the repression that ensued. Even before the Revolution, the elimination of "Steppe Dumas" ["local Dumas"] and the reorganisation of land ownership, as well as the colonisation of Eastern Siberia by peasants from the western regions of the empire, worsened the economic conditions of the Buryat and Evenki. Eastern Buryats were compelled to rent land from the Cossacks. The situation was worsened by further tax collection and the mobilisation of workers to the hinterland in the region of Arkhangelsk during World War I. Revolution, intervention, civil war and the cataclysms of the socialist transformation increased migration flows in border areas. Thus various groups left Siberia through the Chinese border: members and supporters of the defeated groups, people who strove to live in peace and security, who disagreed with the Soviet authorities, who were considered political enemies or who had become the object of revolutionary experiments. An especially powerful factor of outmigration was collectivisation.

Migrations of families with household goods and cattle were extremely arduous and many could not even make it to the border. Lhama-Tsyren of Baruun Somon, who spent seventy-five years in Shenehen, recalls:

> In the winter of 1931, dozens of Buryat families established encampments in the Borzinsky steppe. Once, during a frosty night, a horseman came and announced that Russian soldiers had come from the north and that they were moving towards the Chinese border. To avoid them, it was necessary to cross the boundary line urgently. Hundreds of Buryats had already been arrested. Panic took over the camp. The cattle had to be urgently gathered and driven south. People were divided into two groups: one group rounded up the cattle and drove it south, the second group, composed mainly of women and children, collected belongings onto carts and followed the herds. On the second day, the first convoy crossed the Chinese border,

but the second group never made it. During the year, many Buryats came from the Russian side but our wives and children were not among them. It's only in the 1950s that we learnt how the convoy had been intercepted, everyone arrested, put on freight trains and deported first to Irkutsk, then to Kazakhstan, where, near Semipalatinsk, a camp had been established for women who had betrayed the motherland. Many died within the first few days. It is only in 1959, when the Chinese border was reopened, that we had the opportunity to meet with those who had survived ("Pamyati zhertv repressii": 1)

The group that had escaped from Russia was mostly made up of Agin Buryats (predominantly representatives of eight Khorin clans), but also included some Barguzin and Selenge Buryats, as well as some Evenki and Russians. Relocating with kin to a new site in another state, with cattle as the basis for economic activity, did lead, in spite of enormous difficulties, to the automatic reestablishment of sociality, to the transplantation into a new setting of traditional social structures, systems of power and other relationships, ways of life, property and economic structures. The territories that were allotted to Buryats were "unclaimed" lands unoccupied for about a century. To eliminate the consequences of anthrax, the refugees had to burn the pasture lands repeatedly. However, the proximity of the natural and geographical environment, and the similarity in economic and cultural terms, allowed them to carry out their usual activities.

By 1922, the initial phase of the territorial, administrative and legal registration by the Buryats was completed. The organisation of their local self-government was consistent with the administrative structure of Hulun Buir introduced as early as the Qing period. The ethnic space of Hulun Buir was a multicultural mosaic characterised by a rather complex ethnic and demographic makeup. According to Darima Boronoeva, "it is a place where ethnic and national differences are pronounced, a specificity which is apparently due, to a large extent, to an administrative and territorial organisation along ethnic lines" (2010: 280). The official language of the region was Manchu. Since Buryats were not conversant in that language, the authorities made an exception and gave them permission to use the Mongolian script in administrative documents. This was very important for the economic success of the group.

In Hulun Buir, Bargads, Dagurs, Evenkis, Khamnigans, Horchin Mongols, Russians and Chinese live in compact groups. Interrelationships between these groups are influenced by the duration and depth of contact, as well as by cultural differences. Buryats and Bargads have long been linked through their common historical roots. In addition, the land on which the Buryats came to live was the territory of the Old and New Bargas. The linguistic and ethnocultural affinity between the Buryats and the Bargas continues to have an impact on the formation of a positive setting for ethnic and cultural interaction. The very process of Buryat relocation was seen by the Bargas as an attempt to reunite a single ethnic organism that had been artificially dissected. For this reason, in the first years following Buryat relocation, the Bargas offered them their full support.

The estimated number of Shenehen Buryats in this ethnic group ranges from 6,000 to 9,000 people. This data is so divergent because Buryats are not classified as a separate ethnic group and their numbers are not recorded separately by the authorities: officially they are subsumed under the Mongols of Inner Mongolia. According to the Shenehen chronicler Tsoktyn Zhamso, the number of Buryat people living in China today is about 6,500, and this figure has not changed for decades, although nearly 500 people have returned to Russia in recent years (Fieldwork notes, 7 August 2007).

The consolidation process of the Shenehen Buryats is reflected in their increasing ethnic awareness, the tendency to fuse into a cohesive ethnic group, the pursuit of relative isolation leading to a predominance of endogamous marriages within the ethnic community, and the preservation of their language as well as traditional and material culture. The very existence of the local ethnonym "Shenehen Buryats" bears testimony to the group members' awareness of their special unity, the difference from their original ethnic group and the existence of an autonomous ethnolocal identity. The fact that the immigrant Buryats and the territorialised Shenehen Buryats lived in isolation from the main corpus of Buryats – and were surrounded by other ethnic groups – led to an us/them dichotomy, and an integration of the two groups. While a distinction between regional and local groups remained a characteristic of the mother ethnos, a feature that holds true to this day, for the Buryat ethnic groups of Inner Mongolia, sub-ethnic affiliation has become secondary, given that contradistinction is made, primarily, with non-Buryats.

The Shenehen Buryats are a structured community characterised by a strong internal organisation, a system of power, controls and sanctions with minimal openness to the host society. They remain self-sufficient in terms of economic specialisation, and culturally different from China on account of their Buryat language, their system of clanic ties, customs, holidays and traditions. Adherence to traditional forms of social and cultural ways of life has made the ethnic component the principal vehicle of self-expression. The community is sufficiently large to maintain its social structures – from endogamous marriages to language, education and government. It has relied on the memory of the "historical homeland" – as well as on the notion of being a detached "fragment" of the Buryat people – as evidenced by their carefully preserved myths and folklore.

It is precisely because of these ties to their homeland that no declassification nor marginalisation was witnessed. They also did not merge into culturally-related groups in the host society. This is where the fundamental difference lies with respect to the classic image of the refugee. In the overall context of modernisation processes, all of this led to the formation of new types of sociality and new mechanisms of intergroup relations. We came to the conclusion that the Shenehen Buryats formed a new type of cross-border migration (Baldano and Dyatlov 2008: 171).

However, despite the closed nature of the group, the Shenehen Buryats and the Bargas showed joint activism by participating in the creation and in the activities of the People's Party of Inner Mongolia. The Mongolian People's Revolution of 1921 resonated greatly with the group. At the head of the Barga intelligentsia were Merse and Fumintai, who along with the Buryat Tsyden-Eshe Tsydypov, organised a revolutionary circle. In Barga, all-Barga congresses were held annually. During one of them it was decided to organise a people's cooperative in Hulun Buir. Shenehen *khoshuu*[1] had many old Buryat cooperative members from Tsugol *khoshun*: Ayusha Tugulturov, Shirnin Badmaev, Vanchik Munkuev, on the basis of which the cooperative was formed. In summer 1922 the first cooperative congress was hosted in Shenehen. The number of shareholders grew rapidly. The Chinese Eastern Railways (CER) and Barga princes, including the *amban*, were especially wealthy investors. The members of the cooperative were active in revolutionary agitation activities. During this period, contacts were made with the leaders of Mongolia, namely with Elbegdorj Rinchino. In summer 1923, the Barga Mongols Tsyden-Eshe Tsydypov and Fumintai were sent to Urga in order to establish friendly ties. The Central Committee of the Mongolian People's Revolutionary Party asked them to form a branch of the party in Barga. Consequently the Barga People's Party was born. The party included Shenehen Buryat members and maintained relations with Urga, the Soviet ambassador in Beijing, the Consulate of the USSR in Hailar and the leadership of the CER. The

---

1   A "banner", an administrative unit in Inner Mongolia.

People's Revolutionary Party of Inner Mongolia, headed by Merse, also led an armed uprising even "as China was beginning to recover from internal crises and assert itself not only within its former borders, but also through a consolidation of centripetal forces" ("Escho pro Shenehen": 2).

Shenehen authors have noted that during the Socialist period the Shenehen Buryats survived the formation of collective farms, "the struggle with the old foundations", as a result of which "100% of the population became working people, and the best workers and activists became members of the party" (Tsyrenzhabai Abida 2005: 23). However, "on account of the 'left' deviations, the Cultural Revolution and the destruction wreaked by capitalists and Soviet, Mongolian and Japanese spies, many people suffered. Many continued to work, but some become unable to do so" (Tsyrenzhabai Abida 2005: 25).

Because of developments in the CER at the end of summer 1929, Soviet-Chinese relations became strained. Concentrated at the border from August to November, Chinese troops made repeated attacks, bombing Soviet territory and pursuing an aggressive repressive policy against immigrants from Russia living near the border, accusing them of spying and committing other counter-revolutionary activities. In addition, those immigrants who had fled dispossession, political purges and hardship – despite having crossed the Soviet-Chinese border – remained under Moscow's control, and so waves of punishment followed. Shenehen Buryats were in a no-win position – to the Chinese they were "Soviet spies" and to the Soviet Union they were "Chinese spies". The Chinese authorities not only allowed the police to beat and torture prisoners, but also held executions without trial or investigation. According to eyewitnesses, the representatives of the NKVD felt completely free on Chinese territory: they arrested and sent people to prisons and labour camps – first to Hailar and then to Chita, and still others to Leningrad. During the interrogations, torture and blackmail (threats of reprisals on close relatives) were widely used, and confessions of "anti-Soviet espionage and terrorist operations" were extracted through coercion.

From the early 1930s onwards, Manchuria became the object of Japanese aggression. The Japanese government, seeking to "legalise" its occupation of Manchuria, inspired the creation of the new state of Manchukuo. The period of occupation lasted from 1932 to 1945. During this time, substantial changes were made in the political and administrative structure of the region. During the Japanese period, the Buryat *khoshun*, until then an independent unit with the right to determine and regulate the main issues of domestic life, was abolished and became part of Solon *khoshun*. One of the residents of Shenehen, Dambyn Dambi, said:

> The Japanese were meticulous in giving their orders. Young people were supposed to serve in the Japanese army, and children had to be taught the Japanese language. We learnt it, though during the Manchu period we spoke exclusively in Buryat. Keeping a million-strong Kwantung Army ready for military action in Manchuria caused constant tension on the Soviet-Manchurian border (Fieldwork notes, 14 August 2008).

The policy of integration of all non-Han peoples of Northeast and Western China under the banner of the construction of "Greater East Asia", conducted by the Japanese during World War II, included the Shenehen Buryats. One of them, Urzhin Garmayev, later Colonel-General of the Kwantung Army, served in the government of Manchukuo. On account of his authority and capacity of organisation, he was entrusted with the formation and training of military units of Buryats and representatives of other Mongolian groups, even before the war officers were trained and a cavalry of over two thousand people was formed.

The main thrust of Tokyo's strategy focused on the ideological neutralisation of Inner Mongolia's local population in the event of an outbreak of hostilities between Japan and the USSR. Under the guise of helping the small nations of China, Japan started to recruit and train agents from the various ethnic communities. Not surprisingly, in August 1945, as the Soviet army advanced in China, Buryats were accused of "aiding the enemy". In 1945, several hundred Shenehen Buryats, mostly young men, were taken to the USSR where their traces are lost in prisons and camps (Bazarov 2001: 18).

From the beginning of World War II, the Shenehen Buryats, fearing a Soviet invasion, attempted to move away from the border. Up until 1947, the Buryat migration that occurred within Inner Mongolia, together with emigration, played a significant role in the dynamics of the localisation of the Buryat ethnic population in Shenehen. The life of Buryats in China was wholly determined by the border as people who attempted to move away from it ended up being returned.

The occupation of Manchuria by Soviet troops ended on 28 April 1946. Following liberation from Japanese occupation, the Hulun Buir Autonomous Region was created. After joining up the Inner Mongolia Autonomous Region in January 1948, it became the Hulun Buir *aimag*, and the Shenehen *somon* was established on the same date.[2] The modern

---

2   *Aimag* and *somon* are administrative units in Mongolia and Buryatia.

administrative and territorial structure of governance finds its origins in 1958 when, as a result of the reorganisation of the Shenehen Somon, the three *somons* of Baruun Shenehen, Shenehen Zuun and Mungen Shuluun were created and included within the Evenki *hoshun* of Hulun Buir *aimag*. However, following the liberation from Japanese occupation in China, a new war, this time a civil war, between the communists and the Kuomintang, broke out. Buryats had experienced the brunt of mass terror in 1929 during the events in connection with the CER and, in the 1930s and 1940s, they found themselves the object of counterespionage activities by the USSR and Japan.

The border had become more than simply a watershed between sovereign states. It also acted as a boundary between different societies; the idea of clear and immutable "borders under lock" was increasingly reinforced. In the years of Stalinism and the Iron Curtain, when having a relative abroad threatened one's freedom and even life, numerous kinship ties were lost and severed. In the 1960s, the Sino-Soviet border was considered by China as "unfair". In 1962–63, the Chinese government began to implement an elaborate system of constant and serious violations of the Soviet border. In 1963 there were more than 4,000 violations involving more than 100,000 Chinese civilians and soldiers (Borisov and Koloskov 1972: 229). This was an undeniable factor of stress for the Shenehen Buryats who lived in close proximity to the border. The prospect of such a confrontation between the two countries was simply incomprehensible to them.

At the height of the Cultural Revolution (1966–69), the Shenehen Buryats, living as they did in close vicinity to the Soviet border, found themselves at the epicentre of anti-Soviet political campaigns. Provocations on the border became more frequent: "crowds of provocateurs dressed as soldiers and wielding clubs, axes, crowbars and rocks, not uncommonly attacked Soviet border posts. Violating the border, they refused to obey the orders by Soviet border guards to leave the territory of the USSR" ("Prozrachnye granitsy" 2002: 189). Many were arrested on charges of spying for the Soviet Union and Panmongolism. Both executive and rank and file Shenehen Buryats were subject to political repression. According to informants, "both in the USSR and at home, we were considered traitors and Japanese spies, and during the Cultural Revolution we were seen as Soviet spies and Panmongolists" (Fieldwork notes, 8 August 2007). The history of each Buryat family is an example of their desperate struggle for survival in an atmosphere of sweeping accusations, arrests and punishments.

From the 1980s, a new approach was taken in border negotiations. In 1995, the "Shanghai Five" was established, uniting Russia, China, Kazakhstan, Kyrgyzstan and Tajikistan. As early as the time of Deng Xiaoping, the people who had been victims of repression were rehabilitated, reinstated to their posts and had their property restored. In the period of "socialist modernisation", the Shenehen Buryats finally had the opportunity to return to their familiar way of life. Today they are a fairly prosperous group, with their main economy remaining tied to animal husbandry. In order to run individual farms, large tracts of land were taken on a 30-year lease, and it is possible for them to employ hired labour. Three Buryat schools are in operation and the *datsan* [Buddhist monastery in the Mongolian cultural region] that were destroyed during the Cultural Revolution have been restored.

The border with Russia opened up, along with the opportunity to rebuild ties with the historic homeland: the early 1990s saw a process of repatriation of Shenehen Buryats, and about 300 people returned to Russia. Today their numbers have risen to almost 500, more than 350 of them in Buryatia, and a little less than 150 people in the Aga District. Motives for moving to Russia varied: they were nostalgic (it was still seen as the "birthplace of the ancestors"), economic (seeking new opportunities) and educational (they were offered preferential programs). According to informants in Shenehen, young people were also sent to broaden the range of marriage partners (as the small closed community needed "new blood").

Today we are witnessing the rapid transformation of the border from a wall or barrier into a site of encounters, contacts and interactions. With the development of border trade, some Shenehen Buryats started to engage in service activities, working with the Buryats and Russians who came to Manchuria and Hailar in order to purchase cheap Chinese goods. Contacts with the Buryats of Siberia allowed many Shenehen Buryats to find their relatives who lived on the other side of the border. It was now possible to go and work in the Transbaikal region and in Buryatia. The Shenehen Buryats who had previously settled in the Transbaikal region could facilitate the organisation of such work. Many of them regularly visit relatives in Shenehen, which promotes the development of cross-border linkages.

Cross-border trade in the province reached its peak in the early 1990s, during the period of re-emigration of the Shenehen Buryats. However, from 1993 onwards, trade began to decline on account of a tightening of rules regulating barter and "shuttle trade" imposed by Russia, an increase in tariffs on food imports and the introduction of a mutual exchange visa regime.

At the same time, the reputation of Chinese products has been undermined by the large-scale penetration of substandard products on the Russian market. This has had an adverse affect on the Shenehen Buryats: some of those who had worked with the cross-border trade moved on to new activities, while others found themselves unemployed.

The links, contacts and cooperation established in the vicinity of the border have led to the formation of a complex set of interrelations between people, groups and states. In their own way, both Russia and China have used the border to develop the regions adjacent to it. As a result of an increase in cross-border trade in China, there was a rapid growth in commercial activity, along with a fast development in the infrastructure of border cities, and the construction of roads, hotels, shops and restaurants. In 1991, Russia carried out a key liberalisation of the foreign economic sphere, and, in the subsequent period, federal investments in border regions have been associated mainly with the establishment of checkpoints and transport links appropriate to the border. No special measures for boosting investment activities in border areas have been taken.

The 1991 Sino-Soviet Border Agreement was a treaty between the People's Republic of China and the Soviet Union that set up demarcation work to resolve most of the border disputes between the two states. Initially signed by China and the Soviet Union, the terms of the agreement were resumed by Russia after the breakup of the Soviet Union. The border was finally settled by Sino-Russian agreements in 2004. At the same time, the problems linked to contemporary border contact remain acute. Several years of uncontrolled cross-border trade have led to deeply-entrenched criminality. The Russian-Chinese border zone is characterised by problems such as large-scale smuggling and the importation of cheap Chinese products through the so-called "grey" customs clearance system. Therefore, in recent years, customs inspection of luggage was tightened considerably. Informants in Shenehen have observed that the border has always varied from year to year – sometimes constituting a wall behind which they managed to escape, sometimes an insurmountable obstacle, and at other times a source of danger, from which the Bolsheviks might come and subject them to reprisals. Today, when going over the border, although acting like good citizens Shenehen Buryats are made to feel like perpetrators and are subjected to strict checks.

The border allows the formation of a set of economic and everyday practices. The main activities of Shenehen Buryats in Russia revolve around their role as intermediaries, the use of border resources and living experience in the two worlds (the Chinese language, connections in China, life and relationships in Buryatia, the Buryat language), traditional animal husbandry and traditional cuisine.

In the very beginning of the 1990s, when Shenehen Buryats began returning to the land of their ancestors, a trend of renewal of "cultural Panmongolism" was witnessed in Buryatia and Mongolia. This is a complex phenomenon with a long history. In its classic form, it emerged at the turn of twentieth century and its ideas were revived in the context of discussions within academic circles. The idea of unification of the Mongolian historical and cultural community played various functional roles, both as an immediate goal and an instrument of national consolidation. It is this organic "embeddedness" of irredentist ideas in the context of the objectively important task of nation-building, and in the processes of modernisation, which laid the foundations for its revival in the early post-Soviet years. Part of the discussion was devoted to the issue of cross-border integration of the Mongolian community with the full understanding that practical union was impossible. At times, this integration was perceived as a state association, an important part of which was the idea of "bringing compatriots together". Diaspora groups – in this case the Shenehen Buryats – became, as vehicles of "ideal" and authentic national identity, a preferred object of alignment of ideological and political constructs.

The Congress of Buryat People proposed to create a Buryat refugee return fund, determine levels of compensation and facilitate allocation, and set up a special migration service to facilitate their return (Nimaev 2001: 126). The motivation for this was clearly and minutely grounded in the articles and policy statements of one of the founders and leaders of the Buryat-Mongolian National Party and the Movement for National Unity ("Negedel"), Vladimir Khamutaev. He wrote:

> Fragments of all nations are going home. After two thousand years, Jews are returning to their historic homeland, after 200 years the Germans of Russia are returning to Germany. The Kazakhs of China and Mongolia are going to a homeland in which they've never lived. The Nazarbayev government has adopted a program to return the Kazakhs into the nation's gene pool, through which measures have been allowed for to encourage return to the historical homeland, allocate land to returnees, providing them with compact settlements with their way of life... Weak nations that are not able to regroup around their particular ethnic and national values and interests, dissolve into others..." (2000: 177).

Return to the homeland was not considered a humanitarian issue, but rather a political one. It was part of the issue of "bringing the nation back together", the path towards its consolidation, towards the preservation and development of its "gene pool". Repatriation acted here as a tool of nation building. It was therefore crucial that Shenehen Buryats:

> "...had a traditional economy, that they study, sing, dance, get married. They kept all that was native Buryat: consciousness, language, games, traditions, clothing, ceremonies, the old Mongolian script, the 'Taban Khushun' – the traditional animal husbandry, etc. It was crucial to allocate land to the individual construction and compact – in one locality – resettlement of Shenehen returnees in order to preserve the established worldviews, order, tradition, way of life, economic forms, the traditional 'Taban Khushun', horticulture. The preservation of the established traditional way of life of a unique ethnic and cultural group is in the interest of the entire ethnic group" (Khamutaev 2000: 20).

Viewing the Shenehen Buryats as holders and custodians of ethnic traditions is also typical of China, where they enjoy a positive reputation for being original and traditional. This reputation is also maintained through the media, in particular the Chinese Central Television (CCTV) and Inner Mongolia TV (NMTV). One report about the Mongols of Hulun Buir was "full of admiration for the well-preserved traditional way of life, the beauty of the Buryat national dress, and described poetically the Buryats as the most 'authentic steppe plains Mongols'" (Namsaraeva 2007: 252). If immigrants and their children adapt to their new surroundings, it provokes outrage:

> Buryats come to the Republic from China, and their children, who know only their native tongue, are forced to acquire a foreign culture, language, morality, a loud way of expressing emotions, because they are scattered in different schools. With every day that goes by they lose all that is native to them, their ethnicity, their national essence developed over thousands of years, their manners and behaviour, turning more and more into noisy loudmouth Soviet *mankurts* [a term denoting an individual who has become acculturated, who has lost his or her roots] (Khamutaev 2000: 99).

All of this did not mean that the theme of Shenehen Buryats had been monopolised by the discourse of nation-building. This theme perhaps also began playing such a role in the politico-ideological practices that relied on a completely sincere and selfless public interest. A lot of individuals were simply interested in learning how "our people" lived and still live in a foreign country. The media were willing to address and capture the very nature of this interest. One merely needs to look at the headlines given in the newspapers *Inform Polis* (4 July 2004; 7 September 2005) and *Nomer Odin* (2 June 2004 and others): "Russian Buryat in China.

Shenehen – a small preserve of the Buryat spirit and culture", "Chinese Buryats return home", etc.

This may be somewhat reminiscent of a huge, if not exalted, interest in Russian post-revolutionary emigration in general. In one way or another, the authorities themselves could not remain uninvolved in this problem. Demonstrating an interest in this issue the local authorities showed readiness to enter into a dialogue with the public and give attention to its ethnic needs, without irritating the federal centre and its own opponents of Buryat nationalism. In addition, it represented a good opportunity to arrange working contacts with the authorities of border provinces in China, and to increase the status of an active foreign policy. It also deflected the issue away from the danger of ethno-politics onto the humanitarian and cultural sphere. And this was carried out in the "State National Policy Concept of the Republic of Buryatia" (Resolution of the Government of the Republic of Buryatia No. 336 September, 29, 1997), where the activity outside of Buryatia was considered as:

- help and support to people from Buryatia residing in other regions of Russia, the CIS and far abroad;
- conclusion of intergovernmental agreements with Mongolia and the Inner Mongolia Autonomous Region of China regarding cultural and economic cooperation;
- support of public national and cultural associations of the Buryat diaspora and natives of the Republic of Buryatia in the various regions of Russia, far and near abroad, in their efforts to satisfy national-cultural needs, to preserve and develop their native tongue and national traditions, and strengthen their relations with Buryatia (State National Policy Concept of the Republic of Buryatia 1997: 3).

In the 2007 version of the State National Policy Concept, the issue of co-ethnics already sounds more restrained:

"In the international and regional sphere:

- public support for ethnic and cultural Buryat associations in various regions of Russia and abroad in their efforts to satisfy national-cultural needs, to preserve and develop their native tongue, strengthen their relations with Buryatia;
- development of relations with co-ethnics living abroad" (State National Policy Concept of the Republic of Buryatia 2007: 2).

The first returnees received assistance in terms of accommodation, job placement and temporary shelter from the All-Buryat Association for Cultural Development, the Buryat State University and the Buryat State Academy of Agriculture and Agricultural College, and were allocated quotas for the education of their children. But the republic's authorities were unable to do what was most important of all – to provide them with real assistance in obtaining Russian citizenship. Buryatia did not participate in the programme for the return of compatriots. Alexander Elaev, the then First Deputy Chairman of the Committee for International Relations of the Administration of President of Buryatia, emphasised:

> Our compatriots who relocate here are competitors to our people. In other words, we also have a conflict of interest here. And we must consider, as a priority, the interests of Russian citizens. In addition to federal funds, funds from the republic are also necessary for the resettlement of those displaced. This means housing provision, job provision. And this can constitute a problem as people find themselves in limbo ("Chto meshaet vozvrascheniyu Shenekhenskikh Buryat na istoricheskuyu rodinu?": 1).

Intense initial efforts in this direction changed the implementation of routine bureaucratic procedures. The treaties and agreements concluded in recent years between the governments of Inner Mongolia and Buryatia do not have an impact on the issue of Shenehen Buryats returnees. Overall, immigrants have been left to fend for themselves. They have been faced with a range of problems of adaptation that are typical for migrants. The issue of naturalisation has been and remains problematic, while the question of acculturation has been unexpectedly prominent. As it turned out, Buryat culture in Buryatia and Buryat culture in Shenehen differed radically, with almost a century of separate existence and development having left its mark. In practical terms, this was an interaction between two different Buryat cultures. A common ethnicity was not a guarantor of automatic and seamless integration. Behind a façade of a common ethnicity and common self-identification were hidden social and cultural worlds that diverged drastically.

The "era of national and cultural revival" of the 1990s has come to an end, and the numerous new problems and concerns faced by politicians and bureaucrats have, it seems, diminished the interest of the public toward the Shenekhen Buryats. However, on 6 May 2010, Minister for the Economy of the Republic of Buryatia, Tatiana Dumnova, told the newspaper *Delovoi Mir Baikala* that the issue of resettlement in Buryatia of a further 500 former compatriots from Inner Mongolia, China, had been worked out at the federal level. Tsydenzhap Batuev, a deputy in the People's Hural, supported an initiative by the Ministry for the Economy:

> Before suggesting people should leave, you need to create optimum conditions and conduct outreach programmes for the residents of Tunka and Dzhida. Buryatia has had a similar experience, when settlers from abroad moved into the Mukhorshibir area and were faced with a lack of meadows and pastures. We can not cheat people twice, and punish them twice (*Delovoi Mir Baikala*, 6 May 2010).

Later in 2010, Deputy Prime Minister Alexander Chepik also lamented the issue of Shenehen Buryats:

> Unemployment is high, and they do not let us attract them. Yet they're herdsmen, they will have no effect on unemployment. On the contrary, they will create additional jobs in those vast areas of Siberia and Buryatia that have not been claimed (*Inform Polis*, 2 September 2010).

The history of the Shenehen Buryats demonstrates how the existence of a border can mould a group and define its basic parameters and key features. Changes brought to the status of the border led to changes in the group's position within the host society and transformed their relationship with their homeland. The Shenehen Buryats were and remain a people of the border whose life and everyday practices heavily depend on the situation on this strip of land. They do not merely live near the border, they find themselves on the cusp between two different worlds.

11. The Persistence of the Nation-State at the Chinese-Kazakh Border

Ross Anthony

Within the social sciences today there is a wide-spread understanding that boundaries are not simply lines dividing territorial and cultural entities. Studies that view ethnic boundaries and nation state boundaries as constructed (Barth 1969; Turner 1967; Anderson 1991; Gellner 1983; Gupta and Ferguson 1992) now contend with the assertion that states are a set of overlapping institutional practices (Sharma and Gupta 2006; Mitchell 2002). With the advent of globalisation and the discourses which sustain it, flows of capital, labour and media are viewed as re-organising the territorial dividing lines of nation-states as we know them (Appadurai 2000; Giddens 1999). Additionally, there are a variety of cultural ways (often contested) of conceptualising the notion of the border (see Bulag and Billé in this volume). Within Xinjiang, there is a considerable literature on overlapping ethnic boundaries (Bellér Hann et al. 2007) and trans-national boundary movement (Roberts 2004).

In this chapter, I will argue that while the notion of the border is indeed a multiplicity of discourses, practices and imaginaries, it simultaneously persists as a singular, unambiguous entity. Such persistence, I suggest, is due, in part, to the materials and practices that make up borders (fences, guard towers, walls, maps, check points, military patrols), but also the way that such technologies promote viewing space in a singular way. Using the accounts of several people who live in close proximity to the Chinese border with

 DOI: 10.11647/OBP.0026.11

Kazakhstan in the Xinjiang Uyghur Autonomous Region, I argue that the persistence of the border in absolute terms stems from the relative success of the nationalist project of spatial organisation.

Historical and theoretical considerations

The border I will be discussing covers an area of north-west Xinjiang, stretching from the Ili River Valley in the south to the Altai Mountains in the north, where the border joins up with Russia (the Altai Republic). The region has long functioned as a zone of contestation. In the seventeenth and eighteenth centuries, Zhunghar Mongols ruled the region and dominated the Tarim Basin to the south. Following the fall of the Zhunghars, new Qing borders incorporated the region into China. Laura Newby notes that it was during this period that the "notion of border treaties and mapping of lines to demarcate precise territorial limits" (2005: 12) came into being. That being said, borders were often not enforced; the actual border constitutes the establishment of *karun* – guard posts positioned on routes and passes that were frequently used by travellers entering or leaving Qing territory (ibid.: 12). Still, the establishment of this frontier would have a long lasting impact on how space and identity were to be practiced and imagined. Kazakhs inhabited a somewhat liminal space: dwelling on both sides of the border, they paid allegiance to both the Qing and Tsarist Russia. Although the Kazakhs were classified as tributaries of the Qing, many were beyond their direct control. Following Qing conquest, Uyghurs were moved into the Ili River Basin area in order to form agricultural colonies. In 1871 the Ili River Valley was annexed by Russia when the Qing were driven out by a Muslim uprising led by Koqandi adventurer Yakub Beg.

By the mid twentieth century, the entire region was in revolt due to the warlordism and Han Chinese favouritism under the KMT regime (Forbes 1986). The entire border region, from the Tian Shan to Altai, rose up in revolt to form the East Turkestan Republic which lasted from 1944 to 1949 (Lias 1956; Benson 1990). When Xinjiang fell to the communists, the region re-integrated into China proper. In 1962, following the Sino-Soviet split, between 60 and 100 thousand Kazakhs and Uyghurs, escaping famine and the political purges of the Great Leap Forward, migrated across the border to the Soviet Union. The border was shut shortly after this (Millward 2007: 264). The depopulated areas were re-populated with demobilised People's Liberation Army troops from Inner China. The primary task of these soldiers, known as the *bingtuan* or the Production-Construction

Military Corps (*Shengchan jianshe bingtuan*), was to reclaim desert land, farm it and fortify the border regions (McMillen 1979). By 1955 there were 110,000 personnel assembled (Toops 2004: 246); by the 1990s the figure rose to over one million. A number of events, including the fall of the Soviet Union, Kazakhstan's independence and China's economic turn, have led to the border functioning today as an area of international trade. The *bingtuan*, who own several large border-trading companies, are also heavily invested in border trade. With the rise of the market economy, this border region has also recently developed national parks, the most famous of which is the Kanas Lake Nature Reserve.

As this brief history shows, the construction of the international boundary is multiple. The border has moved place several times and has re-aligned ethnic identities. However, with the rise of the Chinese nation state in the twentieth century we see the increasing emergence, despite the "internationalism" of Socialism, of a more precisely-defined Chinese nation-state space (Dirlik 2008; Duara 1996). Benedict Anderson suggests that the pre-nation state era, in which borders were "porous and indistinct, and sovereignties faded imperceptibly into one another" (1991: 21) have been transformed into entities in which "state sovereignty is fully, flatly and evenly operative over each square centimetre of a legally demarcated territory" (ibid.: 19). This has necessitated a fundamental shift in the articulation of how space is divided. David Sneath *et al.* have used the term "technologies of the imagination" to refer to materials and processes that elicit various ways through which people imagine their relationship to the world. While the authors insist that any such technology is never totalised (2009: 26), it is equally true that large-scale projects, such as that of the nation state, distribute homogenising technologies in an attempt to create collectively stable imaginaries. Billig's notion of "banal nationalism" – the circulation of flags, money, turns of phrase and so on – function as important mediators through which the space of the nation is imagined (1995). One constraint such technologies exploit is a simple limit to which humans are subject: that one cannot simultaneously inhabit various places at the same time; that one is forced to imagine spaces vaster than one's perceptual horizon.

The map of the Chinese nation-state is crucial in this regard. As in most other nation states, maps of China are disseminated through books, television, stamps, propaganda posters and various other media. Although many people in China remain map illiterate, the map of China functions as much as a powerful symbol as it does an actually-existing representation of the nation-state, taken from a vantage point several kilometres above the sky. This top-down gaze – what James C. Scott refers to as the "God's-eye view" – is impossible to comprehend while standing on the earth's surface; it is best perceived via the proxy of the map, the miniature or the aeroplane (1998: 57). For Scott, this is part and parcel of a larger modernist project which strives to produce communities that are unmbiguous and clearly legible. While this paper touches on the multiple affordances of the border in daily practice, we also see that the nationalist discourse of a single, unified, unambiguous border is equally persistent. By way of a conclusion, I argue for the continued importance of the study of the nation-state project and its continuing role in shaping the way in which people think about space.

Ethnography

In the summer of 2007 and the summer of 2008, I travelled to various places along the border of northwest Xinjiang. I travelled to the Ili River Valley, Jimunai and the Altai on both occasions. I visited several border towns and travelled up to mountainous areas near the border. Three episodes from these travels were particularly instructive.

Episode 1

During a trip into the Altai Mountains, in one of the last permanent settlements (some 35km from the Russian border and 55 km from the Kazakh border), I encountered a Han Chinese man who was born in the Altai Mountains and had lived here for most of his life. The man was married to a Mongolian woman and his brother to a Tuvan. He spoke fluent Kazakh and some Mongolian. When I met him, he and his family were living with a Kazakh household. The man would act as a tout for tourists, mostly Han Chinese from Eastern China who would be invited to stay the night in the house. But the man's real job was as a hunter. There was money to be had in the trade of fox, wolf, bear and the gathering of the high-altitude caterpillar fungus.[1] Bear paws were particularly in demand and, I was told, reached their optimal length near the end of the year, when the hunters would set out for lengthy expeditions.

---

1   The man informed me that caterpillar fungus (*dongchong xiacao*) could reach 17–18,000 RMB ($2,700–2,800) per kilo; a bear costs 30,000 RMB ($4,750).

In recent years, several forested river valleys in the Altai have become nature reserves and hunting such animals is now illegal. Nevertheless, hunted animal goods are still traded in the area. Businessmen from the booming Chinese medicine industry in south China purchase goods from hunters by paying bribes to the park officials. Hunting, the man told me, was a difficult, risky affair. Because he and his hunting companions carried out their expeditions in December, the snowy terrain was treacherous and the weather bitterly cold; on one occasion, a member of his hunting team froze to death.

Another risky enterprise was the crossing of the Kazakh and Mongolian borders while tracking bears. During our encounter, the hunter pointed to the mountain slopes at the head of the valley: "that is where the border is" he said, tracing his finger along a snowy ridge. Although some of the valleys had military patrols, the area was remote, lacked roads and was inaccessible in the winter. Thus, it was possible to cross the border undetected. However, it was equally possible to cross and be caught. The man revealed that he had once been captured by Kazakh officials and was forced to hand over his hunting catch in return for release. On another occasion, he was handed over to the Chinese authorities, who made him chop wood for 15 days on the Chinese side of the border as punishment. The hunter informed me that this year would be his last year of hunting. He felt he was becoming too old for such high-risk activity.

Episode 2

Another stop on my trip was the highly under-utilised border town of Jimunai. Although Jimunai aspired to be a thriving border town, the bulk of international trade was conducted in the border town of Khorgos, several hundred miles to the south in the Ili River Basin.

When I visited Jimunai in 2008, the trading area at the border was in the process of being relocated to the town itself, some 20km away. On my way to the trading area at the border, I met a Kazakh man of Chinese nationality in his early twenties who was doing contract work for the government. Every morning he would travel twenty minutes to the border where he was helping to build a new road that led to the border itself. The man told me that he had already tried to make a life for himself in the coastal provinces of China. But before he even managed to leave Xinjiang, he got bogged down in the capital city, Urumqi, where he drank all his money away. He then worked in Turpan for several months to make enough money to travel to eastern China. He finally made his way to the Chinese north-east (*Dongbei*) where he sold kebabs on the side of the road.

This situation not being ideal, he had now returned to Jimunai, where he was working on his next project: to move to Kazakhstan to join relatives who had moved there in the 1990s. The young man informed me that they are now far more prosperous than his family in China. With government assistance, they had started up a chicken farm and now had enough money to buy tractors. He had never been to Kazakhstan but it had now become his dream to go. He explained to me that it was his hope to raise enough money building the border road so that he could enrol in a Russian language programme in Urumqi. From there he would continue on to Kazakhstan where he would join his extended family. He now faced the dilemma of how to return to Urumqi and avoid squandering his money again.

Episode 3

During this same trip to Jimunai, I attempted to visit some glacial valleys in the nearby Muzart Tagh mountain range. A portion of the range straddles the Chinese/Kazakh border. In the town itself, I began to enquire about how to access the glaciers. A local taxi driver said he could take us there the next morning. However the next morning, he arrived with bad news: it was not possible for me to visit the glaciers because the area was out of bounds to foreigners. Usually, a military friend of his who patrolled the border would allow us through the check-point. However, because the Olympic Games were only weeks away, security had become much tighter. If his army friend's superiors found out, the friend could get into trouble because the border administration was subject to inspections from higher authorities.

Later in the day, we spoke to another taxi driver who was a former Bingtuan employee. After hearing of our attempts to get to the glacier, he insisted he could take us there; he had many former colleagues working at the border. However, after a brief phone call, he returned with a similar response: "Olympics!" (*aulinhui*).

Discussion

All three of the above episodes provide evidence that the border is practiced as both multiple and singular. Because this chapter is concerned with the persistence of the singular, I will touch briefly on issues of multiplicity , before providing a more in-depth analysis of the border as a singular, abstract entity.

Regarding the first episode, we can see that the hunter is himself the product of a border region insofar as he is culturally aligned with several different ethnic groups (Mongol, Tuvan, Kazakh). By mainstream Han Chinese standards, this kind of heavily overlapping identity is increasingly rare.[2] Additionally, between his own actions, corruption on behalf of park officials and the resources of big business, the borderland activities are part of a much vaster set of practices which stretch all the way to the metropolises of Hong Kong and Shanghai. There is a phenomenological dimension present: namely that when the hunter is illegally crossing the border, he is not so much crossing an abstract line as he is immersed within a landscape in which the risks of animals, weather, border patrols and the like are all serious elements with which the hunter has to engage.

Of course, this experiential element of the border is something in which the parties of all three ethnographic episodes are engaged: their own unique interactions with the border. Regarding the young Kazakh man, this entails his daily travel to the border and his literal construction of it through his work as a builder. The man's family networks, which extend beyond the border itself and well into Kazakhstan, were another reason to negate the singularity of the border as dividing line. For the taxi-drivers, a dimension of their everyday experience of the border was ferrying travellers to and from Jimunai; as we have seen, it also occasionally involved taking tourists into the glaciated valleys along which the border ran. We can deduce from my trip to Jimunai that entry into the more sensitive of the border regions was itself a question of temporality and flexibility. The efficacy of the taxi drivers' connections with the border authorities was one which was inextricably bound to the nation's calendar of events. The tightening of the border during the Olympics indicates that the literal zone which constitutes the border, at the level of enactment, was an entity that literally expanded and contracted according to context.

However, this being said, in all three instances we also see the persistence of the border in its more traditional incarnation as a singular entity. The hunter stands out as a case in point. It appears as if it was important for him, particularly when crossing illegally, to imagine the border precisely as a singular threshold. Deep in the Altai, there were no border fences and

---

2   During my fieldwork in Xinjiang, interaction between Han and minorities, particularly amongst post-1990 Han migrants, was minimal (Anthony 2012). For a discussion on the complexities of boundary making between Han and non-Han in Gansu and Yunnan, see Hansen (2005).

military patrols were widely interspersed. Therefore, as he explained to me, he had to make estimations as to where the precise location of the border was. Whereas tracking a bear involved imagining its movements coupled with interpreting traces of its presence (pawed trees; fresh dung), engaging with the border entailed imagining not only the potential presence of border patrols and their locations, but also the very real, but also very abstract, line that helped determine his legality at any given moment.

Another instance in which the hunter actualised the line of the border was when he traced his finger along the mountain ridge so as to show me where the border lay. Such a gesture literally re-inscribes the abstraction of the nation-border upon the ridge of the mountain that is, in effect, the border's actually existing double. Imagining and projecting this partially imaginary line as the man recalled his forays into the border region presents an interesting inversion of Tim Ingold's categories of space as abstract and space as lived and practised. Of primary importance to Ingold is how one experiences and recalls the environment as one engages in it – not how it appears in abstract form, such as on a map. Ingold believes that peoples' accounts of moving through space (what he refers to as "mapping") take into account the importance of time as one moves through the environment. Modern maps (referred to as "mapmaking") bracket out this sense of time. He states:

> It is at the point where maps cease to be generated as by-products of story-telling, and are created instead as end-products of projects of spatial representation, that I draw the line between mapping and mapmaking. In effect, mapmaking suppresses, or 'brackets out', both the movements of people as they come and go between places (wayfinding), and the re-enactment of those movements in inscriptive gesture (mapping) (2000: 234).

But what we see in the instance of the hunter is a process of story-telling that draws on and reproduces these very "end-products of projects of spatial representation" as primary content. This suggests that even when an individual engages with the border in the dynamic way that the hunter does, it nevertheless persists as a single dividing line, akin to those drawn on maps themselves.

A similar emergence of the border as a line is also evident in the story of the young Kazakh man. In his case, it was as if the border itself had become a line of desire beyond which lay future prosperity. Whereas before, this future prosperity seemed to lie a great distance away in inner China, it now lay beyond the fence that he lived so close to. While I occasionally met nationalistic Kazakhs who believed that northern Xinjiang should be incorporated into Kazakhstan, their nationalist aspirations were far more diluted than, say, the Uyghur population living predominantly in southern Xinjiang. I never saw, for instance, a map that claimed northern Xinjiang as part of Kazakhstan. Thus, even though the young man had reified Kazakhstan as an almost utopian dream – Chinese Kazakhs are allowed to obtain Kazakh passports – it was the line dividing these two nation-states that was the primary barrier he needed to overcome.

The border possessed a prohibiting function – he could not simply cross it. At the same time, however, the prohibition played a role in the motivation to transgress the border itself. This seemed to be the feeling of several Kazakhs I knew: the notion that Kazakhstan offered good economic prospects for them, particularly in the realm of cross-border trade where Kazakh family connections and a shared language could ease the passage of goods. If there was any irony in the young man's situation, it was the fact that his desire to transgress the dividing line was sustained through his daily work: helping the state fortify and strengthen the very barrier he wished to cross. The man's idea of the nation states of Kazakhstan and China being divided by a line most probably stems in part from the fact that this was a very simple but important element of what the border itself comprised. Thus, the series of straight fences running along the semi-desert steppe function as a technology of the imagination themselves: they invite one, with the supplementary help of maps, flags and so forth, to imagine the continuation of these very fences for thousands of kilometres beyond the immediate place in which one encounters them.

In the third ethnographic description, in which I was unable to visit the Muzart Tagh glaciers, we see the border produced abstractly in a somewhat different sense: people performing an imaginary of the exemplary border during a period of state ritual. Catherine Bell has written that ritual is essentially a "strategic mode of practice" (in Hevia 1994: 193) – that is to say, a repository of performative actions that can be drawn upon during, for instance, significant political events. The 2008 Olympic Games, with its emphasis on presenting China to the outside world as modern, unified, disciplined and welcoming, was a political ritual *par excellence*. This entailed a heavy promotion of what Borge Bakken terms "the exemplary society", (2000) in which models of ideal citizens proliferate; people are encouraged to embody and repeat these exemplars. The exemplary form, promoted in propaganda posers, books, television and so on, promotes modernity, civility, education, middle-income prosperity and a harmonious environment. In regions such as Tibet and Xinjiang, it also heavily promotes another exemplary form: multi-cultural harmony.

To sustain multi-cultural harmony was tricky even at the best of times in Xinjiang, let alone during the run-up to the Olympics. This was mainly due to government fears of Uyghur ethno-separatist attacks, which would use the international attention brought by the Olympics to publicise their causes. In fact, such anxieties were somewhat founded in truth: on 4 August 2008, the first of four attacks occurred on a military base outside Kashgar, in which 11 soldiers were killed. The next evening, in the neighbourhood of Er Dao Qiao, Urumqi, where I lived (some 1,500 km away from where the attack happened), there was a complete lock-down. By sunset, all shops were closed and armed military personnel permeated the neighbourhood. In fact, in the months before the Olympics, the usually chaotic Uyghur trading areas in the Er Dao Qiao neighbourhood were already being "harmonised". Illegal markets were closed and in their place appeared a long desk with a row of chairs upon which a number of government officials sat for months on end. Over the entire city, bags were checked as one entered and exited commercial buildings, busses, markets, mosques and temples; nearer the time of the actual Games, road blocks surrounded the entire city.

This kind of behaviour was reiterated throughout the country and was particularly noticeable at the border. In the year prior to the Olympic Games, when I had travelled up to this region for the first time, the border was more relaxed. There were few roadblocks and the contours indicating where you could and could not travel were not nearly as unambiguous. On the second trip security was far more heightened. For instance, there were far more roadblocks, some carried out by soldiers, some carried out by the police. At every check-point, each person on the bus had to pull out their identity cards for the officials to inspect.

At the Jimunai border, we read on a marble statue of an open book, of the call to "defend the frontier" (*shubian*) and of "protecting", or even "pacifying the frontier" (*zheng guomen*). This call to alertness was embodied during the Olympics through the breaking down of the usual informal relationships (*guanxi*) that structure Chinese social life (in this case, the connections between the border guards and the taxi drivers). This was bound to the promotion of a hyper-vigilance, which was itself tied to the idea of being seen to be performing one's official duties. Those in charge of monitoring were, most likely, themselves subject to inspections from other institutional entities. Thus, the construction of the border during the Olympics period was sustained through a mixture of coercive and ritual means.

In the analysis of these three examples, we see how the idea of borders as singular persists and that such persistence is due in large part to material forms and their subsequent embodiment by the populace. This is not to say, however, that such material structures are themselves not subject to multiple types of interpretation. We saw, for instance, how the border meant very different things for the three informants discussed in this paper (danger, hope and employment security). Nevertheless, we simultaneously see how a common theme – namely a line that divides space – structures the narratives of the three accounts. Caroline Humphrey has argued that the materials that constituted infrastructure within the Soviet Union, such as Socialist living spaces were, on the one hand, ideology embedded in material form. On the other hand, the ways in which people understood and interpreted such forms were bound up with personal ambitions, often refracting "outwards to the very horizon of the ideologized imagination" (43: 2005). Here we see how the play of multiplicity is underscored by a common feature: the ubiquitous and highly repetitive space of the Soviet dormitory that grounded and offered a sense of commonality to the various personalised memories of such spaces. Similarly, technologies of border control, many of which are external to human subjectivity, serve to anchor people's imaginations of the vaster spaces within which they are immersed.

Conclusion

This chapter has discussed how the border as singular and abstract persists in the way that people engage with international boundaries. This is due in part to the proliferation of nationalist symbolism, which persuades people to imagine large-scale spaces. But it is also due to the material nature of borders. Fences and walls that constitute borders effectively attempt to trace abstractions themselves. Thus they function almost as if they were actual abstractions existing in reality. We also saw how people imagine and embody the border as part of a larger imaginary of the idealised nation state. This involves not only imagining idealisations of territorial integrity, but also their enactment and embodiment.

The three cases highlight ways of imagining and practicing the border which are wide-spread within China and beyond. While we might think that people living close to borders would interpret them in fluid and flexible ways – and in many senses, they do – we see here how equally they think of them in quite an unambiguous fashion. While each encounter with the border is structured by its own unique conditions, each encounter is also informed by pre-existing models of what the border ought to look like. There is an overlap between the way space is thought about within nationalist discourses and the way it is thought about by individual border-dwelling people.

12. Neighbours and their Ruins: Remembering Foreign Presences in Mongolia

Grégory Delaplace

This chapter addresses Mongolian people's relationship with their two gigantic neighbours: the Federation of Russia and the People's Republic of China, on the basis of two ethnographic situations. The first one, which will be the point of departure and form the core of this discussion, concerns the discourses and practices surrounding the abandoned Russian mining town of Mardai. The second one deals with a rumour regarding Chinese ghosts, reported to haunt the places where they used to live in Mongolia. I will argue that these two sets of data reveal two very different ways in which Mongols might relate to their neighbours – two opposite technologies of cross-border relationship (see Introduction).

In October 1989, following the policy of "transparency" (*il tod*) initiated by Jambyn Batmönh after the Russian Glasnost', the Mongolian government revealed the existence of a secret town, located in the middle of the far-eastern province of Dornod, next to the borders with Russia and China (Sanders 1989: 64). The town was called Mardai: it had been established in 1981 in the vicinity of an uranium mine exploited by the Russians, as part of a secret agreement with the Mongolian government. Until its gradual opening after the end of the communist regime, the town had been closed to the Mongolian population, and was exclusively inhabited by Soviet nationals

 DOI: 10.11647/OBP.0026.12

coming from all over the USSR.[1] According to memories of people who knew the city at that time, "Russian" (*Oros*) workers worked in the mines and tended the shops, "Russian" teachers taught their children in a school and a kindergarten, and "Russian" policemen patrolled the town. It is estimated that about 50,000 people lived in this secret enclave of the Soviet Union, working in Mongolia, and yet living in a strictly "Russian" environment, completely cut off from the local population (ibid.).

The uranium extracted in Mardai was shipped directly to a processing plant in Krasnokamensk, some 500 km away on the other side of the border (Nuclear Energy Agency 1998: 246), using a railway line that did not feature on any map. Mardai was therefore, as stressed by Uradyn Bulag, who visited the city in the beginning of the 1990s, a "symbol of Russian colonial exploitation of Mongolia" (1998: 23). It was the concrete proof that Mongolia, although an independent state, was not completely sovereign within its own borders; that parts of its territory could be closed off to its own population and exploited by Russians, for Russia's exclusive profit.

However, the revelation of the existence of this secret town, equipped with state-of-the-art Russian infrastructure, and supplied with Russian goods, seems to have elicited less resentment than excitement among the local population. This in spite of the fact that the city and shops remained closed to most, with the occasional exception of Party officials. Many Mongols, however, came to settle around the city, to live off small

---

Research for this work has been conducted in 2008 and 2009 thanks to generous support from the Isaac Newton Trust and the Mongolia and Inner Asia Studies Unit. This chapter could never have been written without Caroline Humphrey's advice and supervision: not only did she suggest I should visit Mardai in the first place, but she also convinced me to revise this paper and submit it as a chapter for our volume; the argument proposed here, moreover, benefited a lot from our discussions before and after fieldwork. The material presented here also owes a lot to Batchimeg Sambalkhundev, who provided crucial help during fieldwork, and who searched the Internet for additional information in the later stage of its preparation. Finally, I wish to thank Ippei Shimamura, Franck Billé, and the two anonymous reviewers of this chapter, for their insightful comments and helpful suggestions.

1   A former inhabitant of Mardai who created a web page dedicated to his childhood memories of this place (http://maxpey.narod.ru/mongol.html), remembers that: "People came here from all over the Soviet Union, from Belarus, Ukraine, Moscow, St. Petersburg, Georgia, Kazakhstan, Uzbekistan and so on. In general, the settlement was quite cosmopolitan." (Translated from Russian by S. Batchimeg). It should be added that there were, according to the memories of current local inhabitants, many Buryat Mongols originating from the Buryat Autonomous Soviet Socialist Republic.

trade with the Russian population or to try and acquire re-sellable pieces of the high quality infrastructure. Mongol people who visited Mardai at that time recall its shops selling clothes of the latest Moscow fashion and other items that were not even available in Ulaanbaatar; its orchard providing fruits in the middle of the desert; its swimming pool; and its fully equipped sports hall – all of which were on display and yet forbidden to them.

In 1995, the Russian government finally decided to close down the mine, and three years later the decision was made to repatriate all the workers (Nuclear Energy Agency 1998: 246). Still vivid in people's minds today is the image of a city emptied of its entire population almost overnight and of Mongol settlers suddenly left alone around deserted buildings. The 1990s were a moment of economic hardship in Mongolia, and Chinese traders at the border, were buying iron at a good price. So very soon after the city was vacated, a process began of methodically removing all metallic structures within the city: lamp posts and all kinds of railings were removed, but also the frameworks of buildings were stripped bare. Before long the city was turned into mere standing ruins.

I had the opportunity to visit the city during the summer of 2009, and to see for myself the ruins of what is still remembered as a beautiful town. More importantly, I met a man who had known it as it used to be, and who had been there through the whole process of bringing it down. Later, I met several other people who had visited the town at some point, or who expressed their feelings about its present state. Here, I propose to draw on these memories of Mardai to retrace the uncommon history of this town and in particular its destruction by the Mongol population. I wish to argue that the stripping of the iron, and the levelling of the city, should not be seen as an aggressive gesture directed at the symbol of a former colonial power. On the contrary, the destruction of the city seems paradoxically to go hand in hand with enduring feelings of respect towards Russian presence and enterprise in Mongolia – even when projects were undertaken behind the back of the local population, within the framework of an asymmetrical, truly colonial, form of economic cooperation.

On the other hand, these respectful feelings stand in sharp contrast to the negative judgments about Chinese people with whom iron is traded, as illustrated by the rumours about Chinese ghosts currently in circulation in Mongolia. People have been reporting apparitions of souls of colonial merchants, which are supposed to have remained attached to the wealth they accumulated during their stay in Mongolia. Contrasting memories of Mardai and stories of Chinese ghosts, I wish to show in this chapter that memory is used as a site to manage cross-border relationships in Mongolia.

This argument could be seen simply as another illustration of the political implications of collective memory – a topic on which references are just too numerous to be even listed here – and in a way the ambition of this chapter is no larger than that. To be more specific, however, the argument made here could claim to pursue the same kind of intellectual project as that outlined by Janet Carsten in her introduction to the collective volume *Ghosts of Memory*, by giving a further illustration of "the subtle and complex interconnections among everyday forms of relatedness in the present, memories of the past, and the wider political contexts in which they occur" (2007: 1).

Drawing on three bodies of literature – on memory and history, on the "politics of memory" in relation to ethnic or nationalistic claims, and on kinship as relatedness – Carsten sets about to study "how, cumulatively and over time, small everyday processes of relatedness – such as narrating stories of past kinship, tracing family histories, constituting small ceremonies of commemorations [...] – have a large-scale political import" (ibid.: 4). The book is mostly concerned with how the haunting memories of disrupted relations and "critical events" might define patterns of relatedness in the present – a point perfectly illustrated in a Mongolian context by Rebecca Empson (2007), who shows with her contribution in the same volume how memories of exiled, deceased, or simply distanced relatives among the Buryat Mongols are embodied in material objects within the domestic space, a relationship with them being thus sustained in spite of their absence.

The argument presented here also envisages the connection between memory, patterns of relations, and their political context. It does so with this slight difference, however, that it takes relationship with foreigners, rather than kinship, as its main object of study. Adopting a technological approach to border studies (see introduction), this chapter explores the "subtle and complex interconnections" between collective memories, relations with foreign neighbours (the closest strangers, the furthest neighbours), as well as the historical and political context in which they are imagined to take place. In this perspective, memories of Russian presence and Chinese ghosts springing up from the past could be seen as elements of a border technology that, although not located right in the border zone, is attached to particular places on Mongolian territory, and defines contrasted styles of relationships with immediate neighbours. I will argue that a crucial role is played here by the *materiality* of foreign presence in Mongolia: while "Russians" (*Oros*) are praised for leaving visible, even conspicuous traces of their presence, "Chinese people" (*Hyatad*, derogatory *Hujaa*) are despised for burying everything underground.

A brief history of Mardai

Uranium exploration started after World War II in Mongolia, when several uranium deposits were found between 1945 and 1960. From 1970 to 1990, a bilateral agreement was signed, allowing the Ministry of Geology of the USSR to lead a geological reconnaissance expedition in Mongolia to inventory its mineral resources. Seventy percent of Mongolian territory was surveyed, and four metallogenetic provinces were identified, one of which was the Mongol Priargun in the eastern part of the country (Nuclear Energy Agency 1998: 240). In 1977, an uranium ore deposit was found near the Mardai river. A secret agreement was subsequently signed, allowing the Soviet government to proceed with its exploitation on Mongolian territory (Mays 1998).

In 1981, a mine was established in Mardai, together with all supporting infrastructure: it was called "Erdes" and was created as a "sub-combine" (*subkombinat*) of Priargunsky Mining and Chemical Works, itself a division of the Soviet Ministry of Atomic Energy. The main combine (*kombinat*), of which Erdes was a sub-section, was located in Krasnokamensk (ibid.). The uranium extracted in Mardai was shipped directly to Krasnokamensk, where it was processed. To this end, a railway line was built that linked the two mining towns across the border. None of these, however, neither the railway nor the town, appeared on maps at that time and until quite recently.

Uranium production began in 1988, ironically less than a year before the existence of Mardai was made public. However, the extraction continued until 1995, providing around 100,000 tons of ore a year, amounting to approximately 100 tons of uranium after refining (Nuclear Energy Agency 1998: 240).

By that date, the settlement had gradually developed into a fully-fledged Russian town (Fig. 1), populated with workers coming from all over the

Soviet Union, including from the nearby Buryat Autonomous Republic. Interestingly, the secrecy of Mardai and its very restrictive access policy created a strict division within the "Buryat" ethnic category: Buryats from the Buryat Autonomous Soviet Socialist Republic, who usually spoke only Russian, were entitled to live in the town from the outset, fully benefiting from its goods, while Buryats living in Dornod province around Mardai, who often spoke both Mongolian and Russian, were excluded.

Fig. 1 Mardai city centre, probably 1980s. Photograph posted by
Wowabruch on Panoramio, ID: 29464337

The town was obviously far better equipped than any Mongolian city of the time. Like any other Soviet town the streets were lined with trees and a social club was located right in the city centre (Fig. 2). Former residents hailing from the Soviet Union also remember the impressive array of goods sold in shops, some of which were not even available back in their hometown (http://www.maxpey.narod.ru/mongol.html). There was also a kindergarten, a school complete with all facilities, a football and even a hockey ground (Fig. 3), where championships were organised in summer and in winter respectively (ibid.). It is reported that at some point a cantilevered wheel was even erected, on which the city and its surroundings could be observed from above (Shimamura, personal communication).

Fig. 2 Mardai's "club" (*klub*), probably 1980s. Photograph
posted by Wowabruch on Panoramio, ID: 29463808

Fig. 3 Mardai's hockey ground, probably 1980s. Photograph
posted by Wowabruch on Panoramio, ID: 29464363

From the beginning of the 1990s onwards, the Mongol population – often
Buryat families who used to live in nearby towns such as Dashbalbar in the
north – began to settle around the city. According to former residents, by
1995, when the uranium production stopped, about 200 households lived

in a separate district. After three years of uncertainty concerning the future of the mine and various attempts to restart production, Russian workers were given leave in 1998, and returned home.

Once emptied of its inhabitants, the city became available for a completely different purpose: as the iron was removed by Mongols settlers and sold at the border to Chinese wholesale dealers, it became a stockpile of saleable parts. Ironically, the mining town itself suddenly transformed into a mine. Everything was removed: all metallic items of course, but also the iron components in buildings, leaving them standing without structure, as well as the metallic framework of the roads (Figs. 4 and 5). Pipes were extracted from the ground for the lead they contained and wires were pulled out for their copper.

Fig. 4 General view of Mardai from the central
square (photo: S. Batchimeg 2009)

Fig. 5 Ruined buildings and roads (photo: S. Batchimeg, 2009)

After the Russian population left, only a few households specialised in iron removal remained in Mardai, occupying more central places in the town, while the rest of the households moved out. Today, a dozen households still live there, often on a seasonal basis, and continue collecting iron to sell it across the Chinese border (Figs. 6 and 7). According to the people interviewed on site, they trade the iron they collect to brokers who then resell it to Chinese buyers, making quite significant profits in the process. Rumour has it that some very wealthy people made their fortune this way at the end of the 1990s. The Mongolian state itself took on some scraping of its own, notably availing itself of railway tracks around Mardai to be reused for its own network.

Fig. 6 Household living next to the central square, living of iron trade
(photo: S. Batchimeg, 2009)

Fig. 7 Iron loaded on a truck (photo: S. Batchimeg, 2009)

Recently Mardai has again made the news when plans for re-exploitation by a new company were made public (Urantogos 2010). The firm, Central Asian Uranium Company, is jointly owned by the former Russian owner (Priargunsky Mining and Chemical Works), the Mongolian government (through a small company called Erdene Mongol LLC), and a Canadian company called WM Mining International Ltd – which later sold its rights to World Wide Minerals Ltd, also known as Khan (Mays 1998; Wu 1999: 154). Newspapers have voiced concerns regarding the status of these mining licenses obtained through opaque agreements between the Mongolian and Soviet governments. Some journalists have called on their leaders not to make the same mistakes and let foreign agents exploit Mongolian resources unilaterally. Locals generally assume that, should uranium be exploited again, Mardai will be rebuilt. And the irony that Russians themselves might take part in this rebuilding was not lost on the people I was able to talk to – I will return to this point.

Memories of Mardai – a forbidden island of modernity

Mongolian people who have known Mardai before its destruction remember it with great excitement, almost enthusiasm. This excitement, in part, comes from the fact that the city had been inaccessible for so long, and that it was brought down to ruins as soon as it became open to the public. This has allowed Mardai to remain some kind of a legend, mostly known by hearsay and clad with the prestige of lost Soviet grandeur; people's memories, intertwined with fantasies, single out Mardai as an archetype of Socialist modernity.

"How do people go about remembering something they have never seen?" asked Morten Pedersen (2010: 245) upon considering narratives of Buddhist temples in Mongolia's northern Darhad region. Following Lars Højer (2009), Pedersen emphasised "the peculiar *enhancement* of occult agency that sometimes grows out of having incurred a religious loss" (2010: 246). He described how the leveling of almost every monastery in the Darhad region spurred people's imagination about the extent and power of Darhad Buddhism. Focusing on the fate of one single artefact, a golden Tara statue extracted from a monastery before it was destroyed during the purges of the 1930s, Pedersen described the legends that flourished in relation to it. The statue, "a condensation of Darhad Buddhism" is now the material anchor point of a "virtual temple" that people carry in their mind (ibid.: 254).

As we will see, the ruins of Mardai could be said to achieve the same kind of effect: a condensation of Socialist ideology and Soviet way of life, they form the material basis of a virtual temple to modernity. What follows confirms what emerges from Pedersen's material, and what has been proposed by anthropologists working on mnemonic techniques (e.g. Severi 2007): it is not so much absence that stimulates recollection as *the salience*[2] *of the last remaining item*. The last remnant spurs imagination and memory, irresistibly filling the void and conjuring up an invisible framework within which the isolated vestige starts making sense again.

When I went to visit Mardai on a day trip in summer 2009, I was lucky enough to meet Tögsöö. Now in his thirties, he was a teenager when the town partially opened in the beginning of the 1990s. He often visited his brother, who had settled there with his family, and worked with him during the summer in small jobs related to the Russian population of the town (selling milk to them, for example). After 1998, when the Russians left, he took an active part in the iron trade.

Fig. 8 Chatting with Tögsöö on the central square (S. Batchimeg, 2009)

---

2   Carlo Severi (2007) highlighted two recurrent features of mnemonic techniques cross-culturally: a principle of salience (a selection of significant components is singled out, the other being left out or pushed to the background), and a principle of order (the selected components are sorted). It remains to be shown whether, and how, this second principle of order could apply to the way Mardai is remembered among the local population.

Fig. 9 High-rises where workers used to be accommodated
(photo: S. Batchimeg, 2009)

Tögsöö remembers Mardai with great emotion, notwithstanding the fact that he himself took part in the destruction of its buildings. After a brief conversation on what used to be the central square (Fig. 8) and serves now as an iron trading market, he took us on a tour around the city. His memories brought the city back to life. Showing us the high-rises where workers were accommodated (Fig. 9), he recalled the daily shuttle bus service that took them to work.[3] Behind these high-rises, Tögsöö pointed out the kindergarten, which was several floors high (Fig. 10); parts of the flowered wallpaper were still visible on the walls in the ruined buildings (Fig. 11). A little further, blue tiles still covering a half-destroyed wall testified to the presence of a swimming pool only a few years earlier – something hard to believe in the middle of the arid Mongolian steppe (Fig. 12). By pointing out details that revealed what was before, Tögsöö transfigured the ruins, helping us picture the lives of people who had lived there, and appreciate how impressive these infrastructures must have appeared in the middle of the plain. At some distance from the town, Tögsöö pointed out a space that looked empty, explaining that it had been the location of a large airfield capable of accommodating planes that would not be able to land in the

---

3   According to a former inhabitant, no private car was allowed in the town, and most people would go around on bicycles when not using public transport (http://maxpey. narod.ru/mongol.html).

capital city Ulaanbaatar's airport today. Now it was nothing but dust, barely distinguishable from the rest of the steppe. What was striking in Tögsöö's memories was their precision, and the obvious fact that he *cultivated* them. These ruins were associated with very vivid recollections of the past, which he let out for us eagerly, almost proudly, for several hours. Throughout our visit to the town, he celebrated it as an island of modernity, unsurpassed in the richness of its infrastructures, even by present-day Ulaanbaatar.

Fig. 10 Ruins of the kindergarten (photo: S. Batchimeg, 2009)

Fig. 11 Detail of the wallpaper still covering the wall of the kindergarten (photo: S. Batchimeg, 2009)

Fig. 12 Ruins of the swimming pool, parts of the tiled walls are still visible
(photo: S. Batchimeg, 2009)

It is not unusual to find among the Mongolian population today such expressions of nostalgia for the communist period in general and for Russian presence in particular.[4] However, Mardai was not really remembered with nostalgia by people I interviewed. Nostalgia is a feeling for something which has been lost, and Mardai was never really Mongolian: until the end, indeed until its destruction, Mardai was a Russian town, whose wonders were strictly reserved to Russian usage – with the exception, as already mentioned, of Party leaders. Moreover, Mardai was not only associated with modernity, but also with the danger of uranium: rumours still circulate today about livestock born with malformations because of contaminated grass. Also present in people's mind was the more immediate danger of being shot if one ventured too close to the city: as Uradyn Bulag reported (1998: 23), "no bird could fly over Mardai". Therefore, the feeling associated with Mardai today is less nostalgia, as other traces of Russian occupation often inspire, than *fear*, or excitement mingled with fear, that is awe.

As an area restricted to Russian population located far behind the borderline, Mardai could be seen as some kind of a proxy for the border

---

4   Even, crucially, coming from the younger generation who has not known this period from first-hand experience (Legrain 2007): once again, "how do people go about remembering something they have never seen?" (Pedersen 2010: 245).

with the Soviet Union, a testimony to the fact that the border is actually more of a frontier area than a line (see Billé, this volume). However, it should be noted that Mardai was far less accessible to Mongols at the time than the Soviet Union itself: whereas Mongolian students would go to universities in Ulan-Ude, Moscow or Saint-Petersburg, "not even a [Mongolian?] bird" could fly over Mardai, although it was located on Mongolian ground. Mardai was not so much a proxy for the Russian border as a *super-border*, a territory of exception, to which access was not regulated according to the usual rules. This, perhaps, contributed in making Mardai even more awe-inspiring than the Soviet Union itself: Mardai is remembered as Socialism itself in a condensed form,[5] *closer* to Mongolia than the Soviet Union ever was, and yet *more closed* to the Mongolian population than the Soviet Union actually was.

Memories of Mardai – "it has become like Chechnya"

Strong feelings of nostalgia, however, are still felt today by the Russian people[6] who used to live there, some of them for over fifteen years, and who had to leave almost overnight. It was reported that Russian inhabitants were very reluctant to leave the city: Tögsöö assumed that they were easy prey to the "Russian Mafia" back in their hometowns. Coming back after fifteen years of comfortable salary abroad, they were not only deemed rich, they were also quite vulnerable.

The Internet, through such media as picture sharing and mapping software (like Google Earth and Panoramio), provides us with testimonies from former inhabitants, who post pictures and comment on each other's recollections. Pictures of the central square, of the social club, and of the school, have been commented on with great emotion by

---

5   This impression is shared by former Russian residents themselves, as conveyed on the web page quoted earlier, which concludes its description of Mardai in the following way: "All in all, it was the village of Socialism as it should actually be, where everyone had what they needed, and everyone was happy." (http://www.maxpey.narod.ru/mongol.html, translated from Russian by S. Batchimeg).

6   "Russian", here, includes Buryats from the Buryat Autonomous Soviet Socialist Republic. As was already mentioned, these were clearly separated from the local Buryat population, as they enjoyed different status in Mardai and often spoke only Russian. When Mongols – whether Buryat or Halh – speak about the Russian population of Mardai, they usually do not distinguish between Buryat and other Soviet nationals.

former residents evoking their years spent as children or workers in the town (Fig. 13):

"– Ramon: My beloved school!

– Ser. Terexov: As for me I have spent the most refined moments under the building of this school. I'd like to exchange photos of this village and its surroundings. My address is [...]

– Elena: The best school ever. How it hurts to see what remains, I wish everything could be there again... So sad...["]7]

Fig. 13 Mardai's School n° 17 – picture posted by Ramon on Panoramio, ID: 14413674

This nostalgia might also turn into deep sorrow when former residents come back to the town and realise what it has become. Tögsöö told me the story of a Buryat foreman who shed tears when he returned to visit only one year after he left, in the autumn of 1999. Tögsöö was there, and he remembers the old man lamenting: "it has become like Chechnya!" as if the city had been destroyed by war. The comparison is interesting, first of all because it illustrates how much Russian settlers, even of Buryat origin, imagined the place as part of Russia, and Mongolia as a potentially dangerous colony.[8]

---

7   Quoted from comments on the picture of Mardai's school linked through Panoramio to its geolocation on Google Earth (http://www.panoramio.com/photo/14413674). Translation from Russian by S. Batchimeg.

8   Although Mongolia was always nominally independent from the USSR, the total subordination of the ruling Communist Party (Mongolian People's Revolutionary Party) to its Soviet counterpart made Mongolia an actual colony. A popular saying in Russia at that time put it in no uncertain terms: "A chicken is not a bird, and Mongolia is not really abroad" ("kuritsa – ne ptitsa, Mongolia – ne zagranitsa" quoted by Sneath 2003: 40).

But it illustrates also that the destruction of Mardai was felt as as a violent act by former Russian and even Buryat residents – something comparable to an act of war.

Interestingly, the image of a "war zone" is also conjured up by a (presumably) Canadian visitor, who describes on a picture sharing website (http://www.pbase.com/buznsarah/mardai) how depressed he or she felt upon seeing the city in such a "distasteful" state: "Unlike a war zone where the destruction takes place through external forces, here it has been internal forces". One can only be surprised with this confident assertion that Mardai was actually "internal" to Mongolia, and this description actually raises several angry comments from (presumably) Mongolian users. Yet, this impression shares with that of the foreman a comparable bewilderment: how could such a large and modern town be demolished so thoroughly? What kind of violence – and directed to whom – does this act of destruction entail?

Certainly, the violent character of bringing down a whole town, unanimously considered a jewel of European modernity, occurred to the local population as well. During my trip, people appeared visibly embarrassed when they recalled such episodes as the one involving the Buryat foreman. I heard a number of discussions regarding the possibility that Russians might come back to restart the mine, and possibly even rebuild the city. The main idea that came out of these discussions was that Russians should be very upset to see their beautiful city brought down to ruins. People assumed they would be reluctant to build it again from scratch.

However, there was notoriously no attempt among the local population to deflect responsibility for this upon other people, and to blame some irresponsible and shameless profit seekers for its destruction. In addition, there was clearly no aggression associated with the dismantling of the city, no suggestion that the destruction of Mardai was an act of revenge wreaked by Mongolian people onto Russians for their exclusion from the city, and no sign whatsoever that scrapping was associated with any kind of violence. We have seen how Tögsöö himself, who took an active part in the ruination of the city, cultivated the memory of its previous state. It seems that the stripping of the iron, Mardai's ruination, was not aimed at erasing the past, at re-conquering Mongolian space. In other words, it would be a mistake to understand Mardai's ruination as an attempt at obliteration.

On the contrary, this whole city left for the local population to make use of was seen as a long-lasting testimony not only to Russian greatness, but crucially also, to Russian *generosity*. This, and the sharply contrasted feelings elicited by Chinese presence in the country, was clearly expressed by our driver, a resident of the regional centre Choibalsan who had already been to Mardai once and seemed happy to have this opportunity to return. Gazing at the ruins, after a long discussion on what each building used to be, he commented to us thoughtfully: "Russians, at least, they left things for us to take… Chinese people would have buried everything underground." Tögsöö could not agree more.

The suspicious neighbour

When prompted to justify their suspicious feelings towards "Chinese people" (collectively and indistinctively referred to as *Hyatad*, or by the derogatory term *Hujaa*), Mongolians consistently summon their history, supposedly replete with "Chinese" attempts at dominating Mongolia and spoiling its resources.

From the mid seventeenth century until the demise of the Qing dynasty in 1911, Mongolia was known as "Outer Mongolia", and formed the northern confines of the Sino-Manchu Empire. Following a period of nominal autonomy after the fall of the Qing, Mongolia declared independence in 1921, thereby putting an end to Chinese political domination. Mongolian revolutionaries were assisted in this task by the newly (self-)appointed rulers of Russia, the Bolsheviks, who saw in Mongolian controlled independence a strategic asset against Chinese alleged ambitions in Manchuria and Siberia (Rupen 1979). Therefore, Mongolia declared itself in 1924 a People's Republic, and was ushered by her new mentor along the path of a "non-capitalist way of development".

Of course, Mongolian people's evaluation of their past as part of the Sino-Manchu empire is undoubtedly influenced by the way it was portrayed by propaganda throughout the communist period. As a feudal system whereby (Mongol) lords levied tax on the population for their own benefit and that of the (Manchu) Emperor to whom they answered, the Qing Empire came to be pictured as the epitome of exploitation; the backward evil to be blamed for Mongolian people's economic stagnation over more than three centuries.

Of concern here in this well-known story is the way Sino-Manchu domination during the Qing period has been linked to, or disconnected from, the question of the relationship between Mongolian and Chinese people *in general*. Official propaganda, especially after the Sino-Soviet split in the beginning of 1960s, has actually gone in two different directions. On the one hand, Chinese people, and by extension the People's Republic of China, were *denied* any responsibility in Qing Empire's political domination over Mongolia (Rupen 1979: 93). According to history, Party officials emphasised, it is the Manchus who conquered and ruled Mongolia, not the Chinese: therefore, China has never had control over Mongolia, and cannot assert any claim over Mongolian territory.

Yet, on the other hand, Chinese people were *blamed* for their economic exploitation of Mongolian people (Bawden 1989: 83): Chinese merchants, backed up by the Imperial administration, were accused of having taken an active part in the pauperisation of Mongolian people through their unfair credit policy. Besides, the individuals who had become renown for looting Chinese shops or even for burning them down, were celebrated as Robin Hood-like figures of social justice (1989: 143). All in all, the massive indebtedness of a great part of Mongolian population to these merchants is widely remembered until today, and vigorously recalled whenever relationships between China and Mongolia are evoked. As a matter of fact, not only is there a very strong sentiment today that Chinese presence in Mongolia has been nothing but exploitative and ruinous, but moreover, Chinese people are seen as essentially greedy, animated by the unique will to selfishly appropriate the resources of Mongolia.

The exact extent to which these ideas are the direct outcome of Soviet inspired propaganda lies beyond the scope of this chapter. Yet, since commercial relations resumed between Mongolia and China in the early 1990s, as Chinese workers came to look for jobs, and as Chinese investors started to express their interest in Mongolian land and resources, the population widely expressed fears regarding Chinese people's appropriative intentions. Neo-nationalist movements such as Dayaar Mongol have given voice to these concerns (Billé 2010: 40, 45), which have also found expression in hip-hop songs – some of which have gone as far as to call for murder (Billé 2010: 37–38; Delaplace 2010: 139). More generally, rumours circulate about continuous attempts by Chinese government or population to exterminate, or at least harm, Mongolian people (Billé 2008).

Chinese ghosts in Mongolia

One of these rumours, which could be heard particularly in Ulaanbaatar, but also in the Eastern region of Dornod where Mongolian, Russian and Chinese borders meet, is particularly telling. People report being haunted by "Chinese ghosts" (*Hyatad süns*): souls of Chinese merchants who allegedly remained attached to the goods – often gold or silk – they have buried under the ground before they died (Delaplace 2010; 2012). These ghosts appear as white-bearded old men, who speak in broken Mongolian and with a distinct Chinese accent. They claim their wealth, and threaten to harm anyone who dares to come too close to it. These stories often insist that although victims ask shamans and lamas to come and perform rituals, none of these are effective: Chinese "envious" (*shunalt*) souls are thought to stick to the place no matter what the new occupants do. Sometimes, the Mongol residents are even forced to satisfy the soul's greed with continuous gifts, until they can bear it no more and decide to move away. In these stories, Chinese people are pictured as some kinds of parasites, who pump up resources and suck out Mongolian people's blood. These stories also tend to equate present-day Chinese businessmen with the colonial merchants of the past – those who are still resented today for ruining the Mongolian population before the Revolution (Fig. 14).

Fig. 14 Chinese merchants in Mongolia, beginning of twentieth century
(©Mongolian National Archives)

These ideas about Chinese people's unbridled greediness and its cosmological implications are further illustrated through an experience related by a Mongolian (Buryat and Halh) shaman I interviewed in 2008 on the topic. She said that she had been contacted two years earlier by the sons and daughters of a Chinese man and a Mongol woman. These "half-breed" (*erliiz*) people, as she called them, had experienced many difficulties since the death of their parents, so they had called the shaman to have a ritual made to remedy the situation. In shamanic rituals, patients are supposed to give offerings to the shaman's auxiliary spirits (*ongod*), and on this occasion, spirits asked for five metres of silk. The family claimed they were poor, and apologised that they could only give a small piece of material. However, when the spirits started to possess the shaman, they became really angry, claiming that the house *did* in fact contain silk. The shaman, under her spirits' influence, started to jump repeatedly in one particular location in the house, and the floor sounded as if there was a cellar below it. The spirits then demanded that the family dug there. They did so, and discovered rolls and rolls of silk, as well as gold and other goods. They swore that they had no idea that there had been silk there. They seemed quite distressed to realise that their Chinese father had kept his wealth secret, even when he had died, and had chosen to bury it in the ground rather than pass it on to his own children.

Given these ideas about Chinese people's low economic morality, it seems quite interesting and indeed rather challenging that Mongols have chosen precisely Chinese people as privileged trading partners for iron and other goods. It is not only at an official level that trading relations have resumed between Mongolia and China:[9] Gaëlle Lacaze's contribution to this volume shows how much cross-border trade owes to individual initiatives from Mongols who start and sustain economic relations with their Chinese neighbours.

Neighbour	Relation	Affect	Status
Russians	(asymmetrical) gift exchange	Respect	'elder brother'
Chinese	(asymmetrical) trade	Contempt	'parasite'

Fig. 15 Model of Mongolian people's contrasted relations with their neighbours

---

9   According to statistics published in a report by the Economic Research Institute for Northeast Asia (ERINA), the People's Republic of China went from receiving 1.7% (amounting to $11.3 million) of Mongolia's total exports in 1990, to absorbing 46.6% of them (amounting to $287 million) in 2003 ; besides, the part of Mongolia's total imports that came from China saw a sharp increase from 2.4% ($22.3 million) in 1990 to 24.5% ($196.3 million) in 2003 (Shagdar 2005: 31). The Bank of Mongolia's 2011 review for Mongolia's Foreign Trade states that 56% (or $6327.5 million) of foreign trade in Mongolia (that is imports plus exports) was made with the People's Republic of China (quoted on http://www.infomongolia.com/ct/ci/3015/). Meanwhile, a 2010 World Bank report contends that the People's Republic of China absorbs no less than 70% of Mongolia's total exports, although it remains unclear whether this figure concerns 2008, before the recession, or 2010 (World Bank 2010: 1).

At this stage, it is possible to sketch a set of oppositions in the way Mongols seem to picture their relationships with their Chinese and Russians neighbours (Fig. 15). Relations with Russians, from Mongolian people's point of view, seem to be regarded as a classic relationship of gift exchange. Russians are thought to have provided Mongolia with modern infrastructure and with resources from the communist world channelled through the Soviet Union; conversely, Mongolians have occasionally provided Russians with raw material, such as minerals. As a result, the plunder of Mardai seems to be understood by the local population as a continuation of this gift-exchange relationship: the buildings appear to Mongols as a *supplementary* gift from Russians. Even though they have initially built Mardai for their exclusive use, Russians are understood to have left the buildings for Mongolian people's profit, thus demonstrating their generosity in the gift exchange process: they have given more than what was planned in the first place by leaving things – indeed the *best* things – behind.[10] The embarrassment felt by people who took part in the stripping process seems to emerge from the idea that they took *more* from the Russians than they had given to them, as if the exchange process had been an asymmetrical one, to the benefit of the Mongols. This, however, fits with and even consolidates the ideology of an "elder brother" relationship elaborated through Soviet propaganda: an elder brother is indeed expected to provide for his younger sibling without insisting on an equivalent return (Sneath 2003: 48).

On the other hand, relations with Chinese are based on trade. It is also deemed an asymmetrical relationship, to Chinese people's benefit this time, as they are considered as parasites on Mongolian resources since the Manchu period. In opposition to the Russians, the Chinese are seen as always taking *more than initially planned* through unfair credit policy, even sucking out resources after their own death while their soul remains anchored in Mongol land.

---

10   There might be an interesting parallel to be made here with the general expectation of Mongolian herding families – which I could observe personally in Uvs province – that travellers staying over will leave some of their belongings behind when they leave. While honorific and often standardised gifts (pieces of silk, candies, biscuits, etc.) are usually expected at the beginning of a visit, it is not infrequent for guests to make more spontaneous and personal gifts at the end of it, particularly in the case of long sojourns. The host himself might occasionally choose what he wants among his guest's belongings, simply by asking for it. The gifts left by foreign travellers to Uvs province herding families, such as torch lights, cameras, or even cooking pans, have been described to me in great details by their recipients, as proof of their generosity.

Conclusion

The two ethnographic situations considered in this chapter thus allow us to draw at least three conclusions:

1. Both situations show that *memory has been used in Mongolia to qualify relations with neighbours across the border* – memories of a Russian town *versus* memories of Chinese merchants;

2. yet, these memories are *embodied in different kinds of vestiges*: material vestiges, in the form of a city falling apart, *versus* immaterial vestiges, in the form of resilient ghosts;

3. and these vestiges *stand for opposite processes of ruination* (Stoler 2008): whereas Russians are credited for erecting buildings *for Mongols to ruin*, sustaining a legitimate relationship of brotherhood, Chinese people are resented for *ruining Mongolian people and territory*, taking advantage of an illegitimate relationship of colonial subjection.

Therefore, while they are not located specifically on the border area with Russia and with China, memories of foreign presences in Mongolia are found to *act as a border* – a device that separates and connects at the same time, that is open to some relations and closed to others, that is programmed to let some things go, and to retain others (see Introduction). In sum, Russian mining towns and Chinese ghosts are part of an apparatus which ties up memories, people and material vestiges into a border technology that qualifies and regulates Mongolian people's relationship with their neighbours.

Appendix 1: Border-Crossing Infrastructure: The Case of the Russian-Mongolian Border

Valentin Batomunkuev

The importance of cross-border cooperation between countries is a topical issue at a time when the increase of cross-border contacts plays an important part in international affairs and economic relations; Russia and its neighbouring countries in East and Southeast Asia are no exception. Yet the development of such cooperation is possible only if the border is seen not as a barrier but as a point of contact between countries. Such an active role, however, is made possible by a degree of border cooperation and is mediated by the border-crossing infrastructure.

In the specific, the border crossings in the Russian-Mongolian region studied in this appendix reveal a gap in the transport chain, a period of time during which the cargo or passengers remain immobile. Such delays bring additional costs which are especially significant at a time of increasing cargo and passenger traffic across the border.

For this reason, the Russian Federation now regards the fitting out and maintenance of border and customs infrastructure as a necessary step in the development of both its economic and diplomatic relations and its cross-border cooperation with Asian countries.

 DOI: 10.11647/OBP.0026.13

Border and customs infrastructure comprise the following:

- Border checkpoints.
- Border zones and the set of border regulations in place within their confines.
- Buildings, constructions, installations, engineering communications, telecommunication lines, power and water supplies, sources of electricity and water supplies, control devices and other technological equipment servicing crossing points.
- Road and railway networks, water transport and air routes.
- Border units, outposts, customs, customs offices, warehouses, terminals, residential houses for staff, etc.

The geographical area under consideration here is the Russian-Mongolian section of the state border, which passes through the territories of the four entities of the Russian Federation located within the Siberian federal district: the Altai Republic, Tuva, Buryatia and the Zabaikalsky Krai. Russia's land borders are 22,170 km long and the border with Mongolia represents 15.7% of the total length (3,485 km). The total length of Mongolia's border is 8161.9 km, 42.7% of it with Russia (along the Altai and Sayan mountain ranges), and the relatively flat section is confined to the valley of the Selenge River.

The Russian-Mongolian section of the border is characterised by a low checkpoint density, the average distance between permanent checkpoints being 387.2 km (Fig. 1).

Border region	Length of the border, in km	Number of checkpoints (permanent)	Distance between checkpoints, in km
Altai Republic	288,7	1	288.7
Tuva Republic	1305	3	435.0
Republic of Buryatia	1275	3	416.0
Zabaikalsky Krai	831,5	2	415.8
Total	3485	9	387.2

Fig. 1 Transport and communication links of Russian and Mongolian border regions

The low checkpoint density in this area is due to the uniform distribution of checkpoints over the border regions of the Russian Federation: three functional checkpoints exist in the Zabaikalsky Krai, the Republic of Tuva and Buryatia. In the Altai Republic only one checkpoint is operational. Of these, four are multilateral, i.e. they allow passage of citizens of third countries. In addition these checkpoints provide the crossing line for vehicles of Kyakhta (Republic of Buryatia), Tashanta (Altai Republic) and Solovyovsk (Zabaikalsky Krai), and the railway crossing of Naushki (Republic of Buryatia).

A change of classification is currently under review for the multilateral road crossing point in Mondy (Republic of Buryatia). In 2009 and 2010, the Federal Agency for the Development of the State Border of the Russian Federation (Rosgranitsa) carried out a series of surveys of the conditions and operational state of checkpoints and other border and customs infrastructure. The study shows that of the 29 crossing points on the Russian-Mongolian border, only ten were properly equipped and fully operational. These ten checkpoints control virtually all freight and passenger traffic between Russia and Mongolia. Since April 2010, fourteen crossing points on the Russian-Mongolian border were closed as a prior study revealed that they were not functioning effectively due to lack of equipment and conflicting requirements by state bodies exercising control over checkpoints.

At present, nine permanent crossing points are operational along the Russian-Mongolian border, seven of them are road crossing points and two are railway crossing points.

Crossing point		Russian entity	Mongolian aimag	Crossing point classification		
Russian	Mongolian			Status	Type	Type of exchange
Tashanta	Tsagaan-Nuur	Altai Republic	Bayan-Ölgii	Bilateral	road	cargo and passenger
Khandagaity	Borshoo	Tuva Republic	Uvs	Bilateral	road	cargo and passenger
Shara-Sur	Tes	Tuva Republic	Uvs	Bilateral	road	cargo and passenger
Tsagaan-Tolgoi	Arts-Sur′	Tuva Republic	Zavkhan	Bilateral	road	cargo and passenger

Mondy	Khankh	Republic of Buryatia	Khövsgöl	Bilateral	road	cargo and passenger
Naushki	Sühbaatar	Republic of Buryatia	Selenge	multilateral	railway	cargo and passenger
Kyakhta	Altan-Bulag	Republic of Buryatia	Selenge	multilateral	road	cargo and passenger
Verkhny Ulkhun	Ulkhun	Zabaikalsky Krai	Dornod	Bilateral	road	cargo and passenger
Solovyovsk	Erdentsav	Zabaikalsky Krai	Dornod	Bilateral	railway	cargo

Fig. 2 Permanent crossing points between Russia and Mongolia

The development of cross-border cooperation is not only a leading factor of regional integration, but it also strengthens the strategic partnership between countries. Figure 3, for example, provides data on the number of people who crossed the border during the period 1995–2008. In 2008, through eight checkpoints on the Russian-Mongolian border the number of arrivals and departures was 513,621. Out of these, 76.2% of passenger traffic crossed through the three checkpoints on the territory of the Republic of Buryatia: 52.3% through Kyakhta-Altan-Bulag, 20.1% through Naushki-Sühbaatar and 3.8% through Mondy-Khankh (Osodoev 2010).

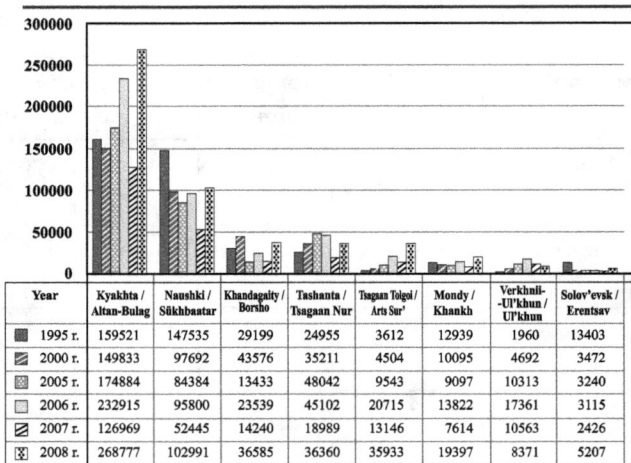

Year	Kyakhta / Altan-Bulag	Naushki / Sükhbaatar	Khandagaity / Borsho	Tashanta / Tsagaan Nur	Tsagaan Tolgoi / Arts Sur'	Mondy / Khankh	Verkhnii- -Ul'khun / Ul'khun	Solov'evsk / Erentsav
1995 г.	159521	147535	29199	24955	3612	12939	1960	13403
2000 г.	149833	97692	43576	35211	4504	10095	4692	3472
2005 г.	174884	84384	13433	48042	9543	9097	10313	3240
2006 г.	232915	95800	23539	45102	20715	13822	17361	3115
2007 г.	126969	52445	14240	18989	13146	7614	10563	2426
2008 г.	268777	102991	36585	36360	35933	19397	8371	5207

Fig. 3 Number of people crossing the Russian-Mongolian border at border crossing points (1995–2008)

Figure 4 shows Mongolia's export and import flux through the Russian-Mongolian border in 2007. The main cargo stream is transported through Naushki-Sühbaatar (90.9%), Kyakhta-Altan-Bulag (4.0%), Solov'evsk-Erentsav (2,7%), Khandagaity-Borshoo (1.7%).

Crossing point		Export	Import	Foreign trade turnover	Share of export and import movement (in percent)
Russian	**Mongolian**				
Tashanta	Tsagaan-Nuur	4.4	0.9	5.3	0.5
Khandagaity	Borshoo	15.1	1.5	16.6	1.7
Shara-Sur	Tes	0.2	0.1	0.3	0.03
Tsagaan-Tolgoi	Arts-Sur'	0.7	1.6	2.3	0.2
Mondy	Khankh	0.2	0.1	0.3	0.03
Naushki	Sühbaatar	833.6	70.3	903.9	90.9
Kyakhta	Altan-Bulag	36.5	3.7	40.2	4.0
Verkhnii Ul'khun	Ul'khun	0.1	0.2	0.3	0.03
Solov'evsk	Erentsav	15.1	11.4	26.5	2.7
Overall movement through checkpoints		905.1	89.8	994.9	100

Fig. 4 Mongolia's exports and imports through checkpoints
(2007, in million US dollars)

The relations between the two countries are currently reaching new heights on the basis of trade and economic partnerships and the development of border infrastructure, which is a crucial factor in cross-border cooperation. Recently a decision was made to give multilateral status to the "Khandagaity-Borshoo" and "Mondy-Khankh" checkpoints, to build customs and logistics terminals in the vicinity of the multilateral checkpoints of "Kyakhta-Altan-Bulag" and "Tashanta-Tsagaan Nuur" and to provide the necessary infrastructure.

A modernised infrastructure will increase traffic capacity while the equipping and modernisation of existing crossing points will enhance efficiency and reinforce a sense of spatial integration between countries. In establishing objectives and identifying the right approaches for the development of a border and customs infrastructure, a number of factors need to be taken into account:

- The current situation of the border and customs infrastructure.
- The existing legal framework governing this sector.
- The presence of specific historical, economic and socio-political conditions.
- The need for degrees of modernisation and allocation of financial resources to each crossing-point depending on its status and type (international, simplified, temporary, permanent, etc.).
- The divergent interests of the parties in the process of modernisation, maintenance and use of border infrastructures.
- Law violations in the operation of the checkpoints due to system faults and insufficient equipment.

The need to solve such challenging and often conflicting objectives led, in 2007, to the creation of the Federal Agency for the Development of the State Border of the Russian Federation (Rosgranitsa) whose mandate is the construction, technical equipment, and modernisation of checkpoints and border infrastructure. In the case of the Russian-Mongolian border, surveys conducted by Rosgranitsa reveal numerous shortcomings in the organisation of checkpoint activities. Although border checkpoints are being modernised they are still not well-integrated in the surrounding infrastructure, which is often obsolete. In particular, poor roads and communications and unreliable water and electricity supply inhibit the smooth functioning of these check-points.

It is difficult to calculate the costs involved in the modernisation of each crossing point due to the lack of reliable technical estimates. However, we can point out the main reasons for inadequate infrastructures, which include:

- Non-compliance to technological plans and practical technical issues.
- Non-compliance to required standards regarding the location of controlling devices, obsolete or faulty equipment, or its absence.
- Inadequate cross-border transport infrastructure for existing levels of traffic.

- Lack of territorial planning at checkpoint locations. This is often a source of conflict between parties during the modernisation work on checkpoints.

The inadequate state of checkpoints, which often stems from the inefficiency of federal agencies and institutions, has a negative effect on the economy of the region. It is crucial that the crossing points ensure a smooth commercial and passenger traffic through the state border. Hence the optimisation of border procedures must be a priority, in particular the shortening of control procedures, which has an immediate impact on checkpoints' efficiency and competitiveness.

In the Russian Federation building, fitting out and equipping checkpoints, as well as opening, closing and limiting their activities are regulated by the law of the Russian Federation ("On the State Border of the Russian Federation"). The Russian State Duma is currently considering a draft bill "On amendments to some legislative acts of the Russian Federation in connection with the transfer of authority for the implementation of state control of the customs authorities by the Russian Federation". The bill proposes that all forms of control at the border (except for issues of border protection such as transport, health, veterinary and phytosanitary control) should be under the jurisdiction of a single body – the Federal Customs Service. It also proposes that border checkpoints are in charge only of customs and border protection services while other types of border control (health, veterinary, etc.) would be handled by different authorities. The purpose of this bill is to reduce the transit time of goods through the checkpoints, and to implement a "one window" structure on the border (on the basis of the "single window" experiment used since 2008 at Pskov customs posts).

In 2011, a new federal law on border checkpoints was adopted across the border of the Russian Federation. The draft bill sets the legal regime of checkpoints along Russia's state border and regulates the establishment, opening, operation and closure of checkpoints. Given the present state of checkpoints' infrastructure, the shortage of budgetary funds and the economic losses incurred, priority should be given to the modernisation of all existing checkpoints, to facilitating cooperation between all federal and regional services concerned, as well as fostering a close collaboration with neighbouring states for the legal resolution of border issues.

Since 2011, the establishment of border infrastructures has been regarded as one of the priority areas in the development of the new federal target program "State Border of the Russian Federation" for the period up to 2017. Previously, within the framework of the programme "State Border of the Russian Federation (2003–2011)" headed by Rosgranitsa, the following major activities have been financed and implemented:

Title	2003	2004	2005	2006	2007	2008	2009	2010	Whole period
Total of federal budget (million Roubles)	800, 0000	1329, 0400	1452, 7196	3814, 6875	11253, 3979	9900, 5552	8476, 8700	1643, 4699	38670, 7401

- Equipment of the state border in new areas; infrastructures were improved on the Russian-Ukrainian, Russian-Kazakh and Russian-Mongolian segments of the state border.
- Preparation of estimates and planning of road checkpoints (RC) on segments of the state border that were not fully equipped.
- Activation of new RC; reconstruction of numerous RC; installation and inspection of monitoring systems (MS); inspection of offices and industrial buildings, production bases and facilities.
- Equipment of numerous RC with systems for the reading and recognition of vehicle size and number plates; purchase and fitting on a temporary basis of portable x-ray inspection systems for checkpoints; acquisition of stationary x-ray inspection systems; provision of various weighing equipment, providing and restructuring state-integrated telecommunication networks.

The fitting out of the state border plays an important part in the Russian Federation's border policy. The modern, technology-oriented look of a border is in the first place given by the checkpoints as they convey the "first impression" of a country, as well as being an important factor in the successful development of its foreign trade. As we have seen, however, the variable levels of technological compliance of checkpoints is slowing down the drive toward the modernisation of Russian borders.

Moreover, the development of cross-border cooperation contributes to the development of democratic processes in Russian-Mongolian relations and, as such, becomes an incentive for strengthening a strategic partnership. The role of cross-border cooperation is regarded by foreign and Russian scholars as a mechanism of socio-economic growth for border regions in the country. The development of modern infrastructures, including checkpoints, needs to be regarded as an area in which bordering countries cooperate. Such international cooperation is also needed for the development of tourism, the creation of trade and economic zones and the improvement of trade and economic activity, such as, for example, the supply of energy resources in Mongolia. The modernisation of border infrastructure (especially transport services, the service sector, the wholesale and retail trade in the municipalities and *aimags*)[1] is thus needed for the socio-economic well-being of the people living in border areas who, by virtue of their geographic location, are in the best position to enjoy the advantages of international cooperation.

---

1   An administrative subdivision in Mongolia.

Appendix 2: Maps

Map 1. The border towns of Zabaykalsk (Russia) and Manzhouli (China). Map created by Philip Stickler.

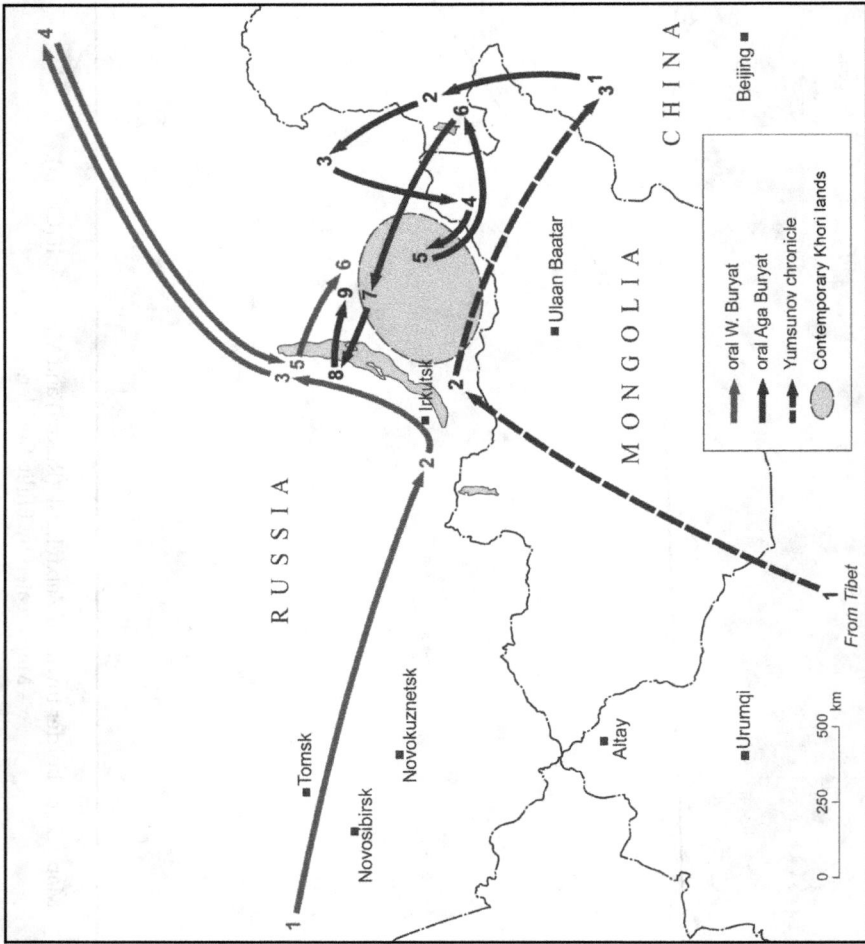

Map 2. Legendary and historical Khori Buryat migrations.
Map created by Philip Stickler.

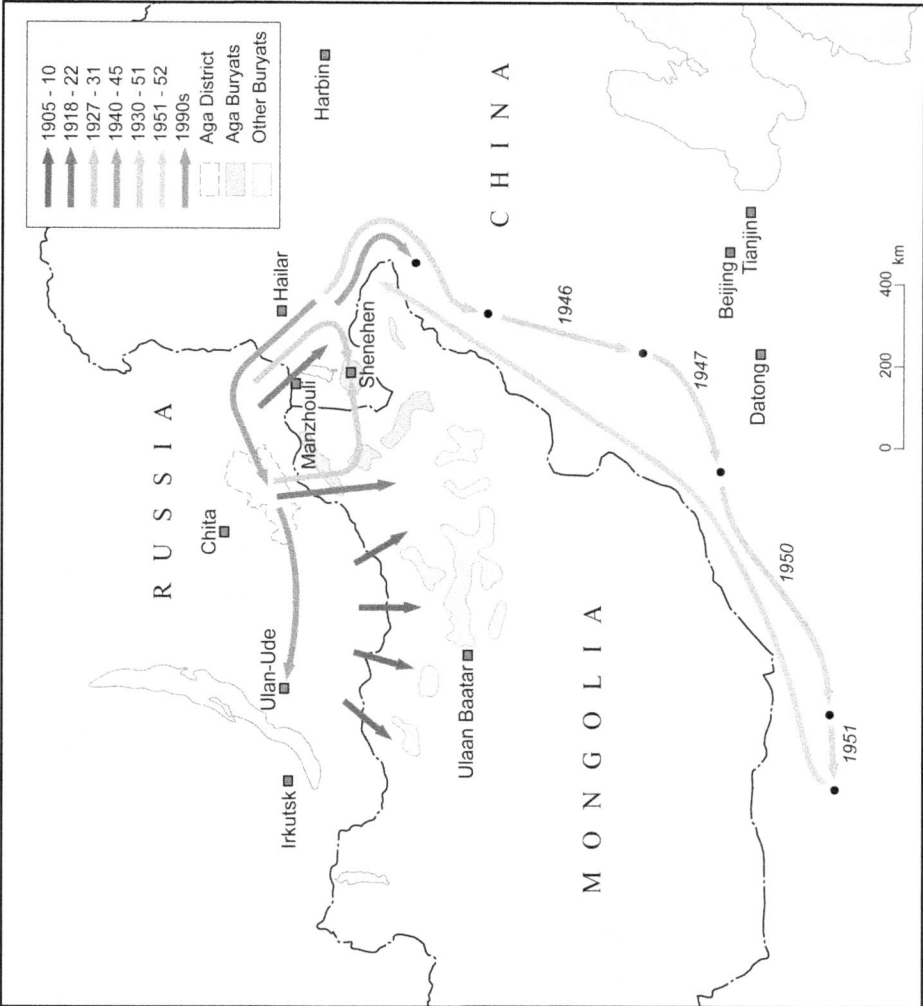

Map 3. Buryat emigrations in the 20th century. Map created by Philip Stickler.

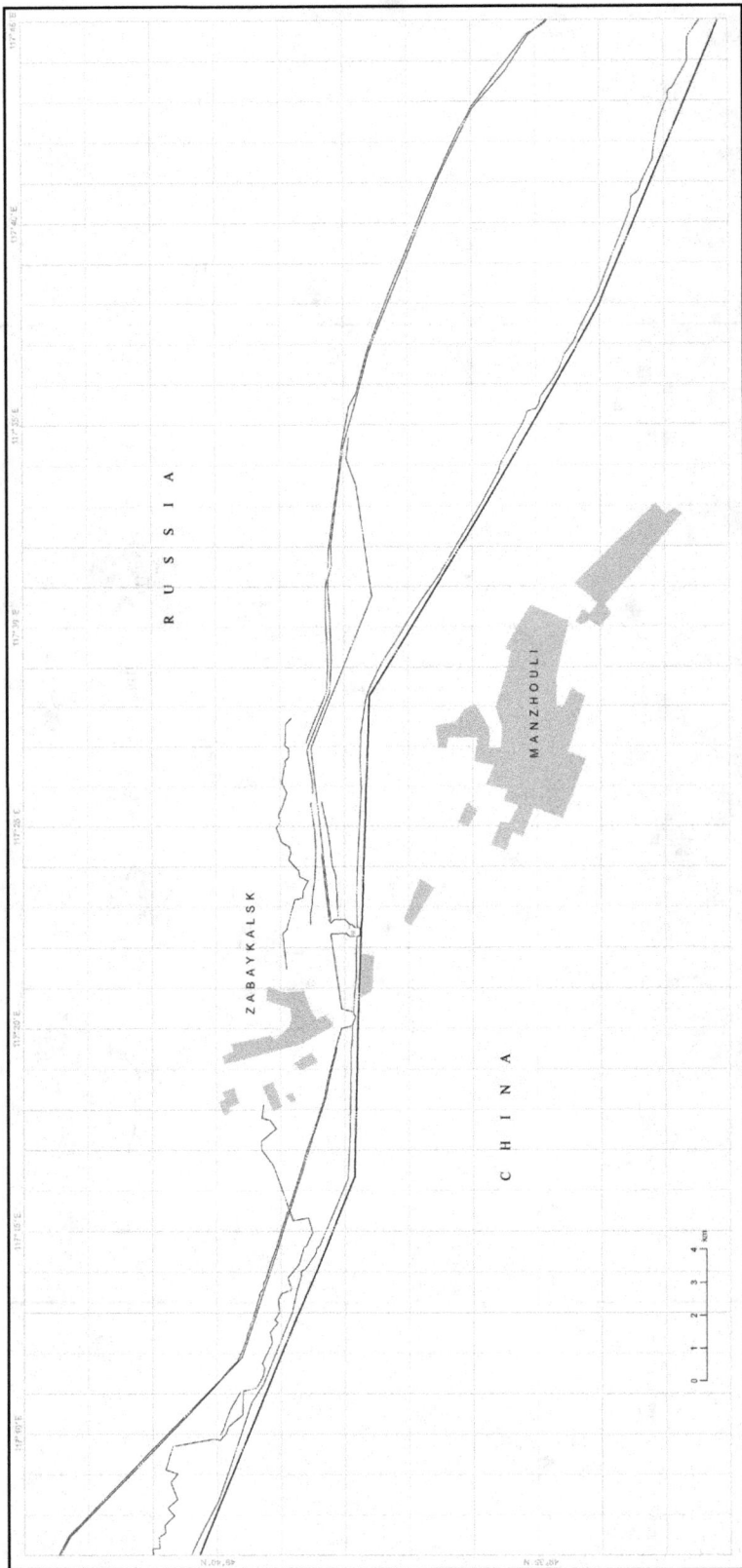

Map 4. Numerous demarcation lines supplement the Sino-Russian international boundary. Map created by Philip Stickler.

Bibliography of Works Cited

Ablazhei, N. I. 2007. *S Vostoka na Vostok. Rossiiskaya emigratsiya v Kitae*. Novosibirsk: SO RAN.

Acheson, James M. 2006. "Institutional Failure in Resource Management", *Annual Review of Anthropology* 35: 117–34.

Alexseev, Mikhail A. 2006a. *Immigration Phobia and the Security Dilemma: Russia, Europe, and the United States*. Cambridge: Cambridge University Press.

–. 2006b. "Migration, Hostility, and Ethnopolitical Mobilization: Russia's Anti-Chinese Legacies in Formation", in *Rebounding Identities: The Politics of Identity in Russia and Ukraine*, eds. Dominique Arel and Blair A. Ruble. Baltimore: The Johns Hopkins University Press, pp. 116–48.

–. 2001. *The Chinese Are Coming: Public Opinion and Threat Perception in the Russian Far East*. PONARS Policy Memo no. 184, January. Available at: http://www.gwu.edu/~ieresgwu/assets/docs/ponars/pm_0184.pdf (accessed 18.4.2012).

Anderson, Benedict. 1991 [1983]. *Imagined Communities. Reflections on the Origin and Spread of Nationalism*. London and New York: Verso.

Andreas, Peter. 2000. *Border Games. Policing the US-Mexico Divide*. Ithaca, NY: Cornell University Press.

Anthony, Ross. 2012. *Repetition and its Discontents: Space, Time and Identity in the City of Urumqi*. Unpublished Ph.D Dissertation. University of Cambridge.

Appadurai, Arjun. 2000. *Modernity at Large: Cultural Dimensions of Globalization*. Minneapolis, MN: University of Minnesota Press.

Aprelkov, V. 2009. *Batiushka Zabaikal*. Moscow: Granitsa.

Arsen'ev, Vladimir. 1914. *Kitaitsy v Ussuriiskom krae. Ocherk istoriko-etnograficheskii*. Khabarovsk (Zapiski Priamurskogo otdeleniya Rossiyskogo geografitcheskogo obschestva). 10/1.

Asiwaju, A. I. and P. O. Adenyi (eds). 1989. *Borderlands in Africa*. Lagos: University of Lagos Press.

Attané, Isabelle. 2005. *Une Chine sans femmes?* Paris: Perrin.

Atwood, Christopher. 2002. *Young Mongols and Vigilantes in Inner Mongolia Interregnum Decades, 1911–1931*. Leiden: E. J. Brill.

Babakulov, Ulugbek. 2007. "Svoimi glazami. Velikii Shelkovyi put' segodnya. Chast' III 'Kitaizatsiya'". Available at: http://www.ferghana.ru/article.php?id=5498 (accessed 18.4.2012).

Baev, Pavel. 1996. *The Russian Army in a Time of Troubles*. Oslo: PRIO, International Peace Research Institute.

Bakken, Borge. 2000. *The Exemplary Society: Human Improvement, Social Control, and the Dangers of Modernity in China*. Gloucestershire: Clarendon Press.

Baldano, Marina and Dyatlov, Victor. 2008. "Shenekhenskie buryaty: Iz diaspory v diaspory?" *Diaspory* 1: 164–92.

Balzhinimaeva, Namzhilma. 2012. "Erelkheg zorigtoi Erdem-Belig Sandiev", *Buriad Ünen – Dyükherig* 6/769. Ulan-Ude: 8.

Bao, Fengyu and Xiang Fusheng (eds.). 2008. *Mengguzhen Lishi*. Shenyang: Liaoning Minzu Chubanshe.

Baoyinchaoketu (Buyanchogt) 2003. "Qingchao Bianfang zhong de Sanzhong Xunshi Zhidu Jiexi: 'Kabing Xuncha', 'Xuncha Kalun', 'Chabian' zhi Lianxi yu Qubie", *Qingshi Yanjiu* 4: 67–73.

Baradiin, Bazar. 1926. "Rozhedenie rebenka u buryat-mongolov: iz starogo byta khori-buryat Aginskogo aimaka", *Zhizn' Buryatii* 7–9: 87–92.

Barnard, Alan and Jonathan Spencer. 2010. *The Routledge Encyclopedia of Social and Cultural Anthropology* (2nd edition). London and New York: Routledge.

Barth, Frederic. 1969. *Ethnic Groups and Boundaries. The Social Organization of Cultural Difference*. London: Allen and Unwin.

Basaeva, Klara. 1993. "Poseleniya i zhilischa alarskih buryat", in *History of Household and Material Culture of Mongol and Turkic Ethnic Groups*, ed. Bulat Zorigtuev. Novosibirsk: Nauka, pp. 109–24

Basharov, I. P. 2010. "Russkie Vnutrennei Mongolii kratkaya kharakteristika gruppy", in *Aziatskaya Rossiya: migratsya, regiony i regionalizm v istoricheskoi dinamike*, ed. B. V. Bazarov, Irkutsk: Ottisk, pp. 301–07.

Bassin, Mark. 1999. *Imperial Visions: Nationalist Imagination and Geographical Expansion in the Russian Far East, 1840–1865*. Cambridge: Cambridge University Press.

–. 2008. "Eurasianism 'Classical' and 'Neo': The Lines of Continuity", in *Beyond the Empire: Images of Russia in the Eurasian Cultural Context*, ed. Tetsuo Mochizuki. Sapporo: Slavic Research Centre, pp. 279–94.

Batbayar, Tsedendamba. 2005. "Foreign Migration Issues in Mongolia", in *Crossing National Borders: Human Migration Issues in Northeast Asia*, ed. Tsuneo Akaha and Anna Vassilieva. Tokyo: United Nations University Press, pp. 215–35.

Bawden, Charles R. 1968. *The Modern History of Mongolia*. London: Kegan Paul International.

Bazarov, Boris. 2001. *General-leitenant Manchzhou-go Urzhin Garmaev*. Ulan-Ude: Buryatskii nauchnyi tsentr.

Bell, Catherine. 1992. *Ritual Theory, Ritual Practice*. Oxford University Press: Oxford.

Bellér-Hann, Ildikó et al (eds). 2007. *Situating the Uyghurs between China and Central Asia*. Aldershot: Ashgate.

–. 2008. *Community Matters in Xinjiang 1880–1949: Towards a Historical Anthropology of the Uyghur*. Leiden: E. J. Brill.

Benjamin, Walter. 1999. *The Arcades Project*. Harvard University Press: Cambridge.

Billé, Franck. 2008. "Faced with Extinction: Myths and Urban Legends in Contemporary Mongolia", *Cambridge Anthropology* 28/1: 34–60.

–. 2009. "Cooking the Mongols / Feeding the Han: Dietary and Ethnic Intersections in Inner Mongolia", *Inner Asia* 11: 231–56.

–. 2010. *Bodies of Excess. Imagining the Chinese in Contemporary Mongolia.* Unpublished PhD dissertation. University of Cambridge.

–. 2012. "Territorial Phantom Pains (and other Cartographic Anxieties)", Presentation given at CRASSH, Cambridge, on 23 May 2012: http://www.crassh.cam.ac.uk/events/2022

Bloch, Maurice. 1999. "Death, Women and Power", in *Death and the Regeneration of Life*, eds. Maurice Bloch and Jonathan Parry. Cambridge: Cambridge University Press, pp. 211–30.

Blyakher, Leonid and Nikolai Pegin. 2010. "Dinamika predstavlenii naseleniya Dal'nego Vostoka Rossii o kitaiskikh migrantakh na rubezhe XX-XXI vekov (na materiale interv'yu s predprinimatelyami)", in *Migratsii i diaspory v sotsiokul'turnom, politicheskom i ekonomicheskom prostranstve Sibiri. Rubezhi XIX-XX i XX-XXI vekov*, ed. V. I. Dyatlov. Irkutsk: Ottisk, pp. 485–501.

Bodiguel, Clotilde. 2002. "Fishermen Facing the Commercial Lobster Fishery Licensing Policy in the Canadian Maritime Provinces: Origins of Illegal Strategies, 1960–2000" *Marine Policy* 26/4: 271–81.

Bogoslovskii, Leonid. 1913. "Krepost'-gorod Vladivostok i kitaitsy", *Vestnik Azii* 13: 20–33.

Bol'shoi akademicheskii Mongolo-Russkii slovar'. 2001. Moscow: Academiya. 4 vols.

Bold, Bat-Ochir. 2001. *Mongolian Nomadic Society: A Reconstruction of the 'Medieval' History of Mongolia*. New York: St. Martin's Press.

Borisov, Oleg and Koloskov, Boris. 1972. *Sovetsko-kitaiskie otnosheniya*. Moscow: Mysl.

Borjigin, Burensain 2004. "The Complex Structure of Ethnic Conflict in the Frontier: Through the Debates around the 'Jindandao Incident' in 1891", *Inner Asia*. 6/1: 41–60.

–. 2007. *Jinxiandai Menggu Ren Nungen Cunluo Shehui de Xingcheng*. Huhehaote: Nei Menggu Daxue Chubanshe.

Boronoeva, Darima. 2003. "Rol' idei 'vozvrascheniya na rodinu' v mirovozzrenii shenekhenskikh buryat", in *Buddhism v kontekste istorii, ideologii i kul'tury Tsentral'noi i Vostochnoi Azii*, ed. Conference Proceedings Ulan-Ude: IMBiT, pp. 184–87.

–. 2006. "Vozniknovenie Buryatskoi diaspory za rubezhom", in *Diaspory v kontekste sovremennikh etnokul'turnykh i etnosotsial'nykh protsessov*, eds. Lyubov' Abaeva, Daba Nimaev and Darima Boronoeva. Ulan-Ude: Buryat State University, pp. 33–46.

–. 2010. "Buryaty v Mongolii i vo Vnutrennei Mongolii KNR: Antropologia perepisi i identichnost'", in *Aziatskaya Rossiya: Migratsii, regiony i regionalizm v istoricheskoi dinamike*, ed. Boris Bazarov. Irkutsk: Ottisk.

Bretell, Caroline (ed.). 2007. *Constructing Borders / Crossing Boundaries. Race, Ethnicity and Immigration.* Lanham, MD: Lexington.

Buchanan, James M. and Yong J. Yoon. 1999. "Generalized Increasing Returns, Euler's Theorem, and Competitive Equilibrium", *History of Political Economy* 31: 511–23.

Bulag, Uradyn E. 1998. *Nationalism and Hybridity in Mongolia.* Oxford: Clarendon.

–. 2008. "Contesting the Words that Wound: Ethnicity and the Politics of Sentiment in China", *Inner Asia.* 10/2: 87–111.

–. 2010a. "Twentieth Century China: Ethnic Assimilation and Inter-Group Violence", in *The Oxford Handbook of Genocide Studies*, eds. Donald Bloxham and A. Dirk Moses. Oxford: Oxford University Press, pp. 426–44.

–. 2010b. *Collaborative Nationalism: The Politics of Friendship on China's Mongolian Frontier.* Lanham, MD: Rowman and Littlefield.

–. 2010c. "Alter/Native Mongolian Identity: From Nationality to Ethnic Group", in *Chinese Society: Change, Conflict and Resistance* (3rd edition), eds. Elizabeth J. Perry and Mark Selden. London and New York: Routledge, pp. 261–87.

–. 2012. "Good Han, Bad Han: the Moral Parameters of Ethnopolitics in China", in *Critical Han Studies: The History, Representation, and Identity of China's Majority*, eds. James Leibold, Stéphane Gros and Eric Vanden Bussche. Berkeley, CA: University of California Press, pp. 92–109; 282–85.

Buraeva, O. B. 2005. *Etnokul'turnoe vzaimodeistvie narodov Baikal'skogo regiona v XVII-nachale XX v.* Ulan-Ude: Izdatel'stvo Buriatskogo nauchnogo tsentra SO RAN.

Buyandelgeriyn, Manduhai. 2002. *Between Hearth and Celestial Court: Gender, Marginality, and the Politics of Shamanic Practices among the Buriats of Mongolia.* Unpublished PhD dissertation. Harvard University.

Carsten, Janet. 1998. "Borders, Boundaries, Tradition and State on the Malaysian Periphery", in *Border Identities: Nation and State at International Frontiers*, ed. Thomas M. Wilson and Hastings Donnan. Cambridge: Cambridge University Press, pp. 215–36.

–. 2007. "Introduction: Ghosts of Memory" in *Ghosts of Memory. Essays on Remembrance and Relatedness*, ed. J. Carsten. Malden and Oxford: Blackwell, pp. 1–35.

Cashdan, Elizabeth. 1983. "Territoriality among Human Foragers: Ecological Models and an Application to Four Bushman Groups", *Current Anthropology* 24/1: 47–66.

Certeau, Michel (de). 1991. *L'invention du quotidien. 1. Arts de faire.* Paris: Gallimard.

Chabros, K. 1998. "Space and Movement in Mongolian Culture", *Journal of the Anglo-Mongolian Society* 11/1: 30–38.

Chen, Ganglong. 2001. "Menggu Zu Shibao Chuanshuo Yanjiu", *Minsu Yanjiu* 2: 84–92.

Chen, Hsin-Yüan. 2008/09. "Local Identity, Popular Autonomy, and Political Authority in the Dragon-boat Festival Celebrations in Ming-Qing China", *Bulletin of the Institute of History and Philology Academia Sinica* 79/3: 417–96.

Cheremisov, K. 1973. *Buriad-Orod slovar'.* Moscow: Sovetskaya entsiklopediya.

Coase, Ronald H. 1960. "The Problem of Social Cost", *Journal of Law and Economics* 3: 1–44.

[n.a.] "Chto meshaet vozvrascheniyu Shenekhenskikh Buryat na istoricheskuyu rodinu?" (1.3.2007). Available at: http://www.arigus-tv.ru/news/detail.php?ID=3468 (accessed 14.5.2008).

Cohen, Robin. 1996. "Diasporas and the Nation-state: From Victims to Challenge" *International Affairs* 72/3: 507–20.

Crews, Robert D. 2010. "Russian Unbound: Historical Frameworks and the Challenge of Globalism", *Ab Imperio* 1: 53–63.

Crossley, Pamela K. 2006. "Making Mongols" in *Empire, Frontier and Ethnicity in Early Modern China*, eds. P. K. Crossley, H. F. Siu and D. Sutton. Berkeley, CA: University of California Press, pp. 58–82.

–, Helen F. Siu and Donald S. Sutton. 1991. *Empire at the Margins: Culture, Ethnicity, and Frontier in Early Modern China*. Berkeley, CA: University of California Press.

Crowley, R. M. 2005. "Stepping Onto a Moving Train: The Collision of Illegal Logging, Forestry Policy, and Emerging Free Trade in the Russian Far East", *Pacific Rim Law & Policy Journal* 14: 425–53.

Dai, Weiyu. 2009. *Teühe-ber Toli Bolyasuyai / Lishi wei Jing*. Hong Kong: Dongfang Caifu Chubanshe.

Davis, Sue. 2003. *The Russian Far East: The Last Frontier?* London: Routledge.

Delaplace, Grégory. 2009. *L'invention des morts. Sépultures, fantômes et photographie en Mongolie contemporaine*. Paris: EMSCAT (Nord-Asie 1).

–. 2010. "Chinese Ghosts in Mongolia", *Inner Asia*. 12/1: 111–38.

–. 2012. "Parasitic Chinese, Vengeful Russians: Ghosts, Strangers and Reciprocity in Mongolia", *Journal of the Royal Anthropological Institute* (Special Issue on The Return to Hospitality. Strangers, Guests and Ambiguous Encounters, edited by M. Candea and G. da Col) 18: 131–44.

Diener, Alexander. 2003. *One Homeland or Two? Territorialization of Identity and the Migration Decision of the Mongolian-Kazakh Diaspora*. Unpublished PhD dissertation. University of Wisconsin-Madison.

–. 2005. "Kazakhstan's Kin State Diaspora: Settlement Planning and the Oralman Dilemma", *Europe-Asia Studies* 57/2 (March): 327–48.

Dijstelbloem, Huub and Albert Meijer (eds.). 2011. *Migration and the New Technological Borders of Europe*. London: Palgrave Macmillan.

Dirlik, Arif. 2008. "Socialism in China: A Historical Overview", in *The Cambridge Companion to Modern Chinese Culture*, ed. Kam Louie. Cambridge: Cambridge University Press, pp. 155–72.

Donnan, Hasting and Thomas M. Wilson. 1999. *Borders: Frontiers of Identity, Nation and State*. Oxford: Berg.

Donnan, Hastings and Thomas M. Wilson. 1998. "Nations, State and Identity at International Borders", in Wilson *Border Identities: Nation and State at International Frontiers*, eds. Hastings Donnan and Thomas, Cambridhe: Cambridge University Press, pp. 1–30.

Duara, Prasenjit. 1995. *Rescuing History from the Nation: Questioning Narratives of Modern China*. Chicago, IL: University of Chicago Press.

Dugarov, Bair. 2004. "Poem Nayan-Nava. *Sibirskie ogni*" (7). Available at: http://www.sibogni.ru/archive/37/420 (accessed 15.6.2011).

Dugin, Aleksandr. 2002. *Osnovy evraziistva*. Moscow: Arktogeya Tsentr.

–. 2004. *Proekt "Evraziya"*. Moscow: Yauza.

Dunn, John. [n.d.]. "Nationalism as a Political Phenomenon", unpublished manuscript.

Dvizhenie. 1997. "Dvizhenie kitaitsev v Rossiyu prinimaet ugrozhayushchie razmery", *Istochnik* 1: 69–71.

Dyatlov, Viktor. 1999. *Kitaitsy v Sibiri: otnoshenie obshchestva i politika vlastei*. Moscow: Rabochie materialy moskovskogo Tsentra Carnegie, June.

–. 2003. "Blagoveshchenskaya 'Utopia': iz istorii materializatsii fobii", in *Evraziya. Lyudi i mify* (Collection of articles from *Vestnik Evrazii"*), ed. S. A. Panarin. Moscow: Natalis, pp. 123–41.

–. 2008. "Rossia: v predchuvstvii chainataunov", *Etnograficheskoe obozrenie* 4: 6–16.

"Escho pro Shenehen" (10.6.2007). Available at: www.buryatia.org, http://taina.h15.ru/index.php?id_cont=16&shot=onestat.php (accessed 12.8.2007).

Edmonds, Richard Louis 1979. "The Willow Palisade", *Annals of the Association of American Geographers* 69/4: 599–621.

–. 1985. *Northern Frontiers of Qing China and Tokugawa Japan: A Comparative Study of Frontier Policy*. University of Chicago, Department of Geography; Research Paper, no. 213.

Elverskog, Johan. 1996. *Our Great Qing: The Mongols, Buddhism and the State in Late Imperial China*, Honolulu: University of Hawaii Press.

Empson, Rebecca M. 2011. *Harnessing Fortune: Personhood, Memory, and Place in Mongolia*. Oxford: British Academy/Oxford University Press.

–. 2007. "Enlivened Memories: Recalling Absence and Loss in Mongolia", in *Ghosts of Memory. Essays on Remembrance and Relatedness*, ed. Janet Carsten. Malden and Oxford: Blackwell, pp. 58–82.

Ettinger, Patrick. 2009. *Imaginary Lines. Border Enforcement and the Origins of Undocumented Immigration, 1882–1930*. Austin, TX: University of Texas Press.

Fairbank, John. 1968. *The Chinese World Order: Traditional China's Foreign Relations*. Cambridge, MA: Harvard University Press.

Farquhar, David M. 1967. "Chinese Communist Assessments of a Foreign Conquest Dynasty", *The China Quarterly* 30: 79–92.

–. 1978. "Emperor as Bodhisattva in the Governance of the Ch'ing Empire", *Harvard Journal of Asiatic Studies* 38/1: 5–34.

Fassin, Didier. 2005. "Compassion and Repression. The Moral Economy of Immigration Policies in France", *Cultural Anthropology* 20/3: 362–87.

FCS [Federal Customs Service of Russia]. 2006. "Vpervye kitaiskii kontrabandist osuzhden na dva goda lisheniya svobody". Available at: http://dvtu.customs.ru/index.php?option=com_content&view=article&id=4639 (accessed 30.4.2012).

–. 2009. "Tamozhenniki presekli kontrabandnyi kanal postavok ryboproduktsii". Available at: http://dvtu.customs.ru/index.php?option=com_content&view=article&id=1923 (accessed 30.4.2012).

–. 2010. "Zaderzhana krupnaya partiya ryby". Available at: http://dvtu.customs.ru/index.php?option=com_content&view=article&id=1206 (accessed: 30.4.2012).

Fei, Xiaotong 1989. "Zhonghua Minzu de Duoyuan Yiti Geju", in *Zhonghua Minzu de Duoyuan Yiti Geju*, ed. Fei Xiaotong et al. Beijing: Zhongyang Minzu Xueyuan Chubanshe, pp. 1–36

Figes, Orlando. 2007. *The Whisperers: Private Life in Stalin's Russia*. London: Allen Lane.

Fiskesjö, Magnus. 1999. "On the 'Raw' and the 'Cooked' Barbarians of Imperial China", *Inner Asia* 1/2: 139–68.

Fitzgerald John (ed.). 2002. *Rethinking Chinese Provinces*. London: Routledge.

Fitzpatrick, Sheila. 1976. "Culture and Politics under Stalin: A Reappraisal", *Slavic Review* 35/2: 211–31.

–. 2000. *Everyday Stalinism: Ordinary Life in Extraordinary Times: Soviet Russia in the 1930s*. Oxford: Oxford University Press.

–. 2006. "Ascribing Class. The Construction of Social Identity in Soviet Russia", in *Stalinism: New Directions*, ed. Sheila Fitzpatrick. London and New York: Routledge, pp. 20–46.

Földhazi, A. 2009. "Activités prostitutionnelles et gestion des violences : les risques du métier", *Genre, sexualité et société*. 2. Available at: http///gss.revues.org/index1020.html (accessed 1.10.2010).

Forbes, Andrew W. 1986. *Warlords and Muslims in Chinese Central Asia: A Political History of Republican Sinkiang* 1911–1949. Cambridge: Cambridge University Press.

Fossé-Poliak, Claude. 1984. "La notion de prostitution. Une définition préalable", *Déviances et société* 8/3: 251–66.

Foucault, Michel. 2004 [1978]. *Sécurité, territoire, population : Cours au Collège de France (1977–1978)*. Paris: Le Seuil.

–. 2007 [2004]. *Security, Territory, Population. Lectures at the College de France 1977–1978*. London: Palgrave Macmillan.

Foucher, Michel. 2007. *L'obsession des frontières*. Paris: Librairie Académique Perrin.

Fravel, M. Taylor. 2008. *Strong Borders, Secure Nation: Cooperation and Conflict in China's Territorial Disputes*. Princeton, NJ: Princeton University Press.

FSS [Federal Security Service of Russia]. 2001. "V Evreiskoi AO Zaderzhali Kitaiskikh Brakon'erov". Available at: http://www.fsb.ru/fsb/comment/ufsb/single.htm!id=10311325@fsbComment.html (accessed 30.4.2012).

–. 2002. "V Birobidzhane sotrudnikami FSB presechena popytka kontrabandnogo vyvoza v Kitai krupnoi partii osetrovoi ryby". Available at: http://www.fsb.ru/fsb/comment/ufsb/single.htm!id=10311774@fsbComment.html (accessed 30.4.2012).

–. 2004a. Na Dal'nem Vostoke na reke Amur zaderzhana gruppa kitaiskikh i rossiiskikh brakon'erov. Available at: http://www.fsb.ru/fsb/comment/ufsb/single.htm!id=10314924@fsbComment.html (accessed 30.4.2012).

–. 2004b. V Amurskoi oblasti osuzhdeny kitaiskie brakonery. Available at: http://www.fsb.ru/fsb/comment/ufsb/single.htm!id%3D10315092@fsbComment.html (accessed 30.4.2012).

–. 2006a. "13 kitaiskikh brakon'erov zaderzhany v khode sovmestnykh reidov rossiiskikh i kitaiskikh pogranichnikov na rekakh Amur i Ussuri". Available at: http://www.fsb.ru/fsb/comment/ufsb/single.htm!id=10313031@fsbComment. html (accessed 30.4.2012).

–. 2006b. "S 15 maya na pogranichnykh s Kitaem rekakh Amur i Ussuri v Khabarovskom krae i YEAO nachalas' spetsoperatsiya 'Putina-Amur-2006'". Available at: http://www.fsb.ru/fsb/comment/ufsb/single.htm!id=10316738@ fsbComment.html (accessed 30.4.2012).

Galdanova, G. 2000. "Rodil'niye obryady" in *Traditsionnaya kul'tura buryat*, eds. K. Gerasimova, G. Galdanova and G. Ochirova. Ulan-Ude: Belig, pp. 85–90.

Galenovich, Yuri. 2001. *Rossia i Kitai v XX veke: Granitsa*. Moscow: Izograf.

Galeotti, Mark. 1995. "The Cossacks: A Cross-border Complication to Post-Soviet Eurasia", *IBRU Boundary and Security Bulletin*. Summer: 55–60.

Gallinat, Anselma. 2010. "Playing the Native Card: The Anthropologist as Informant in Eastern Germany", in *The Ethnographic Self as Resource: Writing Memory and Experience into Ethnography*, eds. Peter Collins and Anselma Gallinat. Berghahn Books, pp. 25–44.

Gantogtoh, G. 2010–2011. *Buriad ayalguunii tol'*. Ulaanbaatar: Anton Mostaerd mongol sudlaliin Töv.

Gellner, David (ed.). Forthcoming. *Borderlands in Northern South Asia*. Durham, NC: Duke University Press.

Gellner, Ernest. 1983. *Nations and Nationalism*. Ithaca, NY: Cornell University Press.

–. 1988. *Nations and Nationalism*. Oxford: Basil Blackwell.

Gertsen, Alexander. 1957. *"Byloe i dumy"*. *Gertsen A.I. Sochineniya: v 9 t.*, Tom 6. Moscow: GIKhL.

Giddens, Anthony. 1999. *Runaway World*. London: Profile.

Goulard, Jean-Pierre. 2005. "Ethniciser le territoire. Mouvements pendulaires transfrontaliers dans un contexte amazonien", *Cahiers des Amériques Latines* 48: 147–68.

Graber, K. and Long, J. 2009. "The Dissolution of the Buryat Autonomous Okrugs in Siberia: Notes from the Field", *Inner Asia* 11: 147–55.

Grave, Vladimir. 1912. *Kitaitsy, koryeitsy i yapontsy v Priamur'e*. St Petersburg: (Trudi Amurskoy expeditsii. Vypusk 9).

Grayson, Robin and Chimed-Erdene Baatar. 2009. "Remote Sensing of Cross-border Routes between China and Mongolia", *World Placer Journal* 9: 48–118.

Gudkov, Lev 2005. "Ideologema 'vraga': 'Vragi' kak massovyi sindrom i mekhanizm sotsial'noi integratsii", in *Obraz vraga*. Moscow: OGI, pp. 7–79.

Gumilev, Lev. 2002 [1989]. *Drevnyaya Rus' i velikaya step*. Moscow: Rol'f.

Gupta, Akhil *and Ferguson,* James. 1992. "Beyond 'Culture': Space identity and the Politics of Difference", *Cultural Anthropology* 7/1: 6–23.

Guseinov, Gasan. 2005. *Karta nashei Rodiny: Ideologema mezhdu slovom i telom*. Moscow: OGI.

Hale, Henry E. 2010. "Eurasian Politics as Hybrid Regimes: The Case of Putin's Russia", *Journal of Eurasian Studies* 1: 33–41.

Halfin, Igal. (ed.). 2002. *Language and Revolution. Making Modern Political Identities.* London: Frank Cass.

–. 2009. *Stalinist Confessions: Messianism and Terror at the Leningrad Communist University.* Pittsburgh, PA: University of Pittsburgh Press.

Hancock, Nelson. 2003. "Regimes of Classification and the Paradox of Kamchadal Heritage", *Polar Geography* 27/2: 159–73.

Handman, Marie-Elisabeth and Mossuz-Lavau Janine (eds). 2005. *La prostitution à Paris.* Paris: La Martinière.

Hangalov, M. N. 1903 [1958–60]. *Sobranie sochinenii v 3-kh tomakh.* Vol. 1. Ulan-Ude: Buryat Book Publishing House.

Hansen, Mette Halskov. 2005. *Frontier People: Han Settlers in Minority Areas of China.* London: Hurst & Co.

Hardin, Garrett. 1968. "The Tragedy of the Commons, *Science* 162: 1243–48.

Henriot, Christian. 2004. "Public Health Policy vs. Colonial Laissez-faire: STDs and Prostitution in Republican Shanghai", in *Sexual Cultures in East Asia: The Social Construction of Sexuality and Sexual Risk in a Time of AIDS*, ed. E. Micollier. London and New York: Routledge Curzon, pp. 159–82.

Hentschel, Thomas, Felix Hruschka and Michael Priester. 2002. *Global Report on Artisanal & Small-Scale Mining.* International Institute for Environment and Development, World Business Council for Sustainable Development. Available at: http://pubs.iied.org/pdfs/G00723.pdf (accessed 30.4.2012).

Hevia, James L. 1994. "Sovereignty and Subject: Constituting Relations of Power in Qing Guest Ritual", in *Body, Subject and Power in China*, eds. Angela Zito and Tani E. Barlow. Chicago, IL: University of Chicago Press.

Hill, Fiona and Clifford Gaddy. 2003. *The Siberian Curse: How Communist Planners Left Russia out in the Cold.* Washington, DC: Brookings Institution Press.

Højer, Lars. 2009. "Absent Powers: Magic and Loss in Post-Socialist Mongolia", *Journal of the Royal Anthropological Institute* 15/3: 575–91.

Huidianguan (ed.) 2006. *Qinding Daqing Huidian Shili: Lifanyuan.* Beijing: Zhongguo Zangxue Chubanshe.

Humphrey, Caroline. 2002. "Eurasia and the Political Imagination in Provincial Russia", in *Postsocialism: Ideals, Ideologies and Practices in Eurasia*, ed. C. Hann. London: Routledge, pp. 258–76.

–. 2002a. *The Unmaking of Soviet Life: Everyday Economies after Socialism.* Ithaca, NY: Cornell University Press.

–. 2005. "Ideology in Infrastructure: Architecture and Soviet Imagination", *The Journal of the Royal Anthropological Institute* 11/1: 39–58.

–. 2007. "Alternative Freedoms", *Proceedings of the American Philosophical Society* 151/1: 1–10.

–. 2009. "Opasnye slova: tabu, uklonenie i molchanie v Sovetskoi Rossii", *Antropologicheskii forum* 3: 314–38.

– and Onon, Urgunge. 1996. *Shaman and Elders: Experience, Knowledge and Power among the Daur Mongols.* Oxford: Clarendon.

Hürelbaatar, Altanhuu. 2000. "An Introduction to the History and Religion of the Buryat Mongols of Shinehen in China" *Inner Asia* 2/1: 73–116.

Il'in, V. N. 1997. *Esse o russkoy kul'ture*. St. Petersburg: Akropol

Ingold, Tim. 2000. *The Perception of the Environment: Essays on Livelihood, Dwelling and Skill*. London: Routledge.

International Labour Office. 1999. *Report for Discussion at the Tripartite Meeting on Social and Labour Issues in Small-scale Mines*. Geneva, 17–21 May.

Iwashita Akihiro. 2004. *A 4,000 Kilometer Journey along the Sino-Russia Border*. Sapporo: Slavic Research Center, Hokkaido University.

–. 2006. *4000 kilometrov problem. Rossiisko-kitaiskaya granitsa*. Moscow: Vostok-Zapad.

Jagchid, Sechin. 1988. "Tibetan Buddhism, the Mongolian Religion", *Common Voice*, vol. 1. Available at: http://www.freedomsherald.org/allied_comm/commonv-1-3.html (accessed 10.10.2010).

Kaganskii, V. L. 2004. "Evraziiskaya kontseptsiya prostranstva Rossii", in *Tsivilizatsiya, Vol 6. Rossiya v tsivilizatsionnoi strukture evraziiskogo kontinenta*, ed. A. O. Chubar'yan. Moscow: Nauka, pp. 201–16.

Kaplonski, Christopher. 2008. "Prelude to Violence. Show Trials and State Power in 1930s Mongolia", *American Ethnologist* 35/2: 321–37.

Khabarovskyi krai. Ministry for Economic and International Relations (2009). "O sostoyanii i ob okhrane okruzhayushchei sredy Khabarovskogo kraya v 2008 godu". Available at: http://www.adm.khv.ru/invest2.nsf/ecology_ru/2731E837E0 8BA4F4CA25767300197269?OpenDocument (accessed 30.4.2012)

Khamutaev, Vladimir. 2000. *Buryat-mongol'ski vopros: istoriya, pravo, politika* (Part 2). Ulan-Ude: Ulzy.

Khramchikhin, Alexander. 2005. "Zheltoe gospodstvo. Zakhvat Kitaem Sibiri – ne "strashilka". Poskol'ku drugogo vykhoda u nego prosto net". *Politicheskii zhurnal* 27: 61–64.

Kobzev, Artyom. 1984. "O protivorechivom obraze Kitaya u V.S.Solovyeva", *Pyatnadtsataya nauchnaya konferentsiya "Obshchestvo i gosudarstvo v Kitae"*. Tezisi dokladov. Part 1. Moscow: Nauka, pp. 189–91.

Koshelev, A. 2000. "Revansh 'zheltyi'", *Alfavit*, 35/93. Available at: http://www.alphabet.ru/nomer.shtml?action=select&a=82 (accessed 18.08.2002).

Kosmarskaya, Nataliya. 2006. *Deti imperii' v postsovetskoi Tsentral'noi Azii: adaptivnie praktiki i mental'nie sdvigi (russkie v Kirgizii, 1992–2002)*. Moskva: Natalis.

Kotkin, Stephen. 1997. *Magnetic Mountain: Stalinism as a Civilization*. Los Angeles, CA: University of California Press.

Kovalevskii, Maxim. 1909. "Porto-franko vo Vladivostoke", *Vestnik Evropy* 255: 423–37.

Kubieck, Paul. 2004. "The Evolution of Eurasianism and the Monroeski Doctrine under Vladimir Putin". Available at: http://www.allacademic.com//meta/p_mla_apa_research_citation/0/7/4/2/5/pages74255/p74255-1.php (accessed 4.5.2012)

Kuhrt, Natasha. 2007. *Russian Policy towards China and Japan: The El'tsin and Putin Periods*. London and New York: Routledge.

Kurto, O. 2009. "Vy russkie? My tozhe. Ili 'Sidya na sopkah Man'chzhurii'". Available at: http://ricolor.org/rz/kitai/rossia/emigr/adaptation/11_09_09 (accessed 19.4.2012).

L.G. [n.a.]. 1916. "Zheltyi trud na Dal'nem Vostoke po dannym 1914 goda", *Voprosy kolonizatsii* 19: 140–71.

Lacaze, Gaëlle. 2010. "Run after Time: The Roads of Suitcase Traders", *Asian Ethnicity* 11/2: 191–208.

Lagrange, Charles. 2008. "Les Compradores, de l'intermédiaire indispensable … à l'homme d'affaire avisé", *La Gazette de Shanghai* 11. Available at: http://www.ambafrance-cn.org/La-Gazette-de-Shanghai-11-Les-Compradores-de-l-intermediaire-indispensable-a-l-homme-d-affaire.html (accessed 11.1.2011).

Lahusen, Thomas. *Harbin and Manchuria: Place, Space, and Identity*. Durham, NC: Duke University Press.

Larin, Victor. 2005. "Chinese in the Russian Far East: Regional Views", in *Crossing National Borders: Human Migration Issues in Northeast Asia*, ed. Tsuneo Akaha and Anna Vassilieva. Tokyo: United Nations University Press, pp. 47–67.

Latour, Bruno. 1993. *Petites leçons de sociologie des sciences*. Paris: La Découverte (Points Sciences).

Lattimore, Owen. 1967. *Inner Asian Frontiers of China*. Boston, MA: Beacon Press.

Lee, Robert. 1970. *The Manchurian Frontier in Ch'ing History*. Cambridge, MA: Harvard University Press.

Legrain, Laurent. 2007. "Au bon vieux temps de la coopérative: À propos de la nostalgie dans un district rural de la Mongolie contemporaine", *Civilisations* 56: 103–20.

Lemonnier, Pierre. 2010. "Technology", in *The Routledge Encyclopedia of Social and Cultural Anthropology* (2nd edition), eds. Alan Barnard and Jonathan Spencer. London and New York: Routledge, pp. 684–88.

Leonard, Mark. 2010. "What Does Russia Think?", *Prospect*. November: 52–5.

Levit, Peggy and Waters, Mary C. 2002. "Introduction", in *The Changing Face of Home: The Transnational Lives of the Second Generation*, eds. Peggy Levit and Mary C. Waters. New York: The Russell Sage Foundation.

Lévy, F. and Lieber, M. 2009. "La sexualité comme ressource migratoire : les Chinoises du Nord à Paris", *Revue française de sociologie*. 50/4: 719–46.

Li, Zhiting 2005. "Kangxi Yuanhe Fei Changcheng", *Renmin Luntan*, no. 9. Available at: http://www.people.com.cn/GB/paper85/15703/1388771.html# (accessed 19.10.2010).

Lias, Godferey. 1956. *Kazakh Exodus*. London: Evans Brothers Limited.

Lifanyuan (edited and annotated by Yang Xiandi and Jin Feng). 1998. *Lifan Yuan Zeli*. Haila'er: Nei Menggu Wenhua Chubanshe.

Lin, Gan. 2007. *Zhongguo Gudai Beifang Minzu Shi Xinlun*. Huhehaote: Nei Menggu Renmin Chubanshe.

Lindgren, Ethel John. 1938. "An Example of Culture Contact without Conflict: Reindeer Tungus and Cossacks of Northwestern Manchuria", *American Anthropologist*. 40/4: 605–21.

Linkhovoin, L. L. 1972. *Zametki o dorevolutsionnom byte aginskikh buryat*. Ulan-Ude: Buryatskoe knizhnoe izdatel'stvo.

Liu, Wei. 1999. "Wanqing 'Sheng' Yishi de Bianhua yu Shehui Bianqian", *Shixue Yuekan* 5: 59–65.

Liu, Xiaoyuan. 2006. *Reins of Liberation: An Entangled History of Mongolian Independence, Chinese Territoriality, and Great Power Hegemony, 1911–1950*. Stanford, CA: Stanford University Press.

–. 2010. *Recast All Under Heaven: Revolution, War, Diplomacy, and Frontier China in the 20ᵗʰ Century*. New York: Continuum.

L-n. [n.a.]. 1904. "Kapitulyatsiya russkogo truda i kapitala v Priamur'e (k zheltomu voprosu)", *Sibirskii sbornik za 1904 god* (supplement of *Vostochnoe obozrenie*): 77–108.

Logvinchuk, Arkadii. 2006. "Val Chingis-Khana – Gosudarstvennaya granitsa imperii Aisin Gurun (Zolotaya Imperia)". *Nauka i priroda Dalnego Vostoka*, 2. Available at: http://www.levking.ru/vals.htm (accessed 17.5.2011).

Lomanov, Alexander. 2005. "On the Periphery of the 'Clash of Civilizations?' Discourse and Geopolitics in Russo-Chinese Relations", in *China Inside Out: Contemporary Chinese Nationalism and Transnationalism*, ed. Pál Nyíri and Joana Breidenbach. Budapest: Central European University Press, pp. 71–98.

Lukin, Alexander. 2009. "Russia and China: The Politics of Solving Problems", in *Living with China: Regional States and China through Crises and Turning Points*, ed. Shiping Tang, Mingjiang Li, and Amitav Acharya. New York: Palgrave Macmillan, pp. 193–210.

Lyapustin, Sergey N. 2006. "Bor'ba s kontrabandoi ob'ektov fauny i flory na Dal'nem Vostoke. Istoricheskii aspect", *Bulletin of the Far East Branch of the Russian Academy of Science* 5: 170–74.

Lyapustin, Sergey N. and Pavel V. Fomenko. 2003. *Bor'ba s kontrabandoi ob'ektov fauny i flory na Dal'nem Vostoke Rossii*. Vladivostok: Apelsin.

Lyapustin, Sergey N., Natalia V. Pervushina and Pavel V. Fomenko. 2010. *Nezakonnyi oborot ob'ektov fauny i flory na Dal'nem Vostoke (2007–2009)*. WWF-Russia. Vladivostok: Apelsin.

Malkki, Liisa H. 1995. *Purity and Exile: Violence, Memory and National Cosmology among Hutu Refugees in Tanzania*. Chicago, IL: University of Chicago Press.

Mamdani, Mahmood. 1996. *Citizen and Subject: Contemporary Africa and the Legacy of Late Colonialism*. Princeton, NJ: Princeton University Press.

–. 2002. *When Victims Become Killers: Colonialism, Nativism, and the Genocide in Rwanda*. Princeton, NJ: Princeton University Press.

Mao, Zedong. 1992 (1935). "Proclamation of the Central Soviet Government to the People of Inner Mongolia (December 10, 1935)", in *Mao's Road to Power: Revolutionary Writings 1912–1949*, ed. Stuart R. Schram. vol. 1. Armonk NY: M.E. Sharpe.

Markowitz, F. and Stefansson, A.H. (eds.). 2004. *Homecoming: Unsettling Path of Return*. New York: Lexington Books.

Martinez, Oscar J. 1994. *Border People. Life and Society in the U.S.-Mexico Borderlands*. Tucson, AZ: The University of Arizona Press.

Mathieu, Lilian. 2000. "L'espace de la prostitution: éléments empiriques et perspectives en sociologie de la deviance", *Sociétés Contemporaines* 38: 99–116.

–. 2007. *La condition prostituée*. Paris: Textuel.

Matsokin, Peter. 1911. "Otsenka dannykh proizvodstv v yaponskikh, kitaiskikh i evropyeiskikh remeslenno-promyshlennykh zavedeniyakh goroda Vladivostoka za 1910–1911 gg.", *Vestnik Azii* 10: 1–20.

Mauss, Marcel. 1979 [1935]. "Body Techniques", in *Sociology and Psychology. Essays by Marcel Mauss*, transl. Ben Brewster. London: Routledge and Kegan Paul, pp. 95–123.

–. 2001 [1930]. *Les Civilisations: elements et formes* (electronic edition). Available at http://classiques.uqac.ca/classiques/mauss_marcel/oeuvres_2/oeuvres_2_13/les_civilisations.html (accessed 4.5.2012).

Mawdsley, Evan. 2007. *The Russian Civil War*. New York: Pegasus.

Mays, Wallace. 1998. "The Dornod Uranium Project in Mongolia. The Uranium Institute Twenty Third Annual International Symposium". Available at: http://www.world-nuclear.org/sym/1998/mays.htm (accessed 18.4.2012).

McMillen, Donald H. 1979. *Chinese Communist Power and Policy in Xinjiang, 1949–1977*. Boulder, CO: Westview Press.

Merkulov Spiridon. 1911. *Voprosy kolonizatsii Priamurskogo kraya. III. Zheltyi trud i mery bor'by s naplyvom zheltoi rasy v Priamur'e*. Vladivostok [n.p.].

–. 1911b. *Voprosy kolonizatsii Priamurskogo kraya. II. (Stat'i, pis'ma, zametki)*. St Petersburg [n.p.].

–. 1912. *Russkoe delo na Dal'nem Vostoke. Doklad S. D. Merkulova Ego Imperatorskomu Vysochestvu Velikomu Knyazyu Aleksandru Mikhailovichu*. St Petersburg [n.p.].

Mezhduvedomstvennoe. *Mezhduvedomstvennoe soveshchanie po delam Dal'nego Vostoka. Spravka po voprosu o merakh bor'by s kitaiskoi torgovlyei v Priamur'e* [n.p.; n.d.].

Micollier, Evelyne. 2007. "Social Inscription of Sexualities in an Era of AIDS", in *Sexuality Research in China (Zhongguo xing yanjiu)*, ed. by Huang, Y. and Pan, S., pp. 105–24. Available at: http://hal.archives-ouvertes.fr (accessed 30.6.2010).

Migdal, Joel S. 2004. "Mental Maps and Virtual Checkpoints: Struggles to Construct and Maintain State and Social Boundaries", in *Boundaries and Belonging. States and Societies in the Struggle to Shape Identities and Local Practices*, ed. Joel S. Migdal. Cambridge: Cambridge University Press, pp. 3–23.

Mikhailev, A. 2008. "'Russki 'kvartal' Ulan-batora: kollektivnaya pamiat' i klassifikatsionnye praktiki", *Vestnik Evrazii* 2: 6–28.

Mikhailov, V. A. 1996. *Religioznaya mifologiya*. Ulan-Ude: Soyol Publishing House.

–. 2004 "Predstavleniya o dushe, smerti i zagrobnoi zhizni", in *Buryaty*, eds. L. L. Abaeva and N. L. Zhukovskaya. Moscow: Nauka, pp. 366–71

Miller, A. I. 2008. "Nasledie imperii: inventarizatsiya", in *Nasledie imperii i budushcheee Rossii*, ed. A. I. Miller. Moscow: Novoe Literaturnoe Obozrenie, pp. 5–22.

Millward, James. 2007. *Eurasian Crossroads*. London: Hurst & Co.

Ministry of Industry and Trade, Government of Mongolia. 2007. *Notification of the Tender Results*. Available at: http://www.zamynuud.mn/en/tender.html (accessed 10.10.2008).

Mitchell, Timothy. 2002. *Rules of Experts: Egypt, Techno-Politics, Modernity*. Berkeley, CA: University of California Press.

Morozova, Natalia. 2009. "Geopolitics, Eurasianism and Russian Foreign Policy Under Putin". Paper presented at the annual meeting of the ISA's 50th Annual Convention "Exploring the Past, Anticipating the Future", Marriott Marquis, New York, 15 February. Available at: http://www.allacademic.com/meta/p311754_index.html (accessed 3.4.2012).

Morris-Suzuki, Tessa. 2006. "Invisible Immigrants: Undocumented Migration and Border Controls in Postwar Japan", *The Journal of Japanese Studies* 32/1: 119–53.

Nadarov Ivan. 1887. *Severno-Ussuriiskii krai*. St Petersburg: Zapiski Imperatorskogo Russkogo geograficheskogo obschestva 17/2.

–. 1896. "Khunkhuzy v Yuzhno-Ussuriiskom krae (ocherk)", *Voennyi sbornik* 9: 184–205.

Namsaraeva, Sayana. 2007. "Kontseptsia 'edinoi kitaiskoi natsii' *zhonghua minzu* i Shenekhenskie buryaty kak ee komponent", in *Diaspory v sovremennom mire: Materialy mezhdunarodnogo kruglogo stola*, ed. Lyubov Abaeva. Ulan-Ude: Buryatskii gosudarstvennyi universitet, pp. 250–56.

–. 2010. "The Metaphorical Use of Avuncular Terminology in Buriad Diaspora Relationships with Homeland and Host Society", *Inner Asia* 12: 201–30.

Nansen Fridtjof. 1915. *V stranu budushchego. Velikii Severnyi put' iz Evropy v Sibir' cherez Karskoe more*. Petrograd: Izdaniye A&P Xido.

Narayan, Kirin. 1993. "How Native is a 'Native' Anthropologist?", *American Ethnologist*, 95: 671–86.

National AIDS Foundation. 2007. *Hamtran ajillatsgaaja* 1/16.

Nelson, Sarah Milledge. 1995. *The Archaeology of Northeast China: Beyond the Great Wall*. London and New York: Routledge.

Nepstad, Peter. 2000. "Fu Manchu and the Yellow Peril", *The Illuminated Lantern* 1/5. Available at: http://www.illuminatedlantern.com/cinema/archives/fu_manchu_ and_the_yellow_peril (accessed 2.5.2012).

Newby, Laura J. 2005. *The Empire and the Khanate: A Political History of Qing Relations with Khoqand c. 1760–1860*. Leiden: Brill.

Newsland. 2010. "Brakon'ery prodayut tonny rossiiskoi ryby yapontsam". (Online Video). 12 August. Available from: http://www.newsland.ru/News/Detail/ id/544600/cat/86 (accessed 25.4.2012).

Nimaev, Roman. 2001. "Delegat ot Kongressa buryatskogo naroda. Vystuplenie", *Materialy II s"ezda narodov Buriatii*. Ulan-Ude: KBN.

North, Douglass C. 2003. "The Role of Institutions in Economic Development", *UNECE Discussion Paper Series* 2. Available at: http://www.unece.org/fileadmin/ DAM/oes/disc_papers/ECE_DP_2003–2.pdf (accessed 30.4.2012).

Novomodnyi, German, Sergey Zolotukhin and Peter Sharov. 2004. *Amurskie ryby: bogatstvo i krizis*. Vladivostok: Apelsin.

Nuclear Energy Agency. 1998. "Uranium 1997: Resources, Production and Demand". Paris: OECD Publishing.

Osodoev, P. V. 2010. *Prostranstvenno-integratsionnye protsessy sotsial'no-ekonomicheskogo sotrudnichestva prigranichnykh territorii Rossii i Mongolii*. Unpublished dissertation. Buryat State University, Russia.

Ostrom, Elinor. 1990. *Governing the Commons: The Evolution of Institutions for Collective Action*. Cambridge: Cambridge University Press.

"Pamyati zhertv repressii" (7.2.2011). Available at: http://yvision.kz/post/117478 (accessed 17.2.2011).

Pan, Junwu. 2009. *Toward a New Framework for Peaceful Settlement of China's Territorial and Boundary Disputes*. Leiden: Martinus Nijhoff.

Pan, Suming. 2004. "Three 'Red Light Districts' in China", in *Sexual Cultures in East Asia: The Social Construction of Sexuality and Sexual Risk in a Time of AIDS*, ed. E. Micollier. London and New York: Routledge Curzon, pp. 23–53.

Panov, A. 1906. *Gryadushchyee mongol'skoe igo. Otkrytoe pis'mo Narodnym Predstavitelyam.* St Petersburg.

–. 1910. "Zheltyi vopros v Priamur'e", *Voprosy kolonizatsii* 7: 53–116.

–. 1912a. "Zheltyi vopros i mery bor'by s 'zheltym zasil'em' v Priamur'e", *Voprosy kolonizatsii* 11: 171–84.

–. 1912b. "Bor'ba za rabochii rynok v Priamur'e", *Voprosy kolonizatsii* 11: 241–82.

Pedersen, Morten Axel. 2007. "Multiplicity without Myth: Theorizing Darhad Perspectivism. Perspectivism", *Special Issue of Inner Asia* 9/2: 311–28.

–. 2010. "The Virtual Temple: The Power of Relics in Darhad Mongolian Buddhism" in *Representing Power in Modern Inner Asia: Conventions, Alternatives and Oppositions,* eds. I. Charleux, G. Delaplace, R. Hamayon and S. Pearce. Bellingham, WA: Western Washington University, pp. 245–58.

People's Daily Online, 2005. "China helps Mongolia to Build Road along Border City", *Erlian City Inner Mongolian News.* Available at: http://English.peopledaily.com.cn/200511/11/eng20051111_220662.html (accessed 10.1.2011).

Perdue, Peter. 1998. "Boundaries, Maps, and Movement: Chinese, Russian, and Mongolian Empires in Early Modern Central Eurasia", *International History Review* 20/2: 263–86.

Perepiska. 1923. *Perepiska Vil'gel'ma 11 s Nikolaem 11. 1894–1914.* Moscow and Petrograd: Gosudarstvennoye izdatel'stvo.

Perminov, V. V. 2008. *Nakazanie bez prestupleniya.* Chita: Press-sluzhba upravleniya Sudebnogo Departamenta v Chitinskoi oblasti.

Peshkov, I. 2008. "Zakładnicy 'wyobrażonej przeszłości'. Problemy tożsamości etnicznej i kulturowej Guranów Zabajkalskich w Syberii Wschodniej", *Lud* 92: 27–41.

–. 2010a. "Rosjanie z Mongolii Wewnętrznej w cieniu projektowanej i praktykowanej przeszłosci. Pułapki rosyjskości retrospektywnej na pograniczu rosyjsko-chińskim", *Lud* 94: 243–63.

–. 2010b. "Granitsa na zamke postsovetskoi pamiati. Mifologizatsiya frontirnykh soobshhestv na primere russkikh iz Trekhrech'ya", in *Migratsii i diaspory v sociokul'turnom, politicheskom i ekonomicheskom prostranstve Sibiri. Rubezhi XIX-XX i XX-XXI vekov,* ed. V. Dyatlov. Irkutsk: Ottisk.

–. Forthcoming. "Social Crisis, Ethnic Distance and Memory along the Chinese–Soviet Border. The Chinese Russian Old-Settlers Narratives about the 'Chinese' Famine and Cultural Revolution in Inner Mongolia".

Pheterson, Gail. 2001 (1996). *Le prisme de la prostitution.* Paris: L'Harmattan.

Pickering, Sharon and Leanne Weber (eds.). 2006. *Borders, Mobility and Technologies of Control.* Dordrecht: Springer.

Pimin, Alexander. 2000. "Osobennosti kitaiskoi natsional'noi rybalki". *Pacific Ocean Star,* 28 October.

Podolskyi, Sergey. and Veniamin Gotvinskyi. 2007. "'Dorogie gosti' Priamur'ya ili 'kitaiskaya ugroza' Rossii?" *Russian House* 3. Available at: http://www.perspektivy.info/print.php?ID=36246 (accessed 10.9.2010).

Popkova, L.I. 2001. "Etnograficheskaya situatsia v prigranichnykh rayonakh Rossii i Ukrainy (na primere Kurskoi i Sumskoy oblastei). Available at: http://www.erudition.ru/referat/ref/id.48838_1.html (accessed 3.7.2011).

Posner, Richard. A. and Eric B. Rasmusen. 1999. "Creating and Enforcing Norms, With Special Reference to Sanctions", *International Review of Law and Economics* 19: 369–82.

Potter, Pitman B. 2007. "Theoretical and Conceptual Perspectives on the Periphery in Contemporary China", in *The Chinese State at the Borders*, ed. Diana Lary. Vancouver: UBC Press, pp. 240–70.

Poulain, Richard. 2003. "Prostitution, crime organisé et marchandisation", *Revue Tiers Monde* 44/176: 735–70. Available at: http://www.persee.fr (accessed 10.01.2010).

Predvaritel'nye 1924. *Predvaritel'nye itogi byudzhetnogo obsledovaniya rabochikh i sluzhashchikh Dal'nego Vostoka v marte 1924 g.* Khabarovsk [n.p.].

Prescott, J. R. V. 1987. *Political Frontiers and Boundaries.* London: Unwin Hyman.

Prozrachnye granitsy. Bezopasnost' i transgranichnoe sotrudnichestvo v zone novykh pogranichnykh territorii Rossii. 2002. Moscow: Nauchno-obrazovatel'ny forum po mezhdunarodnym otnosheniam.

Qi, Zhi 2010. *Nei Meng Wenge Shilu: 'Minzu Fenlie' yu 'Wasu' Yundong.* Hong Kong: Tianxingjian Chubanshe.

Qingdai Guanxiu 1985. *Qing Sheng Zu Shi Lu.* Beijing: Zhonghua Shuju.

Qu, Yanbin. 2007. "Qite de 'Kezhang Doushi' Minsu: Guanyu Ma'an Shan Duanwujie 'Kezhang Doushi' Minsu de Tianye Diaocha", *Wenhua Xuekan* 2: 157–68.

Radu, Cosmin. 2010. "Beyond Border 'Dwelling': Temporalising the Border-Space through Events", *Anthropological Theory* 10/4: 409–33.

Rangsimaporn, Paradorn. 2006. "Interpretations of Eurasianism: Justifying Russia's Role in East Asia", *Europe-Asia Studies* 58/3: 371–89.

Remnev Anatoly 2004 "'Krest i mech'". Vladimir Solov'ev i Vil'gel'm 11 v kontekste rossiiskogo imperskogo orientalizma", in *Evropa. Mezhdunarodnyi al'manakh.* Vyp. 1V. Tyumen': Mandrika, pp. 56–78.

Riasanovsky, Nicholas V. 1972. "Asia through Russian Eyes", in *Russia and Asia: Essays on the Influence of Russia on the Asian Peoples*, ed. Wayne Vucinich. Stanford, CA: Hoover Institute Press.

Ritter, William S. 1985. "The Final Phase in the Liquidation of Anti-Soviet Resistance in Tadzhikistan: Ibrahim Bek and the Basmachi, 1924–31", *Soviet Studies* 37/4: 484–93.

Roberts, Sean, R. 2004. "A 'Land of Borderlands'", in *Xinjiang: China's Muslim Borderland*, ed. Frederic S. Starr. New York: M.E. Sharpe.

Rosaldo, Renato. 1988. "Ideology, Place, and People without Culture", *Cultural Anthropology* 3/1: 77–87.

Rösler, Michael and Tobias Wendl. 1999. "Frontiers and Borderlands. The Rise and Relevance of and Anthropological Research Genre", in *Frontiers and Borderlands. Anthropological Perspectives*, eds. Michael Rösler and Tobias Wendl. Frankfurt Am Main: Peter Lang, pp. 1–27.

Rupen, Robert. 1979. *How Mongolia is Really Ruled. A Political History of the Mongolian People's Republic, 1900–1978*. Stanford, CA: Hoover Institution Press (Histories of Ruling Communist Parties).

Russko-Kitaiskie otnoshenie 1972. *Materialy i dokumenty*. Vol. 2 1969–72. Moscow: Nauka.

Rybakovskii, Leonid, Olga Zakharova and Vladimir Mindogulov. 1994. *Nelegal'naya migratsiya v prigranichnykh raionakh Dal'nego Vostoka: istoriya, sovremennost', posledstviya*, Moscow: Institut sotsial'no-politicheskikh issledovaniy RAN.

Safran, William. 2004. "Deconstructing and Comparing Diasporas", in *Diaspora, Identity and Religion: New Directions in Theory and Research*, eds. W. Kokot, Kh. Tllyan and C. Alfonso. London: Routledge, pp. 9–29.

Sahlins, Peter. 1989. *Boundaries: The Making of France and Spain in the Pyrenees*. Berkeley, CA: University of California Press.

–. 1998. "State Formation and National Identity in the Catalan Borderlands during the Eighteenth and Nineteenth Centuries", in *Border Identities: Nation and State at International Frontiers*, ed. Thomas M. Wilson and Hastings Donnan. Cambridge: Cambridge University Press, pp. 31–61.

Sanders, Alan. 1989. "Mongolia in 1989: Year of Adjustment", *Asian Survey* 30/1: 59–66.

Sanders, R. (forthcoming) "Memory and Identity of Germans in Kazakhstan" in *Memory, History, Morality: The Socialist Past Today*, ed. A. Gallinat.

Sanzhieva, T. 2006. "Istoricheskie faktory formirovaniya buryatskih diaspor", in *Diaspory v kontekste sovremennykh etnokul'turnykh i etnosotsial'nykh protsessov, eds*. Lubov' Abaeva, Daba Nimaev and Darima Boronoeva. Ulan-Ude: Buriad State University, pp. 26–33.

Schimmelpenninck van der Oye, David. 2009. *Navstrechu voskhodyashchemu solntsu: Kak imperskoe mifotvorchestvo privelo Rossiyu k voine s Yaponiyei*. Moscow: Novoe literaturnoe obozrenie.

Schmidt, M. 2005. "Is Putin Pursuing a Policy of Eurasianism?" *Demokratizatsiya* 13/1 (Winter): 87–99.

Schmitt, Carl. 1991. *Political Romanticism*. Cambridge, MA: The MIT Press.

–. 2007. *The Concept of the Political*. Chicago, IL: University of Chicago Press.

Scott, James C. 1998. *Seeing Like a State: How Certain Schemes to Improve the Human Condition Have Failed*. New Haven, CT: Yale University Press.

Serebrennikov, I. I. 1977 [1922]. *The Albazenes*. Translated by G. Nekranov. Vostochnoye Prosveshcheniye Company Printing and Lithographic Works of the Russian Orthodox Mission Beijing. Available at: http://www.orthodox.cn/localchurch/1922albazene_en.htm (accessed 3.4.2012).

Sergeev Ilia. 2005. "Demarkatsiya amurskikh osetrov. Kitaiskie brakon'ery uzhe ne boyatsya rossiiskikh pogranichnikov", *Vremya Novostei*. Available at: http://www.vremya.ru/2005/104/51/127551.html (accessed 15.10.2010).

Severi, Carlo. 2007. *Le principe de la chimère. Une anthropologie de la mémoire*. Paris: Editions Rue d'Ulm. Presses de l'Ecole Normale Supérieure.

Shagdar, Enkhbayar. 2005. "Mongolia's Foreign Trade, 1985–2003", *Erina Report* 62: 29–36.

Shami, Seteney. 2007. "Prehistories of Globalization: Circassian Identity in Motion", in *Caucasus Paradigms* (Halle Studies in the Anthropology of Eurasia 13), eds. B. Grant and L. Yalçın-Heckmann. Berlin and Münster: Lit Verlag, pp. 191–218.

Shanskii, Nikolai M. and Bobrova, Tatiana A. 1994. *Etimologicheskii slovar' russkogo yazyka*. Moscow: Proserpina.

Sheingaus, Alexandr S. 2005. "Prirodopol'zovanie rossiiskogo Dal'nego Vostoka v aspekte svyazyei s Severo-Vostochnoi Aziyei: problemy i perspektivy", *Bulletin of the Far East Branch of the Russian Academy of Science* 3: 11–27.

Shemyakin, Ya. G. and O. D. Shemyakina. 2004. "Spetsifika formoobrazovaniya v rossiisko-evraziiskoi tsivilizatsii", in *Tsivilizatsiya*, Vol 6. *Rossiya v tsivilizatsionnoi structure evraziiskogo kontinenta*, ed. A. O. Chubar'yan. Moscow: Nauka, pp. 32–64.

Sherbina, Galina P. (ed.). 2008. *Mezhdunarodnyi oborot ob'ektov dikoi prirody Dal'nego Vostoka Rossii*. Vladivostok: Apelsin.

Shirokogoroff, S. 1979 [1929]. *Social Organization of the Northern Tungus*. London: Garland.

Shlapentokh, Dmitry. 2005. "Russia's Foreign Policy and Eurasianism", *Eurasia Insight*, 1 September. Available at: www.eurasianet.org/departments/insight/ articles/eav080205a_pr.shtml (accessed 10.10.2010).

Shryeider, David. 1897. *Nash Dal'nii Vostok*. St Petersburg.

Sidorov, Dmitrii. 2006. "Post-imperial Third Romes: Resurrection of a Russian Orthodox Geo-political Metaphor", *Geopolitics* 11: 317–47.

Simmel, Georg. 1971. "The Stranger", in *Georg Simmel: On Individuality and Social Forms*, ed. Donald N. Levine. Chicago, IL: University of Chicago Press, pp. 143–50.

–. 1997 [1903]. "Bridge and Door", in *Rethinking Architecture. A Reader in Cultural Theory*, ed. N. Leach. London: Routledge, pp. 66–69.

Simmons, Beth A. 2005. "Rules over Real Estate: Trade, Territorial Conflict, and International Borders as Institution", *The Journal of Conflict Resolution* 49/6: 823–48.

Simonov, Eugene A. and Thomas D. Dahmer (eds.). 2008. *Amur-Heilong River Basin Reader*. Hong Kong: WWF. Available at: http://www.wwf.ru/resources/publ/ book/eng/299 (accessed 25.4.2012).

Skinner, Barbara. 1994. "Identity Formation in the Russian Cossack Revival", *Europe-Asia Studies* 46/6: 1017–37.

Skocpol, Theda. 1988. "Social Revolution and Mass Military Mobilization", *World Politics* 40/2: 147–68.

Slezkine, Yuri. 2006. "The Soviet Union as a Communal Apartment, or How a Socialist State Promoted Ethnic Particularism", in *Stalinism: New Directions*, ed. Sheila Fitzpatrick. London and New York: Routledge, pp. 313–47.

Smirnov, Sergei. 2011. "Ugrozy priblizhayutsya", gazeta.ru. Available at: http:// www.gazeta.ru/politics/2011/07/14_a_3695649.shtml (accessed 14.7.2011).

Sneath, David. 2003. "Beyond the Willow Palisade: Manchuria and the History of China's Inner Asian Frontier", *Asian Affairs* 34/1: 3–11.

–. 2003. "Lost in the Post. Technologies of Imagination, and the Soviet Legacy in Post-Socialist Mongolia", *Inner Asia* 5: 39–52.

–, Martin Holbraad and Morten Axel Pedersen. 2009. "Technologies of the Imagination: An Introduction", *Ethnos* 74/1: 5–30.

Sobel, Joel. 2006. "For Better or Forever: Formal versus Informal Enforcement", *Journal of Labor Economics* 24/2: 271–98.

Sodnompilova M. 2005. *Semantika zhilischa v traditsionnoi kul'ture buryat.* Irkutsk: MION.

Solovyev, Vladimir. 1990. "Tri razgovora o voine, progresse i kontse vsemirnoi istorii". *Solov'ev V. S. Sochineniya v dvukh tomakh.* Tom. 2. Moscow: Mysl', pp. 635–762.

–. 1993. "Panmongolizm", in *Rossiya mezhdu Evropoi i Aziyei: Evraziiskii soblazn.* Moscow: Nauka, p. 233.

Sorokin, Konstantin. 1996. *Geopolitika sovremennosti i geostrategiya Rossii.* Moscow: ROSSPLEN.

Starikov, E. N. 1996. *Obshchestvo – kasarma ot faraonov do nashikh dniei.* Novosibirsk: Sibirskii Khronograph.

State National Policy Concept of the Republic of Buryatia. *Resolution of the Government of the Republic of Buryatia no. 336 September, 29, 1997* in *Buryatia* 199, October 17, 1997.

–. *Resolution of the Government of the Republic of Buryatia* № 179, May 29 2007 in *Buryatia* 98, June 2, 2007.

Stepanova, I. Zh. 2009. ""Nekotorye osobennosti mentaliteta potomkov russkih v Mongolii", in *Rossiya v Mongolii: istoriya i sovremennost'. Perspektivy sotrudnichestva. Materialy mezhdunarodnoi nauchno-prakticheskoi konferentsii.* Ulan Bator: Arvai Print.

Stephan, John J. 1994. *The Russian Far East: A History.* Stanford, CA: Stanford University Press.

Stoler, Ann L. 2008. "Imperial Debris: Reflections on Ruins and Ruination", *Cultural Anthropology* (Special Issue on Imperial Debris) 23/2: 191–219.

Strathern, Marylin. 2005. *Kinship, Law and the Unexpected: Relatives Are Always a Surprise.* Cambridge: Cambridge University Press.

Su, Quanyou. 2009, "Lun Sun Zhongshan de Shengjie Guannian", *Guangdong Gongye Daxue Xuebao* 9/1: 9–13.

Su, Xiaokang and Wang Luxiang. 1991. *Deathsong of the River: a Reader's Guide to the Chinese TV Series Heshang* (introduced, translated, and annotated by Richard W. Bodman and Pin P. Wan). Ithaca, NY: Cornell University East Asia Program.

Sunderland, Willard. 1996. "Russians into Iakuts? 'Going Native' and Problems of Russian National Identity in the Siberian North, 1870s-1914", *Slavic Review* 55/4: 806–25.

Suphachalasai, Suphachol. 2005. "Development, Environmental Policy, and Mass Media: Theory and Evidence", *Environmental Economy and Policy Research Working Papers 15.* University of Cambridge. Department of Land Economics. Available at http://ideas.repec.org/p/wpa/wuwppe/0502014.html (accessed 30.4.2012).

Tabet, Paula. 2005. *La grande arnaque.* Paris: L'Harmattan (Bibliothèque du féminisme).

Tagliacozzo, Eric. 2005. *Secret Trades, Porous Borders. Smuggling and States along a Southeast Asian Frontier, 1865–1915*. New Haven, CT: Yale University Press.

Tai, Sheng and Yushan Jin (eds.). 2008. *Mengguzhen Wangfu*. Beijing: Zhongguo Shehui Chubanshe.

Tang, Shiping, Li, Mingjiang and Acharya, Amitav. 2009. *Living with China: Regional States and China through Crises and Turning Points*. New York: Palgrave Macmillan.

Tinguy, Anne de. 2004. *La grande migration: la Russie et les Russes depuis l'ouverture du Rideau de fer*. Paris: Plon.

Titarenko, M. L. 1998. *Rossiya litsom k Azii*. Moscow: Respublika.

Toops, Stanley, W. 2004. "The Demography of Xinjiang", in *Xinjiang: China's Muslim Borderland*, ed. Frederick S. Starr. New York: M.E. Sharpe

Topin, David 2011. "Competing Communities: Ethnic Unity and Ethnic Boundaries on China's North-West Frontier", *Inner Asia* 13/1: 7–25.

Tserenhand, G. 1993. "Traditsii kochevogo stoibischa u mongolov", in: *History of Household and Material Culture of Mongol and Turkick Ethnic Groups*, ed. Bulat Zorigtuev. Novosibirsk: Nauka, pp. 62–74.

Tsydendambaev, Ts. 2001. *Buriatskie istoricheskie khroniki i rodoslovnye*. Ulan-Ude: Respublikanskaya tipografiya.

Tsymburski, Vadim. 2000. *Rossiya – Zemlya za Velikim Limitrofom: Tsivilizatsiia i ee geopolitika*. Moscow: Institut ekonomicheskikh strategii.

Tsyrenzhabai Abida, Khalzain Bolod, Badmyn Dimchig, and Sambuugai Lhamsüren. 2005. "Sovremenny istoricheskii ocherk buryat Shenekhena", in *Lokalnyie osobennosti buryatskoi etnicheskoi obschiny Vnutrennei Mongolii*. Materialy pervoi nauchnoi ekspeditsii NGI. Ed. by Vasilyeva, Mariya Samsonovna. Ulan-Ude: Buryat State University, pp. 23–28.

Tu, Weiming. 1994. "Cultural China: The Periphery as the Center", in *The Living Tree: The Changing Meaning of Being Chinese Today*. Stanford, CA: Stanford University Press, pp. 1–34.

Ukhtubuzhskii, P. 1913. *Russkii narod v Azii. 1) Pereselenie v Sibir' 2) Zheltaya opasnost'. Izdanie Russkogo narodnogo soyuza Mikhaila Arkhangela*. St Petersburg, Izdaniye Russkogo Narodnogo Soyuza Mikhaila Archangela

Urantogos, O. 2010. "Mardain ord 'am' orj' ehellee". Available at: www.sonin.mn (www.sonin.mn/2010/02/23/). Accessed 18.4.2012.

Urbanaeva, I. S. 1994. *Chelovek u Baikala i mir Tsentral'noi Azii: filosofiya i istoriya* Ulan-Ude: BNTs So RAN.

Vachtin, J. V., P. Golovko and P. Shvaitcer. 2004. *Russkie starozhyly Sibiri: sotsial'nie i simvolicheskie aspekty samosoznaniya*. Moscow: Novoe izdatel'stvo.

Vaisman, Alexey and Pavel Fomenko. 2006. *Siberia's Black Gold: Harvest and Trade in Amur River Sturgeons in the Russian Federation*. Brussels: TRAFFIC Europe. Available at: http://www.wwf.ru/resources/publ/book/eng/287 (accessed 25.4.2012).

van der Ploeg, Irma and Isolde Sprenkels. 2011. "Migration and the Machine-Readable Body: Identification and Biometrics", in *Migration and the New Technological Borders of Europe*, eds. H. Dijstelbloem and A. Meijer. London: Palgrave Macmillan, pp. 68–104.

van der Ploeg, Irma. 1999. "Illegal Body: 'Eurodac' and the Politics of Biometric Identification". *Ethics and Information Technology* 1: 295–302.

van Gennep, Arnold. 1991 [1909]. *Les rites de passage*. Paris: Picard.

van Houtum, Henk and Anke Strüver. 2002. "Borders, Strangers, Doors and Bridges". *Space & Polity* 6/2: 141–46.

van Schendel, W. 2005. *The Bengal Borderland: Beyond State and Nation in South Asia*. London: Anthem.

Verezhnikov, A. 1911. "Kitaiskaya tolpa", *Sovremennik* 3/4: 124–34.

Vil'gel'm, 11. 1923. *Memuary. Sobytiya i lyudi. 1878–1918*. Moscow and Petrograd: Izdatel'stvo L.D. Frenkel.

Vila, Pablo. 2005. *Borders Identifications. Narratives of Religion, Gender, and Class on the U.S.-Mexico Border*. Austin, TX: University of Texas Press.

Vishnevsky, A. 1998. *Serp i rubl. Konservativnaya modernizatsiya v SSSR*. Moscow: O.G.I.

Vitkovskaya, Galina and Sergey Panarin (eds). 1999. "Vynuzhdennaya migratsiya i migrantofobiya v Rossii", in *Neterpimost' v Rossii: starye i novye fobii*. Moscow: Carnegie Moscow Center, pp. 151–91.

–. 2000. *Migratsiya i bezopasnost' v Rossii*. Moscow: Carnegie Moscow Center.

Viveiros de Castro, Eduardo. 1992. *From the Enemy's Point of View. Humanity and Divinity in an Amazonian Society*. Chicago, IL: The University of Chicago Press.

Waldron, Arthur. 1990. *The Great Wall of China: From History to Myth*. Cambridge: Cambridge University Press.

Wang, Guojun 2006. *Menggu Jiwen*. Huhehaote: Nei Menggu Renmin Chubanshe.

Weber, Eugen. 1976. *Peasants into Frenchmen: Modernization of Rural France, 1870–1914*. Stanford, CA: Stanford University Press.

Weber, Leanne. 2006. "The Shifting Frontiers of Migration Control", in *Borders, Mobility and Technologies of Control*, eds. S. Pickering and L. Weber. Dordrecht: Springer, pp. 21–43.

Williams, John. 2006. *The Ethics of Territorial Borders. Drawing Lines in the Shifting Sand*. London: Palgrave Macmillan.

Wilson, Thomas M. and Donnan, Hastings. 1998. "Nation, State and Identity at International Borders", in *Border Identities: Nation and State at International Frontiers*, ed. Thomas M. Wilson and Hastings Donnan. Cambridge: Cambridge University Press, pp. 1–30.

Wishnick, Elizabeth. 2005. "Migration and Economic Security: Chinese Labour Migrants in the Russian Far East", in *Crossing National Borders: Human Migration Issues in Northeast Asia*, ed. Tsuneo Akaha and Anna Vassilieva. Tokyo: United Nations University Press, pp. 68–92.

Wolff, K. H. (ed.). 1950. *The Sociology of George Simmel*. New York: Free Press.

Woodside, Alexander. 2007. "The Centre and the Borderlands in Chinese Political Theory", in *The Chinese State at the Borders*, ed. Diana Lary. Vancouver: UBC Press, pp. 11–28.

World Bank. 2010. *Mongolia Economic Retrospective: 2008–2010*. Washington, DC: The World Bank.

Yadritsev, N. M. 2000. *Sochineniya: t. 1, Sibir' kak koloniya: Sovremennoe polozhenie Sibiri, ee nuzhdy i potrebnosti. Ee proshloe i budushchee.* Tiumen': Izdatel'stvo Yu. Mandriki.

Yu, Qiuyu. 1995. *Yige Wangchao de Beiying: Chuanyue Zhongguo Lishi de Sanwen zhi Lü.* Chengdu: Sichuan Wenyi Chubanshe.

Yurchak, A. 2006. *Everything Was Forever, until it Was no More: The last Soviet Generation.* Princeton, NJ: Princeton University Press.

Yuzefovich Leonid. 2010. *Samoderzhets pustyni: baron R.F. Ungern-Shternberg i mir, v kotorom on zhil.* Moscow: Ad Marginem.

Zatsepine, Victor. 2007. "The Amur: As River, as Border", in *The Chinese State at the Borders,* ed. Diana Lary. Vancouver: UBC Press.

Zenkova T. M. 2007. "K voprosu o traditsionnoi kul'ture Trekhrech'ya", in *Uchenye zapiski "Kuznetsovskie chteniia"* (Issue 1), ed. N. N. Zakablukovskaya. Chita: Poisk, pp. 11–13.

Zhamtsarano, Ts. 2001. *Putevye dnevniki*: 1903–1909. Ulan-Ude: BNTs.

Zhang Zhirong. 2005. Zhongguo bianjiang yu minzu wenti: Dangdai zhongguo de tiaozhan ji qi lishi youlai. Beijing: Beijing Daxue Chubanshe

Zhirinovsky, V. V. 1993. *Poslednii brosok na yug.* Moscow: TOO Pisatel' and IK Bukvitsa.

Index

This book does not end here...

At Open Book Publishers, we are changing the nature of the traditional academic book. The title you have just read will not be left on a library shelf, but will be accessed online by hundreds of readers each month across the globe. We make all our books free to read online so that students, researchers and members of the public who can't afford a printed edition can still have access to the same ideas as you.

Our digital publishing model also allows us to produce online supplementary material, including extra chapters, reviews, links and other digital resources. Find *Frontier Encounters* on our website to access its online extras. Please check this page regularly for ongoing updates, and join the conversation by leaving your own comments:

http://www.openbookpublishers.com/isbn/9781906924874

If you enjoyed this book, and feel that research like this should be available to all readers, regardless of their income, please think about donating to us. Our company is run entirely by academics, and our publishing decisions are based on intellectual merit and public value rather than on commercial viability. We do not operate for profit and all donations, as with all other revenue we generate, will be used to finance new Open Access publications.

For further information about what we do, how to donate to OBP, additional digital material related to our titles or to order our books, please visit our website.

OpenBook Publishers

Knowledge is for sharing

www.ingramcontent.com/pod-product-compliance
Lightning Source LLC
Chambersburg PA
CBHW061719270326
41928CB00011B/2038